MORE U~~NCOMMON LAW~~

A. P. Herbert was born in 1890 and educated at Winchester and New College, Oxford, and was called to the Bar in 1918 but never practised. He contributed regularly to *Punch* from 1910 onwards and wrote eight novels, including *The Water Gipsies* and *Holy Deadlock*, fifteen musical and dramatic pieces, eighteen volumes of *Misleading Cases in the Common Law*. He became Member of Parliament for Oxford University in 1935, made his maiden speech in defence of Private Members' time on the second day of the new Parliament and remained there as an active reformer until the University seats were abolished. He fought gallantly and successfully for many causes including the abolition of Entertainments Tax and the reform of the licensing, divorce and obscenity laws. He was President of the Society of Authors. He was also a lifelong waterman and lover of the Thames. He was knighted in 1945. He died in 1971.

Methuen Humour Classics

MORE UNCOMMON LAW

A. P. HERBERT

METHUEN . LONDON

Originally published as
CODD'S LAST CASE first published 1952
by Methuen & Company Ltd and

BARDOT MP? first published 1964
by Methuen & Company Ltd

This first combined edition
MORE UNCOMMON LAW
published simultaneously in hardback and paperback 1982
by Methuen London Ltd
This paperback edition published in 1989
by Methuen London
Michelin House, 81 Fulham Road, London SW3 6RB

ISBN 0 413 50880 3

Made and printed in Great Britain
by Cox & Wyman Ltd, Reading
Filmset in Monotype Baskerville by
Northumberland Press Ltd, Gateshead

British Library Cataloguing in Publication Data

Herbert, A. P.
    More uncommon law.
    I. Title
    828'.91207   PR6015.E58

WITH GREAT RESPECT
TO
MY LEARNED BRETHREN
OF
THE INNER TEMPLE,
AND EVEN
THE OTHERS

ACKNOWLEDGMENTS

MOST of these Cases were originally reported in the pages of *Punch*. My thanks to the Editor, and the Proprietors for their courteous permission to publish them again. I also thank the Controller of Her Majesty's Stationery Office for permission to include some quotations from *Hansard*. Also my thanks to my long-suffering and industrious secretary Miss Priscilla Gaisford.

A.P.H.

INTRODUCTION

THIS volume, comprising *Codd's last Case* and *Bardot M.P.?*, with *Uncommon Law* completes the *corpus* of Misleading Cases, 114 in all, which has been slowly growing since 1924. One or two of the judgments have been quoted on the Bench of the Supreme Court of Justice in the United States. Others I have heard respectfully read or recited by members of the Canadian Bar. Where the first stage only of a difficult case has been reported judges and jurists across the Atlantic have written to inquire about the final decision. British professors and tutors have recommended many of the judgments to the young.

Students of the earlier collection will find the same pleasures here, but perhaps in finer flower than before. In elegance and lucidity of language, acuity of argument, and shrewdness of decision, the judges of to-day need fear no comparisons with the past. The range of subjects is remarkable too, and reaches many questions of interest to the ordinary citizen as well as to the lawyer. No other book that I know reveals in such detail the impact of 'the Common Market' on the British way of life—official and individual. Can Mlle Brigitte Bardot now be elected to the House of Commons? and, if not, why not? Must British courts, even the House of Lords, take orders from Brussels on such a question? A Lord Chancellor, who shall be nameless, said that the ordinary citizen would not be affected. But 'common transport' will mean a 'common time', imposed by Brussels. What time—German Time? or Greenwich Time? Continental Time would mean Perpetual Summer Time in Britain. Will this mean nothing to the Common Briton? Must he accept it on orders from abroad? And would it be the best solution? Again, will the

European Economic Community always share the British tenderness for tea, or approve the Treasury attitude to wine and spirits? These are subjects of more than high-level or academic interest.

'How much may you kill a burglar?' should be studied in every home. 'The Law of Sitting' turns on the citizen's duty to assist the police—and women in distress: and Strool's Case demonstrates the dangers of running to the psychiatrist on a criminal charge.

What exactly is meant by 'With all my worldly goods I thee endow'? Mr. Justice Puce, with remorseless reasoning, makes it clear that the wealthy bridegroom should be as cautious about these words as some brides are about 'obey'. 'Who giveth this woman?', another wedding case, will bring some comfort to any father of marriageable daughters. In 'Stamp out Stampery' the veteran Haddock strikes one more blow—this time at the Hague—for all those who suffer from the International plague of 'redundant passportery'. 'The Law of the Pin' is concerned with the old charge that 'the Pools' are, in effect, nothing but a lottery: and in the *Note* to this case a similar charge against 'the Phantom Pools' is considered and dismissed. 'The Law of Sunday' shows the promoters of Sunday charity enterprises how to deal with the 'Lord's Day' snoopers. 'A Tent in the Road' is another case with an appeal to almost every home, especially to those old-fashioned folk who feel that they have a kind of right to keep their own car at their own front door. There are two or three important legal skirmishes with the Inland Revenue: but a *Note* to the 'Bottle' Case gives an authoritative and congenial answer to the question 'Can you pay income tax with a cheque written in (not very polite) verse?' Other questions answered are: 'What happens at the Old Bailey when the Queen enters the City?' 'What is the strength of a pound note—"genuine" or counterfeit—if you want a pound'? 'What is the constitutional effect of a rise in M.P.'s salaries?'

No student of legal history must fail to read the Trout

Case, where the House of Lords are heard at their best on the law of libel and slander. The Toppest People will be shocked to learn that most of the good actions of the Arts Council are not authorized by its Charter. They will be shocked again (in 'Cheap Literature') by the long history of the Privileged Libraries and the statutory depredation of the book-producers. In the last case a computer issues defamatory statements, is joined as a party, gives evidence, and dominates the Court. A fearless judge faces the menace of these machines, which, he foresees, in unscrupulous hands, may grow to be a cosmic mischief. Whether for instruction or entertainment—generally both together— these Reports are warmly recommended. Some of them may, like many before them, bear fruit in policy and practice. *Ex lite lax*.

The Editor

TABLE OF CASES

(1) HOGBY, E. A. *v.* HOGBY, W. M.

The Price of Justice

(Before Mr. Justice Plush)

His lordship to-day delivered an important judgment on the meaning of Magna Carta. He said:

There is not much left of the Great Charter to-day, and what remains is little known to most of the King's subjects, who in these days appear to be more interested in the liberties of Letts, Sudeten Germans, and Czecho-Slovakians than in their own. But members of the legal profession at least still dwell with reverence and contentment on Chapter 29 of the Magna Carta. Many a tired judge or gentleman of the long robe falls decorously to sleep at last with this much-loved enactment under his pillow and in his mind the unforgettable promise of 700 years ago:

To no man will we sell, to no man deny, to no man delay, justice or right.

'To no man will we sell justice....' It is not to be supposed that the enlightened monarch who set his hand to these words had in his mind to diminish or destroy the meagre remuneration of the legal profession. Barristers and solicitors—and even, I suppose, judges—are as well entitled as others to keep body and soul alive by selling their services and their learning to the people. Moreover, like the medical profession, they give much free advice and service to the poor without much gratitude or even acknowledgment from the public.[1]

No, the meaning of the Monarch, I think, is plain. King John undertook, for his heirs and assigns, that the *Crown*

---

[1] His Majesty's Judges, though their salaries have not been raised since 1832 (when they were free of income-tax), are constantly called upon for heavy extra work on Committees, Commissions of Inquiry, etc.

would not sell justice—that is, that neither the possession of wealth nor the readiness to bribe should be a necessary passport into the Royal Courts of Justice.

This case, not for the first time, reveals how very far we have fallen to-day below the lofty ideals and undertakings of King John. Mr. Hogby has been successful in a law-suit, but he has been required to pay the costs of the unsuccessful party. This at first sight shocking statement is easily explained. The suit was a divorce suit; he is a husband; the other party was his wife; and by a bizarre tradition in this department of justice a husband, innocent or guilty, victorious or not, must always pay the costs of his wife, though the action be erroneously originated by her. This is called the Equality of the Sexes.

To that queer point I shall reluctantly return.

Now, of the costs in question here, some represented the modest fees of barristers and solicitors, some the expenses of witnesses (on both sides), and some the necessary out-of-pocket charges incurred by solicitors in the ordinary conduct of a case. To none of these could Mr. Hogby make reasonable objection, except that under a system of genuine justice they would be paid by his wife, who brought against him a charge of cruelty and was unable to sustain it to the satisfaction of the Court.

But there was also a minor, though, to Mr. Hogby, at least, a substantial charge for what are called court fees. These are the very numerous fixed fees charged by the Crown at various stages of a suit at law. For example, on the filing of each affidavit there is a charge of 2s. 6d., and upon each swearing another half-crown. Here in the bill before me is 'Alimony; application for appointment, each hour or part thereof, 10 shillings. Questions for jury, 10 shillings; settling question for jury, 10 shillings; re-settling questions for jury, 10 shillings. Appeal to Court of Appeal, filing notice and entering, £7; notice of entering, £3'; and so on. At every preliminary stage of the dispute money passes to the Crown; and when at last the litigant is admitted to the Temple of Justice, he is charged by the hour for the time that he spends there. 'Hearing, or trial, of cause—first five hours £2' (or 8s. an hour) 'and for each additional complete hour, 10 shillings.'

It was well said in the House of Commons recently by Mr. Haddock (Ind. Nat.) that, if the Crown must charge for justice, at least the fee should be like the fee for postage: that is to say, it should be the same, however long the journey may be. For it is no fault of one litigant that his plea to the King's judges raises questions more difficult to determine than another's, and will require a longer hearing in court. He is asking for justice, not renting house-property.

Well, if all this is not selling justice, I do not know what is. In the ordinary course, it is true, the party who loses will have to meet these charges, upon the theory that he deserves to pay for taking the time of the Court with a plea now proved to be wrong. But can even this be defended as equitable? He was not to know that he was wrong; and even now it is not certain that he was wrong. For the Court of Appeal might say that he was right. Only the House of Lords can say with certitude and finality that he is wrong; and few of the King's subjects can afford to ask them. Right or wrong, he is entitled to ask for justice (unless he is a frivolous or vexatious litigant, when there are effective ways of dealing with him): and the Crown ought not to make it more difficult for him to obtain justice by charging fees for it. I am told that the Crown makes a profit out of the Courts.

The Attorney-General (Sir Anthony Slatt): Milord, with great respect, I am not sure that that is strictly accurate.

The Judge: It's a very near thing, is it not?

The Attorney-General: If the fees for non-contentious probate business be included, I believe that may be so, milord: but no profit is made from litigation. As to that, milord, may I suggest one possible line of thought? The Crown, in this connection, means the whole body of taxpayers. Would it be fair and equitable if the general taxpayer had to provide all the facilities of the Courts for the benefit of the litigant?

The Judge: Why not? Everybody pays for the police, but some people use them more than others. Nobody complains. You don't have to pay a special fee every time you have a burglary, or ask a policeman the way. I don't follow you, Sir Anthony.

I will go further. I hold that the Crown not merely ought not, but is unable, to act in this way, by reason of the passage in the Great Charter which I have quoted. The Rules of Court, then, which purpose to impose these charges are *ultra vires*, unconstitutional, and of no effect: and Mr. Hogby may continue to decline to pay them.

That, however, does not dispose of his difficulties. There remain the other costs which I have mentioned. These amount to a much larger sum; and they are much larger than they should be in a country which prides itself on its administration of justice. This, again, is the fault not of Parliament but of the Crown.

Mr. Hogby resides in a town in Yorkshire. This is an Assize town—that is to say, it is visited from time to time by two of His Majesty's Judges for the purpose of delivering justice there. If Mr. Hogby had been sued for fraud, for libel, for embezzlement, or for breach of promise, the case could have been heard there, near his own home. But it was a suit for divorce. Now the only divorce cases that can be heard at some Assize Courts (not all of them) are (*a*) undefended cases and (*b*) Poor Persons' cases, defended or not. Mr. Hogby, though poor (he is a school-teacher), is not poor enough to qualify for free legal assistance as a Poor Person. Therefore, if he defends the case, he must travel to the High Court in London, and suffer all the additional expense that that involves.[1]

He must pay not only his own solicitor in Yorkshire but in addition an agent in London—not to mention his wife's

[1] Not now.

solicitor and agent. He must pay for the transport to London, and their accommodation there, not only of his own witnesses but his wife's. He must leave his home, and occupation, for two or three days, for there will be no certainty that his case will be called immediately after his arrival. While they are waiting, though he and his witnesses may be content with a modest hotel and reasonable cuisine, his wife, who knows that she has not to pay, and *ex hypothesi* is not at present well-disposed towards him, has no reason to stint her comfort or that of her witnesses.

Mr. Hogby, he tells us, had saved little, and he was appalled by the prospect of such expenditure. One way out was to allow his wife's case to succeed by default. It would then be heard in his own town as an undefended suit at comparatively small expense. He would be divorced, but not bankrupt. Many men, it is believed, confronted with the same dilemma, have taken that course.

But Mr. Hogby is a school-teacher. If he were to make no answer to a charge of marital cruelty, and for that suffer divorce, he would, he was persuaded, no longer be permitted by the Education Authority to have the care and teaching of children.

It is interesting, by the way, and will be gratifying to many that there is still one profession where divorce is regarded as a handicap. Isn't it, Sir Anthony? Are you awake?

The Attorney-General (Sir Anthony Slatt, K.C.): Yes, milord.

The Judge: Accordingly he fought the case, and, necessarily, in London. He won. The charges against him were struck out. He is not divorced; but he is, to all intents and purposes, bankrupt.

I am now asked to issue a judgment summons against him for the outstanding costs of this unfortunate affair; and, if he does not pay, I suppose that he will go to prison. Two questions will leap at once to the mind of the humane observer: (1) for what good reason am I requested to condemn and punish the husband who was successful in his appeal for justice instead of the wife, who was not? and (2) for what reason could not this comparatively simple case have been heard by one of the King's Judges in Yorkshire, where the costs and inconveniences of Mr. Hogby would have been considerably less?

It is not for me to furnish reasonable answers, if such can be found. It is vain, if it were seemly, to blame Parliament in this affair, for Parliament, I believe, in both cases, has already entrusted the necessary powers to the proper authorities. The remedy, if any, is in the hands of the administration—in other words, of the Crown. All kinds of profound and mystical arguments are used, I know, for the retention of the present system. Since I am dealing with the Crown, which in this case means the learned and illustrious heads of the profession which I adorn, I must not, and shall not, attempt to meet those arguments, though one or two comments may quietly possess my mind.

But here is Mr. Hogby, who declines, for one reason or another, to pay these costs; and, for one reason or another, I am bound to say that in my opinion he is damn well right.

The application is dismissed.

27 July, 1938

NOTE—(1) His Lordship's second ground of complaint was later removed: and defended divorce suits (to the disgust of His Majesty's Judges) can be heard at Assizes. (2) The system of court fees remains, and has recently been laboriously considered by the Committee on Supreme Court Practice and Procedure (Chairman, Sir Raymond Evershed, Master of the Rolls), of which the editor is a humble member. This Committee were informed by the Lord Chancellor (see their Second Interim Report, 1951, Cmd. 8176) that 'The proposal that court fees should be entirely abolished would involve the abrogation of a principle which has been accepted by Parliament and the country for many generations, *viz.* that suitors in the Courts are properly required to bear some proportion of the costs of the machinery of the administration of justice. The taxpayer already contributes a substantial proportion of the costs, and the transference of the whole financial burden of the machinery (which would have to be not only for the Supreme Court, but for all other courts of law) would, we feel, involve questions of public finance which are far beyond the scope of the Committee's enquiry.' But they were permitted, and encouraged, to consider the question 'whether the Supreme Court Fees Order requires overhauling' and did so.

They found (p. 56) that 'in an average small action in the King's Bench Division, where the total bill of costs is in the neighbourhood of £200, court fees

THE PRICE OF JUSTICE

7

may be expected to account for about 6 per cent. of the total. In the case of larger actions, where the total bill of costs is greater, the percentage attributable to court fees is likely to be smaller, and in very big cases considerably smaller. It is obvious, therefore, that even the total abolition of court fees would bring no great relief to the litigant, and the degree of relief which we feel entitled to recommend can only be comparatively small. We cannot afford, however, to neglect any possible means of reducing the costs of litigation, by however small an amount, and being satisfied that some relief from court fees can be given to the litigant without injustice to the taxpayer we think that such relief should be given.'

Detailed recommendations were made: for which you must buy this fascinating Report. It is marked 1s. 9d. net. In other words, though a Government production, it is governed by one of those Retail Price Maintenance Agreements on which His Majesty's Ministers have recently frowned. And see *Rex* v. *Lambert* where a publican, to attract custom to his overtaxed house, sold stamps below the Government price, and without a licence.

(2) REX v. REINSTEIN

The Wizardry Case

There was a dramatic turn to the Palmistry trial to-day. Doctor Reinstein, the fashionable 'futuropath', has appealed to Quarter Sessions against his conviction by the Burbleton magistrates as a rogue and vagabond under the Vagrancy Act, 1824, for 'pretending to tell fortunes by palmistry or otherwise'. The court was full of mink and pearls, for many of the doctor's Mayfair clients had come to see his final duel with the law. Lady Vague, the Hon. Mrs. Marsh-Mallow, and Mr. Edward Sonnet have already testified to the comfort they have received from his estimates of their character and forecasts of their future.

After a severe cross-examination by the Attorney-General, Mr. Mould rose to re-examine the doctor. He handed the witness a blue book:

Kindly turn to page 112. Do you see any predictions there?

Yes. It is stated here that at exactly 12.0 noon on September 1st the planet Venus will be over the meridian of Greenwich. The book also says that Venus will then be 41·2 minutes of arc below the celestial equator.

41·2 minutes? About 40 miles? That is fairly precise, is it not? What else do you find?

The book is full of predictions—300 pages of them. On page 148 we are told that on December 19th the planet Mars will pass less than 1 degree (42 minutes) South of Saturn.

Do you believe these predictions?
Certainly.
Have you the faintest idea how they are arrived at?
None.

The Chairman (Sir Philip Crow): What is this book, Mr. Mould?

Mr. Mould: The *Nautical Almanac*, milord, published by order of the Lords Commissioners of the Admiralty.

The Chairman: It is not illegal, is it, to predict the movements of the heavenly bodies?

Mr. Mould: No, milord. That is the extraordinary thing.

Counsel then handed to the prisoner a small black box, about the size of a cigar-box.

Kindly lift the lid of that box, Doctor.

The Doctor did so. A shrill soprano voice was heard, singing a melancholy song.

The Chairman: God bless my soul! What is this?

Prisoner: That is Gracie Fields, sir, singing 'Sally'.

He turned a small wheel and the voice filled the court.

The Chairman (shouting): WHAT—HAS—MISS—FIELDS—TO—DO—WITH—THIS—CASE?

Mr. Mould: MILORD—SHE—IS—AT—MANCHESTER.

The Chairman: BUT—IF—SHE—HAS—ANYTHING—TO—SAY — SHE — OUGHT — TO — BE — HERE. I — CAN'T—ALLOW —— WILL — YOU — STOP — THAT — FRIGHTFUL —NOISE?

(The prisoner closed the lid.)

Really, Mr. Mould! Perhaps you will now explain the purport of your examination?

Mr. Mould (to the prisoner): Do you believe that the sound emerging from that small box was the voice of Miss Gracie Fields singing at Manchester, 180 miles from this court?

Prisoner: In a sense, no. It does not seem to me to be possible. I cannot imagine how it is done. But I have to accept it, like other wonders I do not understand.

Mr. Mould glanced at his watch and said: Reduce the volume, please, and raise the lid again.

The Chairman (anxiously): Mr. Mould——!

A refined voice said: 'Here are the weather forecasts. Outer Hebrides ...'

The Chairman: You need not go on with that, Mr. Mould. We see the point.

I have one more witness, milord. Call Ebenezer Mole.

When Mr. Mole, a rustic type, had been sworn, Mr. Mould asked if the witness might be permitted to walk about the court. He carried a forked twig.

The Chairman (wearily): If you think it will help, Mr. Mould. You are not, I hope, going to call any performing bears?

No, milord.

The witness walked about, holding the twig in front of him. At the back of the court he halted and said: 'There be water below, dang Oi if there bein't.'

The Chairman: What *is* all this?

The witness is a water-diviner.

The Chairman: Yes, but—— Usher, *is* there any water there?

Usher: Yes, milord, the lavatories are just below.

The Chairman: Bless me! But I don't see—— Does the Crown wish to question this witness?

The Attorney-General: No, milord.

Mr. Mould: That concludes the case for the defence.

Milord, you will forgive, I hope, the unconventional methods I have been compelled to use in this case. My client is charged with 'pretending to tell fortunes by palmistry and otherwise with intent to deceive' under an Act of 1824. Only a hundred years before, in 1716, a woman and her child were hanged for witchcraft. Anyone in that century who had claimed to produce from a small box the voice of a woman singing 180 miles away would certainly have been hanged as well. Now we know better. But fragments of the old ignorance remain embedded in our laws: and with one such, I submit, we have to deal to-day. Our ancestors suspected and shrank from any person who did anything which they could not understand: for the conclusion was that the person was possessed by, or falsely claimed to possess, some supernatural power. We know

now that many good things are done by mortal men which
the rest of us are quite unable to do, explain, or even
understand. How fantastic, how unbelievable, it is that a
simple peasant with a forked hazel twig should be able to
detect the presence of water, or minerals, under the
ground! Yet this piece of wizardry is now so well accepted
that my learned friend the Attorney-General did not think
it worth while to cross-examine the witness Mole. Our
fathers frowned, our law still frowns, on any claim to predict the future—especially if the prediction is said to de-
pend upon the heavenly bodies.

The Judge: You mean all that stuff about being 'born
under Libra', with Venus in the ascendant, and so forth?
It decides your character, they say.

Mr. Mould: Yes, milord.

The Judge: My gardener says you should always sow
under a waxing moon. The full moon pulls the things out,
he says, and you get a better quality.

Mr. Mould: Something of the sort, I believe, is now being
taught in certain agricultural colleges.

The Judge: Is it indeed? Well, perhaps, the astrologers
are not so far out. Bulbs and babies—much the same thing,
I dare say. .

Mr. Mould: Who knows, milord? Then there are the
tides. Every year the Admiralty publishes elaborate tables
predicting the height and the time of the tides at every port
in the Kingdom, and these tables are founded on the movements of the sun and moon.[1] Then there are the weather
reports——

The Chairman: The law distinguishes, does it not, Mr.
Mould, between predictions of a general character and
predictions concerning the future of an individual? You
may say, 'There will be war next year', but not 'Colonel X.,
you will go to war in January.'

Mr. Mould: The predictions I have mentioned, milord,

[1] Lord Mildew said in *Orient Line* v. *Port of London Authority* (1913): 'I never
believed that the moon had anything to do with it.'

are highly selective and particular—the weather in the Hebrides, the Isle of Wight, the Dogger Bank, and so forth. The tides at Southampton, the tides at Harwich. Venus will be in such-and-such a place at 12 noon. If it is lawful to predict the future of a particular planet——

The Chairman: Venus pays no fees—that is the difference. What have you to say about palmistry?

Mr. Mould: Palmistry, milord, is said to have existed in China three thousand years before Christ, and is lawfully practised over vast areas of the earth to-day. The hand, the constant tool of man, could hardly fail to receive important imprints. The hand of the sailor, the clerk, the housewife (in these days), can be recognized by the amateur observer.

The Chairman: They say you can tell a male frog by his thumb.

Mr. Mould: If your Lordship pleases. To the expert, of course, the hand reveals mysteries which are beyond us, like those of radio and water-divining and astronomy. But my client, as he has said, does not rely on the palms only. He uses also all those other indications of character which help my learned friend to sum up a witness so successfully. On these he founds an estimate, a chart of behaviour, probable conduct in a probable future, so far as he can forecast it. 'Forecast' is the word he uses to his clients: and, like the weather-men, he admits that he may be wrong. But he pleads not guilty to the charge of 'pretending to tell fortunes'. Within the limits I have named, he says that he can and does tell fortunes—and is proud of it. In the light of what we have seen and heard to-day, can any of you be sure that that is a baseless claim?

The Attorney-General made a long speech. But the Doctor was acquitted.

31 October, 1951

NOTE—But see *Rex* v. *Oates* (1950), 2 A.C., a test-case, where a 'tipster' was charged as a 'rogue and vagabond' for 'napping' a horse called *Mameluke* to win the 3.30 at Sandown Park (a 'nap' meaning, according to the Crown, 'I predict with certainty that *Mameluke* will win'). The magistrates convicted on the ground that the prediction was not 'general', but referred to an 'individual'. Moreover, the accused, in support of his prognostication, mentioned the hocks and other portions of *Mameluke*'s anatomy, which, said the justices, put the affair in the domain of 'palmistry'. On appeal, Quarter Sessions confirmed the conviction. *Held*, in the Court of Appeal, (Wedderburn L. J. dissenting) that a horse, though an 'individual', was not a man, and that his movements, as those of a star, might freely be predicted by anyone. The conviction was quashed. Wedderburn L. J. said: 'The point is not the subject, but the object, of the prophecy. Money passed. The prediction was erroneous. I can perceive small difference between saying "I see by your hand, Mrs. X., that you will be happy next year," and saying "I see by his hocks that the horse *Mameluke* will win to-day." Of the two assertions the second seems to me to be the more anti-social and difficult to justify.'

(3) INTEGRATED PRESS *v.* THE POSTMASTER-GENERAL

WHAT IS A NEWSPAPER?

(Before Mr. Justice Codd)

SITTING in the Vacation Court, his Lordship to-day gave judgment in *The Swim Girl* case. He said:

This is an unusual action. In form it is an application to make absolute a rule *nisi* vaguely in the nature of the old *mandamus* calling upon the Postmaster-General and the Newspaper Registry Office at Somerset House to show cause why they should not register *The Sunday Sensation* as a newspaper.

In these days, when so much is heard about the 'Freedom of the Press', it is as well to remember that the proprietors and publishers of newspapers are still compelled to register (under the Newspaper Libel and Registration Act, 1881), though not, as in the first half of the reign of Queen Victoria, to deposit a sum of money when they do so. Further, since a newspaper counts as a 'book', a copy (sometimes two) must be sent to the British Museum, the Bodleian Library and other statutory libraries, where they are received, no doubt, with ill-concealed delight by the librarians.

In return they enjoy certain special advantages. A newspaper 'registered at the General Post Office' may be despatched through the post at lower rates than ordinary communications or even 'printed papers'. Further (though this, I think, is not a statutory privilege), they are allowed to market their wares in the streets, through stationary or itinerant salesmen, and to advertise them by the making of loud cries, in a manner which would not be permitted to any other trade, except at a recognised market. It is odd, by the way, that our Parliament and people should take so strong an objection to the quiet negotiation of bets in a public street when they do not mind the loud selling of sensations, disasters and scandals in the same street.[1]

Now, for many years *The Sunday Sensation* has been registered as a newspaper both by Somerset House and the General Post Office. In the present year both have refused to do so on the sole and simple ground that *The Sunday Sensation* (with which is now incorporated *The Swim Girl*) is no longer a newspaper.

The proprietors reply, with indignation and surprise, (a) that their publication *is* a newspaper, and (b) that that question (whatever the correct answer) does not concern the two offices named, whose simple duty it is to register upon demand.

Let us consider the second point first. No doubt in the past the registration of *The Sunday Sensation*, as of *The Sunday Times*, has in fact been almost automatic. But is there any necessity or justification in law for saying that it must be automatic? I cannot think so. Suppose, for example, that someone were to put forward as a 'newspaper' a publication which consisted entirely of extracts from the Bible on the one hand, or of obscene pictures on the other. For different reasons both would be illegal. No one, surely, would suggest that either Somerset House or the Post Office was bound to register such sheets as newspapers simply because the proprietors gave to them that honourable name. It follows that registration is not a matter of right but of fact or reason, and that the authorities have a power to say, in certain cases, what is and what is not a newspaper. The two cases posited are, admittedly, extremes, but they indicate the kind of reasoning which should be applied to all cases on the wrong side of the borderline, and the task of determining where that borderline lies is very familiar to

[1] And see *Sabatini* v. *Sale*, where an organ-grinder, having been 'warned off' for annoyance, complained that his nerves were lacerated by the yelling of a news-vendor. The case was dismissed as frivolous.

our courts of law and, in this affair, is by no means uncongenial to me.

I turn, then, to the question of fact. Assuming that some publications can rightly be described and registered as newspapers, and some cannot, in which class ought the King's Courts to place *The Sunday Sensation* (and *Swim Girl*)?

'News' is a wide and general term. *The Oxford English Dictionary* offers the following description (heading 2): 'TIDINGS: the report or account of recent events or occurrences, brought or coming to one as new information: new occurrences as a subject of report or talk.' It may include events of every kind and degree of importance, from the declaration of a war to the termination of a marriage. It may be of cosmic, continental, national, local or merely professional interest. The information that a new type of potato-chipper has been perfected is not less 'news' because it is exciting only to the readers of *The Fish Friers' Gazette*. But if, say, seventy per cent. not of one but of every issue of that paper were occupied by photographs of potato-chippers the question would arise whether *The Fish Friers' Gazette* had not ceased to be a newspaper in the proper sense and was now a mere circulating photograph album.

What applies to potato-chippers may be thought to apply with at least equal force to swim-girls. Let it be remarked at once that this Court has no objection to photographs of young ladies in bathing-dresses, as such. On the contrary, the Court enjoys them as much as ever. How about you, Sir Roger?

Sir Roger Wheedle, K.C.: Milord, I take *The Times*.

The Judge: How about Sundays?

Sir Roger: The Sunday Times, milord; and I try to keep up with the *Economist* and the *Bilious Weekly*.

The Judge: Well, well. Nor is the Court much impressed by the contention that the frequent contemplation of young ladies in bathing-dresses must tend to the moral corruption of the community. On the contrary, these ubiquitous exhibitions have so diminished what was left of the mystery of womanhood that they might easily be condemned upon another ground of public policy, in that they tended to destroy the natural fascination of the female, so that the attention of the male population was diverted from thoughts of marriage to cricket, darts, motor-bicycling and other occupations which do nothing to arrest the decline of the population. But the Court expresses no opinion on that. And, apart from that, the photographs appear to be socially beneficial—at all events they are beneficial to the Court. For at least the young ladies are radiantly happy, which is more than can be said of most of those whose doings are recorded in the papers. And whether they are poised upon a rock or diving-board, bounding into the ocean, or coyly teasing their companions in the water, it is evident that they are healthy and it is assumed that they possess or will acquire some skill in swimming. All this must surely provide a useful example to other young persons, and, in a country so much dependent on mastery of the sea, might even prove valuable for the defence of our shores.

But that is not the point in issue. The evidence, as I have already hinted, is that in the summer months some seventy per cent. of the space of *The Sunday Sensation* (and *Swim Girl*) is filled with blithe young ladies in similar but scanty costumes. Even in the winter the proportion does not fall by as much as might be expected, for swimming still continues in swimming-baths and tropical waters, and the new models for next year's costumes must of course be exhibited for the judgment of the public. All this may be admirable in its way: but, in any strict sense, in such proportions, can it be said to be 'news'?

It would be fair at this point to turn to the small remainder of the paper, for here perhaps may be found, though in miniature, the essential elements of a newspaper. What do we find? One witness unkindly said that the remainder of the paper consisted entirely of headlines and hysteria. The headlines are abnormally large (indeed, where it is thought necessary to employ headline-type an inch in depth to announce that a lady has been divorced, one wonders what would be required for the outbreak of a world war). But the messages below the headlines are printed in type abnormally small. There is evident here not merely a deficient sense of proportion but, I should say, an elementary technical blunder. For it is the purpose of the headline to attract attention to the full story below—it is, as it were, the label on the meat. But when the labels are so large and loud and numerous as here the general effect in the end must be distracting. The eye is dutifully prepared to accept the flaring invitation to the bigamy at Surbiton when it is diverted by another beacon, equally brilliant and alarming, to the latest banned book. But in the next column or page another scandal, not less distressing, again seduces the attention. And in each case the actual story is printed in type so small and difficult to read that any distraction is doubly powerful.

However, once more, that is not the question before the Court. Do the 'events and occurrences' thus presented, wisely or not, constitute news in such a proportion as to make the paper a newspaper? The weight of the evidence is against that view. No one has suggested that every newspaper should give an equally full and laborious account of all the major events and movements of the day, the work of Governments and Parliaments, the situation and relations of foreign governments, the achievements of art, literature and the sciences; nor, on the other hand, that any paper should be bound to ignore those painful but enjoyable stories of misfortune, scandal and corruption which are so large a part of the tale of mankind. But it was powerfully urged that a habitual concentration upon the latter, coupled with a habitual exclusion of the former, would raise a presumption so strong as to shift the onus of proof on to the complainant in these proceedings. It was said also by counsel for the Crown that, allowing for the many and desirable differences in the class and character of newspapers, every newspaper claiming privileges as such ought at least to offer to its readers some small scrap of authentic information on the most important of the events of the day, and, if possible, some modicum of helpful comment or guidance.

The head of an advertising firm said bluntly that in his opinion *The Sunday Sensation* (and *Swim Girl*) provided no such thing. That suited him; and that was why he used the paper. There were some good articles in it, but nothing you could call news. There were no leading articles at all. That was grand.

This piece of evidence, coming from one who had no axe to grind (whatever that may mean), was for me the last link in a solid and impressive chain. If I find for the Crown in this case the familiar cry will, no doubt, be heard that the liberties of the Press so hardly contested and finally won in the last century are being whittled away. That cry will here be wholly inappropriate. In the first place the liberties of the Press were won for the kind of Press that then existed, for organs of thought, of character and refinement. Most of our great papers deserve that description to-day; and one might censure the black sheep without casting a single shadow upon them. But, in the second place, there is no question here of tampering with anyone's liberties. The proprietors of this paper will still be at liberty to print and disperse their entertaining album of photographs and anecdotes, but they will not be permitted to call it a newspaper and so to enjoy the privileges attached to that name by the Crown and Parliament. I find for the Crown. The rule is discharged.

10 August, 1938

NOTE—See also *Cute Publications* v. *Rumble* (1951), 2 A.C., where it was held that registration had been rightfully refused to the *Daily Delight* on the ground that more than 50 per cent. of its space was given to 'comic strips', advice on football pools and betting, and pictures of attractive women. 'To look at a page of "comic strips",' said Rutt L. J., 'is to despair of Progress. They take us back to an age when man could only express himself by drawing crude pictures of animals on the walls of caves, or making marks in the sand or snow. It may be that this is the kind of entertainment the people desire and deserve, but clearly it does not merit the special privileges reserved for a "newspaper". We were told that a strip called "Jane" won the Election of 1945. The Court remains unimpressed.'

(4) GREENWICH WOMEN'S ROWING CLUB v. HADDOCK

WHAT IS A ROWING BOAT?

A POINT of high importance to mariners was discussed, if not decided, in the Admiralty Court to-day. The action arose out of a collision between a ladies' eight and a motor-boat navigated by Mr. Albert Haddock.

After a long learned argument the President, Sir Thomas Bowline, said:

This case raises a question which, so far as I know, has never come before a British court of law, and, but for the inconsiderate and loathsome conduct of the defendant, would not have troubled us now. But here it is, and it must be considered.

The question, simply put, is: 'What is a rowing boat?' What is the status of a rowing boat in the grand hierarchy of vessels known to the law; and what, in particular, are the duties of those who navigate or approach such a vessel in the open sea or upon tidal waters? (There is no doubt, by the way, that before the law a rowing boat is a 'vessel', however much the description may shock the practical mariner.)

Now, in the Regulations for the Prevention of Collisions at Sea, one of the most celebrated, sound and vital codes of conduct in the English tongue, the relations and the duties (it would be wrong to say 'rights') of the various types of vessel are very clearly defined for almost every conceivable situation.

'A steam vessel', for example, 'shall keep out of the way of a sailing vessel' where there is risk of collision (Article 20): and a steam vessel 'shall include any vessel propelled by machinery.' A sailing vessel which is close-hauled on the port tack shall keep out of the way of a sailing vessel which is close-hauled on the starboard tack (Article 17). Sailing vessels under way shall keep out of the way of fishing vessels (Article 26). Other regulations direct what lights shall be carried by trawlers, pilot boats, and even rowing boats (Article 7).

In the Port of London River Bye-laws, which are additional to but not inconsistent with the General Regulations, there are special rules concerning lighters, barges, dredgers, vessels towing and towed, and so forth. Each class has its appointed signs and duties for all occasions, and under the Steering and Sailing Rules the master of any steam or sailing vessel who sights another knows at once (if he knows his business) which of the two has a duty to 'keep out of the way of' the other, if necessary by altering course, and which, on the other hand, should maintain her course and speed. But he does *not*, from the Rules at least, know what he ought to do if he sights a rowing boat 'approaching him so as to involve risk of collision': for except in the section governing lights, there is no mention of rowing boats, either in the International Regulations or in the Port of London River Bye-laws.

This singular omission, especially in a river which is the scene of so much oarsmanship, has long been the cause of wonder and dispute among the mariners: but good sense has hitherto kept the discussion out of the courts. It will be convenient now to consider the perverse behaviour by which the defendant has brought it here to-day.

The defendant, while navigating down Blackwall Reach on the ebb, on or about the Prime Meridian, saw a vessel rowed by eight ladies on his port bow. She was shaping a south-easterly course obliquely across the river, at about 6 knots, and was likely (if both vessels held on) to cross his bows at a short distance or to collide with him. Both vessels did hold on; there was a collision; the ladies were thrown into the water, and were extricated, one by one, by the defendant, a process which, he said in evidence, he greatly enjoyed. This deplorable comment, unfortunately, has no juridical significance, and the Court must reluctantly ignore it—that is, until the question of costs comes up.

The rowing club sued Mr. Haddock for negligent navigation causing the loss of their boat and some sickness among her crew. Mr. Haddock put in the impudent defence that a rowing boat counted as a steam vessel, and that in the circumstances the ladies ought to have kept out of his way according to Article 19 of the Regulations. It is perfectly true that if the eight had been in fact a steam vessel it would have been her duty to stop or alter course so as to avoid a collision, according to the old mnemonic lines:

> *If to your starboard red appear*
> *It is your duty to keep clear.*

But *is* a rowing boat a steam vessel within the meaning of the Regulations? As I have said, they give us no clear guidance in such a case. It is difficult to accept the contention of defendant's counsel, ably though it was argued, that an eight-oared rowing boat, at least, is 'a vessel propelled by machinery'.[1] The plaintiffs, on the other hand, say that a rowing boat counts as a sailing vessel, and therefore the defendant had an absolute duty to keep out of the way. One of the defendant's witnesses, a very ancient mariner, went even farther than the defendant. He said that there was a very good reason why the rowing boat was not mentioned in the steering regulations; that morally the rowing boat did not exist, and practically the honest mariner was entitled to behave as if it were not there. It was a nuisance; it was a something nuisance; and, like the cat or dog, must look out for itself.

I was not impressed by any of these opinions: and in the absence of precise guidance I must look to the principles

[1] But, with respect to the learned President, there is much to be said for it. *The Oxford English Dictionary*, under heading 5 of 'Machine' gives: '(*In Mechanics*) Any instrument employed to transmit force or to modify its application. *Simple Machine*: one in which there is no combination of parts, e.g. a lever....' A quotation follows from D. Argill, *Reign Law*, ii (ed. 4), 90: 'A man's arm is a machine' (1866). Is not an eight-oared boat a vessel propelled by eight 'simple machines'? See, *passim*, in the sporting sheets: 'The Cambridge boat moved like a machine.' Consider, too, the 'bathing-machine' which was drawn by a horse.

upon which all these Regulations are founded. Why is it that the steam vessel, however mighty, must give way, must alter course, must stop her engines, must go astern, in order to avoid a collision with a sailing vessel, however small? Because the steam vessel has the greater power and ease of manœuvre. She can turn aside (at least in the open seas, though not in the Thames) without effort or danger, where the sailing ship, at grips with wind and tide, can not. Might has its duties as well as its privileges, we are fond of saying: and this Regulation is one of the finest applications of it to be found in our written codes of conduct.

Now, if this be the principle, how is it to be applied to the present facts? How does an eight-oared boat, in power and progress, compare in fact with Mr. Haddock's motor vessel? On this point the defendant's evidence was clear, and I accept it. He says that his vessel is modestly equipped with two 9-horse-power engines and, being at least six tons (he does not seem to know exactly what his tonnage is), proceeds at most at about nine knots (with a good tide under him). Eight-oared boats, he says, whether driven by men or women, go past him with the utmost ease; and he reminded the Court that the University Boat Race, in a bad year, is rowed and won at the rate of about 12·75 land miles per hour. On these facts it seems impossible to say that the eight-oared boat (male or female) is a kind of Cinderella, requiring special privileges. She has more power than Mr. Haddock, not less; she draws very little water; she is steered by a skilled coxswain. In many situations she might well have more ease and power of manœuvre than Mr. Haddock's more solid and cumbrous craft; and in fact, in the present situation, there is no doubt that by stopping or altering course she could without difficulty have avoided the collision. All these considerations inclined me strongly to the view that Mr. Haddock ought to succeed.

But then, as counsel for the plaintiffs very properly reminded me, an eight-oared boat is not the only class of vessel 'under oars'. There is, for example, especially in

London River, the great lighter, driving or drifting on the tide, and arduously steered by a single man with a single monstrous sweep. Here, it is obvious, Mr. Haddock, though he has eighteen horses only at his command, has the greater power of manœuvre and must, at his peril, keep out of the way.

Where are we, then? If I found my general rule upon the nature of the eight-oared boat it must prove inapplicable to the lighter 'under oars', and *vice versa*; and between the two lies the ordinary small boat, propelled by oars or sculls, which, according to circumstances, may or may not be easily manœuvred. It is now, perhaps, a little more clear why the authors of the Regulations said nothing about vessels under oars. It was too much for them.

Like them, I decline to pronounce any general answer to the problem. Practically, on the facts of the case, I think that Mr. Haddock should succeed. But, morally speaking, I should be reluctant indeed to come down on the side of this ungallant mariner and contumacious litigant. Fortunately, the Regulations provide me with an honourable exit from this dilemma. I refer to Article 27. It is one of the merits of this austere code that it confers no rights upon anyone—only duties. Even the mariner whose duty it is in a given situation to maintain his course and speed, the other vessel giving way, is not thereby relieved of responsibility. For Article 27 ingeniously and admirably provides that he may still be wrong. That Article is headed 'SPECIAL CIRCUMSTANCES', and says:

> 'In obeying and construing these Rules, due regard shall be had to all dangers of navigation and collision, and to any special circumstances which may render a departure from the above Rules necessary in order to avoid immediate danger.'

That Article, in my judgment, is applicable in the present case, even assuming, as I do not in terms assume, that the plaintiffs were, in the first instance, at fault. I find therefore that Mr. Haddock was possibly right but practically wrong. Judgment, and every kind of costs, for the plaintiffs.

6 November, 1940

NOTE—It is now the general opinion among sea-faring men that this case was wrongly decided. For one thing, under the Port of London Regulations, a vessel crossing the river, even a ferry, should keep out of the way of a vessel passing up or down the river. The ladies' boat was *crossing the river*. But this point does not appear to have been taken. The ladies (see the print in the National Maritime Museum) were attractive, and attended the trial.

(5) HADDOCK v. SILKWORM

Books into Bombs

Mr. Justice Mouse, sitting without a jury, to-day gave judgment in this libel action. He said:

This is a suit for damages for defamation brought by Mr. Albert Haddock, an author, against Mr. Andrew Silkworm, head of the well-known multiple stores.

The circumstances of the complaint are unusual. The defendants prominently exhibited a book by the plaintiff in the window of one of their stores in one of the principal streets of the Metropolis, the Strand. In the ordinary way most authors would be glad and grateful to have the attention of the public drawn to their works in such a place and manner. But the window in question was devoted to a praiseworthy display in aid of a 'Salvage Drive' at that time being conducted by the Ministry of Supply. It contained a great number of old tooth-paste containers and milk-bottle tops, a pile of rags, a heap of waste paper, and other objects designed to show the people how they can contribute to the Allied cause by salving and surrendering any waste matter suitable for the making of munitions of war. And in the middle of the window were placed five or six books as a kind of centre-piece to the entire display. One of these books was by George Eliot, another by Lord Lytton, one by Mr. André Maurois, one by an eighteenth-century philosopher, and two by Mr. Haddock and another modern author.

Not far off, in Trafalgar Square, the centre of the 'Salvage-Drive', bands were playing, flags flying, and public men from time to time were making speeches. Leaflets were distributed explaining in some detail the kind of scrap and waste matter the good citizens should surrender, to what processes it would be subjected, and what sort of munitions of war it would make or help to make. Four milk-bottle tops, he was told, will make one cartridge-cap plug. Three comic papers make two 25-pounder shell cups. One daily newspaper makes three 25-pounder shell cups. And six old books make one mortar-shell carrier.

Waste paper, the leaflet continues—and it seems clear that old books surrendered as salvage fall into the category of waste paper—is sent to the pulping-mills, where it is thrown into a stream of hot water which carries it to the breaker-beater. This machine contains revolving knives which shred the paper and reduce it to a coarse brown pulp with a consistency like that of pease-soup.

Sir Ambrose Wett: Milord, with great respect, in fairness to my clients, the consistency, in fact, is described as being like that of *porridge*.

The Judge: Thank you, Sir Ambrose. I beg your pardon. The pulp then passes on to the sand-trap channels, where dirt and grit are deposited—and so on.

Now, it will be at once conceded by any sensitive mind that an author is likely to feel pain at the thought of the children of his brain being torn to pieces with revolving knives and reduced to a coarse brown pulp with a consistency like that of porridge. The assurance, however, that six of his books will go to the manufacture of one mortar-shell carrier and so contribute to the destruction of tyrants must be some comfort to any patriotic writer. Indeed, to do him justice, the plaintiff told the Court that, if that were all, he would no more shrink from a necessary sacrifice than the rest of his gallant fellow-countrymen.

Question 1,453: Would it be fair to say that at the crisis in your country's fortunes, when all classes are making sacrifices, you begrudge your books to the national defences?

Witness: No, Sir Ambrose. If the supply of mortar-shell carriers should ever fall short of the nation's requirements, I would willingly sit down and write more books to make good the deficiency.

The Court commended him.

But that, he says—and there is a good deal of evidence to support him—is not quite all. There seems to be some confusion of purpose among His Majesty's Departments in the matter of books. The plaintiff told the Court that he himself has more than once been desired by persons in authority to make appeals to the public to give up books, not for the pulping-machine but for the entertainment and refreshment of our soldiers and sailors in distant parts; and special arrangements were made for the collection and distribution of such books. The supply of new books is sharply limited by the shortage of paper, and therefore any old book of good quality acquires a new importance. A simultaneous injunction to throw all old books into the dust-bin with the tooth-paste containers does suggest, at first sight, the presence of divided counsels among those who govern us, a suggestion which must always be wounding to the loyal subject. And, as the plaintiff observed, if the needs of the nation demand the general destruction of old books it would surely be administratively simpler to requisition public libraries and second-hand bookshops *en bloc*. It is believed, for example, that there are many volumes at such institutions as the Bodleian Library and the British Museum whose 'practical' value would be questioned by many.

We were glad, therefore, to hear the evidence of an official of the Ministry of Supply. He said that the policy of the salvage authorities was not, in fact, the wholesale destruction of books. The books received are 'sorted out' and those considered suitable are sent to the fighting forces and the Mercantile Marine. This process is called Book Recovery. Who makes the selection of books to survive and upon what grounds, or what proportion of the books surrendered go to the troops and what to the porridge-makers was by no means clear. Some may think that a somewhat sinister form of Government censorship of thought has come into being; for what man is fitted to say what books are 'suitable' for his fellow-men? And is there any reason to suppose that persons skilled in the general business of salvage have any special aptitude for literary criticism?

Some may be of a narrow way of thought and condemn to the breaker-beater works of lively fancy like the plaintiff's: others, appointed to their posts without due examination of character, may despatch to our innocent fighting men works which none of us would care to see them enjoy.

But these questions, say the plaintiff's counsel, are only the background of his case. For whether or not the Ministry's policy of Book Recovery be wisely conceived and carried out, *there is no mention of it in the defendants' window*. The books, including the plaintiff's, are not displayed there as examples of the kind of work which the citizen, however much he prizes them, should cheerfully surrender for the comfort of the fighting men. At least, if that is in the mind of the defendants, it nowhere appears. They are displayed in the company of old rags and tooth-paste containers; they are displayed, according to him, as *ejusdem generis* with such articles: and the message, for any ordinary and reasonable citizen, must be that the plaintiff's book is fit only to be torn to pieces and converted into a brown porridge. The defendants, while they deny the innuendo, say that it is a compliment to any author in time of war to suggest that a book of his may make the sixth part of a mortar-shell container. The plaintiff replies that though that might be held a compliment by those who provided the paper and the binding, it would not add anything to his reputation as a writer. On the whole I think that he has sustained this part of his case. If the defendants mean to say: 'This is the sort of book you should give to the troops' they should say so clearly. What they have said, if they have said anything, is: 'This book is no better than an old tooth-paste container.'

But then, I have to ask myself, have they, in effect, said anything? The plaintiff's doctrine of *ejusdem generis* would carry us rather far. Many small traders sell books whose main business is not the selling of books, stationers, and so forth: and this must be 'good', I presume, 'for trade'. I asked the plaintiff:

Question 2,001: Would you object to seeing your books exposed for sale with note-paper, blotting-paper, ink-stands, and typewriters?

Witness: No, milord. The more the merrier.

Question 2,002: Then, to take, perhaps, a fanciful case: suppose that a greengrocer chose to sell books, and exhibited your works for sale in the same window as his fruit. Would you complain that this was as much as to say that your books were no better than a cabbage or vegetable marrow?

Witness: No, milord, I suppose not.

On that frank answer, I am afraid, the plaintiff's case must be held to have foundered: and I find for the defendants. If it be asked why I spent so much time on the first part of the case, the answer is that I enjoyed it.

30 June, 1943

(6) HADDOCK v. MOLE

The Case of the Orange Globes

Mr. Justice Codd to-day delivered a considered judgment in the Orange Globes Case.

His Lordship said:

The plaintiff in this enthralling dispute is a Mr. Albert Haddock, who, although a mariner, is solicitous for the safety of the pedestrian ashore. He has assured the Court that he brings this action as a 'test' case for the guidance of all road-users, and does not in fact desire to receive for his own benefit the very substantial sum of damages which has been delicately suggested by his counsel. This somewhat improbable story is no concern of the Court, whose only business is to ascertain the truth of the facts in dispute and the law, if any, which applies to them.

The plaintiff, whose evidence, though unconventionally delivered, I take to be trustworthy, was crossing the Strand at one of the official 'pedestrian crossings' instituted by Regulations made under the Road Traffic Act, 1934. These crossings were the invention of a Minister of Transport who, after many years of increasing slaughter on the roads, formed the new and startling opinion that the safety and comfort of pedestrians were of at least equal importance as the impatience of those who were fortunate enough to travel by car: and, though it is not for the Court to look behind an Act of Parliament to any personality, we were informed that they will always be gratefully associated with the name of a Mr. Hore-Belisha.

Now, the duty of any driver approaching such a crossing is defined in the Regulations as follows: 'He shall, *unless* he can see that there is no foot-passenger there, proceed at such a speed as to be able, if necessary, to stop before reaching such crossing.' So that at these crossings the visible foot-passenger, at least, has a statutory right to life and limb.

But, for the Regulations to be effective, it was necessary that the crossing as well as the foot-passenger should be distinguishable by the motor-driver. For at other points, it is generally understood, the motorist is entitled to mow the foot-passenger down in the usual way. Therefore, they were marked by two rows of studs on the carriage-way, and, at each end, by a post painted alternately in black and white and surmounted by a globe of a distinctive orange colour, reminding the romantic of a harvest moon.

Unfortunately, in the years 1940 and 1941, many of these orange globes were destroyed by enemy action: others were removed or shattered by the impulsive soldiery of other lands, or by that type of indigenous citizen which delights to place unwanted perambulators in the emergency water-supply tanks thoughtfully provided against the burning of the capital.

It was by such a crossing, clearly indicated, that is, by the posts and the studs but not by orange globes, that Mr. Haddock lawfully elected to cross the Strand. He used, he assured the Court, all due consideration towards the drivers of motors, who in such a thoroughfare are not without anxieties of their own. With many other pedestrians, he patiently permitted about thirty vehicles to rush by, and when at last he stepped on to the carriage-way, raising his hand by way of additional warning, the nearest vehicles, he says, were not less than seventy-five yards away. Two of them bore on notwithstanding, the drivers laughing heartily, and at such a speed that the plaintiff was compelled to retreat in haste and ignominy to the pavement. A little later he made a second attempt, again, he says, with all due caution and consideration. This time the defendant was at the wheel of the leading vehicle; and he too continued on his course without slackening speed. Mr. Haddock, fortunately, was able to preserve his life, and to gain the 'refuge' by a sudden swift leap upward and forward, 'in the manner', to use his own vivid phrase, 'of an elderly chamois'. But life is not everything, and the exceptional effort severely aggravated a leg injury sustained elsewhere, which otherwise might not have troubled him much.

What was the trouble, Mr. Haddock? You used a long word I never met before.

Mr. Haddock: My Lord, I tore the gastrocnemious muscle, at the back of the calf.

The Judge: Just so. Mr. Haddock's own impression, he said, was 'that the car passed underneath him', possibly an exaggeration. It is clear at least that for the safety of the plaintiff, lawfully 'there', it was necessary for the defendant to stop before he reached the crossing, and that he did not stop, and, moreover, that he was unable to stop, according to the Regulations.

But, says Mr. Haddock, the defendant heaped insult upon injury; for as he whizzed away he shouted back '*Can't you see there ain't no orange balls?*'

This impudent plea he actually maintained, though with less and less conviction, at the hearing of the action. The plea is that the absence of the orange globes deprives the Regulation of effect and the crossing of consideration. But there are still the studs and the black-and-white posts. And even if such a suggestion had any practical or ethical validity, it would not, clearly, assist a driver who recognizes the posts sufficiently to remark that they support no orange globes.

Further, unfortunately for the defendant, the sly excuse has been anticipated by those in authority, and the Regulations have been so amended as to make it plain that the driver's duties are the same whether orange globes are visible or not. The defendant says that he did not know of that amendment; but he has been driving for a very long time, and it is his duty, at his peril, to know the law. None the less, it is for consideration whether, for the benefit of impetuous drivers and their victims, some additional sign, as prominent as the orange globe though less expensive, should not soon be provided at these crossings.

For they are valuable; they should be used by the walker,

and respected by the driver. And when I say 'respected', I mean respected fully, in letter and in spirit. The walker's right at these crossings is not a mere right to escape with his life, after a moment of fear, by leaping into the air 'like an elderly chamois' or mountain goat. It is a right to proceed across the road without anxiety at a normal pace, or even, if he be infirm or elderly, at a slow pace; and if motor-cars are compelled thereby to go slow or even stop, so much the better. The more cars stopped or slowed the less work for the doctor and the undertaker. That is the sad and sobering fact. On every day of 1943 three hundred and thirty-five persons were killed or injured on the roads of England and Wales. For the month of December the figure was 394. Only 850 fewer persons were killed in 1943 than in 1938, when the motor-vehicles were immensely more numerous. There is, I know, a notion current that those who dart about at high speed are exhibiting their loyalty to the cause of the United Nations and somehow assisting that cause to victory. This is not necessarily so; and very strong evidence will have to be produced in this Court before that easy assumption is accepted. The defendant must pay the plaintiff £5,000 damages; and in my opinion he should be executed. For reasons, however, which are hidden from the Court, the Legislature is more concerned for his life than he is for others.

16 February, 1944

NOTE—See also Mr. Haddock's verse-translation of paragraph 37 of the Highway Code:

Pedestrian Crossings

37. 'Look out for pedestrian crossings. Learn and observe the Regulations relating to them. (*See* p. 28.)'

> Here are the beacons, here the studded ground
> Where bodies must on no account be found.
> Our duties here the Traffic Laws define:
> You should be 'stoppable' before the line;
> But rare indeed, I much regret to say,
> The motor-drivers who approach that way.

Call us 'jay-walkers' if we rove elsewhere:
But use us kindly if we walk with care.
Can you expect a chap to play the game
If he is chased and chivvied just the same?
It's not enough, sir, not to do us harm:
We have a right to cross without alarm.
So do not whizz an inch behind my back;
For all you know I'll have a heart-attack.
We, for our part, must make our purpose clear,
Not loiter on the studs, not stop to jeer.
If both of us have gumption and goodwill
The population will be higher still.

(7) HADDOCK *v.* TOMKINS AND ISAAC

WHAT IS A REACTIONARY?

MR. JUSTICE ROTE, summing up to the jury in this case, said:

This action for defamation is brought by Mr. Albert Haddock, a Member of Parliament, against the editor of a journal called the *Tumbril* and a writer who contributes to that paper over the pseudonym of 'Culex'.[1] As the hearing of the case proceeded the fact emerged that both the defendants were Members of Parliament also, and that the true name of Culex was Isaac—the Member for Bottlehithe. It might well be thought, therefore, that the dispute could have been settled at less expense in the Chamber, or even the Smoking-room, of the House of Commons, by one of those brisk and lively exchanges of abuse which clear the air so quickly and delight the populace so much. The plaintiff, however, has an answer to that, which I consider it is my duty to impress upon the jury. He says that if the second defendant, the writer 'Culex', who, as he says, attacked him, had used his proper name he, Mr. Haddock, would not have considered this action at law necessary or justifiable. For, he says, it is an honourable tradition of the House of Commons that its Members, however much they may disagree with each other, or dislike each other, owe to each other certain decencies of behaviour. Any Member is entitled, within the rules of procedure and deportment, to say what he likes about another Member.[2] But that Member is entitled, and indeed expected, to make a reply if he has one. So highly valued is the right of reply that the courteous custom is for Member A to give notice to Member B that he intends to make an attack upon him in the House, so that B may have the opportunity to be in his

[1] A gnat.
[2] He must not 'make a personal charge' or 'impute motives'.

place and defend himself or his policy. And even when the attack is casual and unpremeditated Member B is still not without remedy. 'Suppose, for example,' the plaintiff said, 'that the defendant, speaking in debate, suggested in an unrehearsed parenthesis that I was an embezzler, a "Fascist", a vested interest, a rodent operative—or whatever might be the favourite insult of the moment. I could at once interrupt him and deny that I was an embezzler or a Fascist. Or I could bide my time and later, if I caught the Speaker's eye, I could answer the accuser in a speech. Failing that, if the charge were serious enough, I could ask for and obtain a special opportunity for a "personal explanation" in which I could assure the House that, however much I looked like a vested interest, I was not one in fact. Or, failing that, I could accost the defendant in the Smoking-room and say in a friendly manner, "Look here, old boy, what nonsense is this? You know perfectly well that I am not a rodent operative. Please do not say this again." Or I could approach him, less politely, in the corridor, and say "Sir, you are erroneous. If you do not apologize I shall knock your block off." None of these remedies, however, is open to me when I am attacked by a fellow Member writing an account of proceedings and personalities in Parliament under a false name: for the simple reason that I do not know who he is. For all I know, the gentleman for whom I am buying liquid refreshment in the Smoking-room is the same one who has just pseudonymously described me as an embezzler or vested interest. If I knew who the writer was I should be able to tell how much the accusation was prompted by prejudice or venom, and could expose in Parliament or in public the presence of these motives. Not knowing who he is, I have no remedy of a Parliamentary character, and outside Parliament I can only write to the journal: but my letter will not be displayed as prominently as the accusation, and at the end of my letter "Culex" in a slippery footnote will have the last word. This is not good enough: and therefore I have gone to law, chiefly to ascertain the real name of "Culex", and also to make a formal protest against the growing custom by which Members of Parliament, over high-sounding bogus Latin names,[1] criticize their fellow——' At this point I stopped the witness, for the Court has nothing to do with the somewhat complicated niceties of Parliamentary behaviour. I mention the matter only because it may be relevant to the question of damages, and in case you have been influenced by the suggestion that this is one of those actions which 'ought never to have been brought'. I do not think it is.

What the defendant 'Culex', or Isaac, wrote about the plaintiff was that he was 'a reactionary'. At the close of the plaintiff's case the defendant's counsel asked me to say that there was no case to go to the jury, on the ground that the word 'reactionary' was incapable of bearing a defamatory meaning. The dictionary is not of much assistance upon this point—'Reaction—retrograde tendency, especially in politics, whence "reactionary".' A 'retrograde tendency' can only mean a tendency to go back. Well, many wise and patriotic persons think that we should go back, after the war, to some form of League of Nations, to normal lighting in the streets, to Free Trade: but no one describes them as reactionaries. Russia shows a tendency to go back into Poland, and has done so for a long time: but all men know that she is the most 'progressive' of nations. That the inten-tion of the defendants is offensive there can be little doubt in the minds of any who heard their evidence or have read their writings: for 'the forces of reaction', 'reactionary government', and so on, occur in every paragraph, and they are invariably applied to persons or parties of whom they disapprove. But I have to inform you that intention is not the whole matter. The question is: Does the word tend to bring the plaintiff into hatred, ridicule or contempt? Will the ordinary reasonable man think the worse of him?

I had no doubt about my answer. This is one of many

[1] *Cato, Junius, Seneca, Flavus, Cicero, etc.*

expressions which, colourless and even meaningless at first, have been developed into recognized terms of abuse by sloppy writers, prejudiced thinkers and powerful evangelists. The ordinary reasonable man has been trained to shudder away from a 'reactionary' as he does from a 'vested interest', though he may have no clear notion of the nature of either.

I therefore directed that the case must proceed; and the question you now have to answer is: 'Is the plaintiff a "reactionary" in any sense, or not?'

The evidence of the defendants here becomes important. According to them, the main mark of a 'reactionary' is that he is opposed to progressive changes; and by the word progressive they mean changes which they themselves desire. It is necessary to emphasize the latter point, because some of the changes they advocate might almost be thought to have 'a retrograde tendency'. A reactionary, they said, would leave the House of Lords as it is. One of them would replace it by an elected Second Chamber; the other would abolish it and put nothing in its place. To adopt Single Chamber government, it may be remarked, would, without doubt, historically, be a retrograde step, moving back towards the most primitive stages of political life; but to this witness the change would be 'progressive'.

The plaintiff, on his own record and opinions, was clear and credible. He entered Parliament, he said, to advocate certain changes, in his view, 'progressive', a long list of which was given in his election address.[1] Most of these he

[1] The laws of divorce, drink, betting, libel, Sunday entertainments, income-tax, entertainment-tax, and much besides. And see the anecdote in Haddock's *My Life and Letters*:

'Three days after I made a speech against the Fascists my house was burgled. Or, rather, my study was burgled. No other room was touched, and nothing, I believe, was taken. Even an envelope full of Treasury notes was left. But all my files and drawers were emptied, and all my political papers scattered on the floor. I formed two theories about this felony. One was that it was a political burglar, seeking ammunition for blackmail. The other was that it was an ordinary respectable burglar who, for some queer reason of his own, began at the study. He pulled out the files and read in swift succession "Divorce—Adultery—Cruelty—Insanity — Connivance — Collusion — Conduct Conducing — Nullity — Drink—Betting—Adultery", cried, "What sort of place am I in?" and ran screaming from the house.'

had in fact advocated since his election, by speech or otherwise, some with success. He could hardly recall a single speech he had made in Parliament which had not been designed to produce a change of some kind or another. In nearly every instance the condition of things at which he aimed was one which had never existed in these islands before: so it could not be said that his proposals had a retrograde tendency; and therefore they must be progressive. He did not choose to confine himself to the particular matters which were dear to the hearts of the defendants; but there were quite enough people doing that; and in any case it was a free country. Finally, he said that he had just completed a detailed scheme for the renaming of the stars. Was that the action of a reactionary?

The jury found for the plaintiff, with damages of £10,000.

22 March, 1944

NOTE—This case had a powerful effect. The 'bogus Latin names' are now much less numerous: and most Members of Parliament who write critical accounts of Parliamentary debates now do so openly, and creditably, over their own names.

(8) FESTER *v.* THE KING; FESTER *v.* PHILPOTT, RORY AND COMPANY LTD.; FESTER *v.* PLATT

The 'Law of the Land'

(Before Mr. Justice Cheese)

His Lordship, giving judgment in these important proceedings to-day, said:

Mr. Ambrose Fester, the plaintiff in these three suits, which, for convenience, have been taken together, is at least to be congratulated on his pertinacity, and he is to be assured at once that he has the sympathy of the Court, though, as Lord Mildew said in *Glass against the Metropolitan Water Board*, 'Sympathy pays no costs'.

The facts are these. Mr. Fester, a patriotic citizen, 'invalided' out of the Army, was employed by Messrs. Philpott, Rory and Company as an inspector at their important factory. It is admitted that he was a good and skilful servant and received what some would call, insanely, a 'sizeable' salary.

A Mr. Rice, another inspector, but a Government official, and not a member of the firm, addressed to the firm a letter which Mr. Fester was asked to sign to show that he had read it.

The letter began thus: '*Recent circumstances have created a chronological coincidence of two correlated occurrences calling for immediate comment.*'

Except that the author of this communication is fond of the letter 'C' the Court can form no clear opinion of its significance. Mr. Foster, a keen follower, as he told us in the box, of the good Mr. Haddock, took, in his own words, a 'dim view' of it, and wrote to the Government inspector as follows:

'Sir—In reply to your letter regarding Wip Valves, I suggest that you omit the ridiculous blank phraseology and state what you wish to convey in plain English.'

The 'blank' represents an expression which, while not often used in drawing-rooms, even to-day, is familiar to all men with Service experience, is not blasphemous, or sexually indecent, and, in short, in my opinion, is no more than a vivid vulgarity.

Mr. Fester was then called before the general manager of his firm and invited to apologize to Inspector Rice. He refused. He was at once dismissed from his office.

Such is the reward, in the sphere of influence of Government Departments, of an independent mind and a respect for the English language.

Mr. Fester, however, was familiar with the long and, on the whole, honourable history of British justice. He knew that the first word is not always the last: and he appealed, in due form, to the local Appeal Board.

Now, under the Essential Works (General Provisions) Order, the purpose of which, the Court presumes, was to secure the highest possible efficiency in the factories and workshops of the nation in time of war, a man cannot, in effect, leave his employment without permission, and an employer, without permission, cannot summarily dismiss a man except for 'serious misconduct'.

I should mention in passing that the local Appeal Boards were at one time presided over by members of the legal profession, a wise arrangement, but we are informed that already, at the date of the proceedings in question, the Ministry of Labour had decided, and decreed, that no lawyer should sit on these tribunals. This is but one more illustration of a tendency and practice which must be deplored by all thinking men, the exclusion from affairs of justice of persons schooled in the arts and manners of justice. In passing, may I say, it surprises me that the Attorney-General, who appears for the Crown in this case, has been unable to use his persuasive powers to prevent or modify such arrangements.

Sir Anthony Slatt, K.C.: Milord, I have to obey orders, like others.

The Judge: Yes, but you are the head of the Bar: and the Ministry of Labour, I should have thought, would pay some attention to you as a trade union leader, if nothing else. However, all this, the Court supposes, is a sample of the fruits of 'the Century of the Common Man'. But, much as we admire within due limits the Common Man, and the Average Man, and the Man in the Street, and even that repellent figment of the jurist's imagination, the Reasonable Man, we own that in any medical or legal trouble we should rather commit ourselves to the care of a professional adviser than to any of these well-meaning but uninstructed amateurs.

In this case the worthy (but lay) chairman of the Appeal Board, and his colleagues, had to answer this question. Did the conduct of the plaintiff amount to 'serious misconduct'?

In the Order there is no definition of 'serious misconduct' (nothing to cause surprise in an enactment devised by a Government Department). But that omission would not dismay a trained lawyer, who would turn with confidence to the Common Law. And indeed the case-law is clear. Deliberate disobedience to orders, gross neglect of work, and so on, justify instant dismissal. But the theory that a boyish impertinence, or even an adult insult, to a Government official not in the same employ will justify instant dismissal is not supported by any recorded decision of any of His Majesty's Judges.

Of what avail is it, however, to quote the Common Law in proceedings where no trained lawyer is permitted either to sit among the judges or to represent the litigant or accused person? The Chairman, in this case, on being reminded that the Order did not define 'serious misconduct', held himself entitled to put his own interpretation upon the phrase. Mr. Fester's appeal was rejected; and he is now employed at half his former wage, in a position where his technical accomplishments are not being used, and cannot be used, for the benefit of the nation.

In these circumstances Mr. Fester has come to the King's

Courts for justice, or failing that, as he frankly said, to advertise his wrongs and the system which produced them.

The first writ which the young victim impulsively discharged was against Messrs. Philpott, Rory and Company for wrongful dismissal. This suit cannot be entertained for a moment, for the local Appeal Board has decided that the dismissal was rightful, and by the quaint provisions of the Order, approved by Parliament, there is no appeal from their decision.

Then he proceeds against Mr. Platt, his general manager, for slander. Well, Mr. Platt, it is true, informed the Appeal Board that the plaintiff had been guilty of serious misconduct. If there had been any evidence of malice I should have ruled that this bizarre tribunal was not a Court of Law and therefore that there was no absolute privilege for statements made before it. But I found no evidence of malice. The wretched Mr. Platt said simply that the Government Department concerned was now his only customer and therefore he had to do as he did to defend the honour and soothe the feelings of its wounded inspector, Mr. Rice. It is no part of my duty to comment upon such a state of affairs; but, if it were, I confess that I should discharge that part of it with alacrity and enjoyment.

Lastly, the injured youth, with touching faith in the ancient bulwarks of the British Constitution, has asked the Court for a declaration that the treatment he has received is contrary to the provisions of Chapter 29 of Magna Carta. It is perfectly true that in that famous Chapter 'we', that is, the Crown, undertake, among other things, that 'we will not proceed against a freeman, nor condemn him but by lawful judgment of his peers, or by the law of the land'. But I am surprised and saddened to learn that there is any of the King's subjects so innocent as to suppose that these words have any practical significance to-day. Hardly anyone is condemned by his peers in these times, except such malefactors as are sensible enough to go in for murder or incest, and the 'law of the land' is regarded by most of our rulers as a kind of joke, to be evaded or excluded. In this case, as we have seen, the practitioners of the 'law of the land' were deliberately kept away, and the law itself was not even considered by the tribunal. But what can I do? This is the work of Parliament, supporting a despotic Executive, for the sake of a just war. Magna Carta, I regret to say, is dead 'for the duration', at least; and only supreme exertions will renew its life at the termination of hostilities.

But there are still alive some remnants of our ancient rights and principles. It is not for me to advise the plaintiff or correct his solicitors. But I should have thought, without having studied the various Orders that govern us now, that it might still be possible to apply to the High Court for the issue of one of the prerogative writs in the nature of *mandamus* or *certiorari*, calling upon the local Appeal Board to show cause why they acted as they did and to justify their proceedings according to the still indestructible principles of natural, and even British, justice. That, no doubt, is a highly improper, and perhaps erroneous, suggestion: and I withdraw it at once.

I must, with regret, dismiss all the plaintiff's suits, and perhaps that will teach him to bother about the English language. Costs, however, to be paid by everybody, except Mr. Fester.

18 April, 1945

NOTE—His Lordship's hint was taken. A writ of *mandamus* did issue. The Appeal Board were torn to pieces by a strong court (Rammer L. C. J., Codd J., and Plush J.), and Mr. Fester was restored to his office.

(9) THE CORPORATION OF BURBLETON *v.* STANISLAVSKI

How Free is a Freeman?

MR. JUSTICE PLUSH to-day gave judgment in this unusual action which raises a question of interest to many townships at the present time. His Lordship said:

In this action the Corporation of Burbleton City are proceeding—reluctantly, as they have assured us, and we can well believe—against Marshal Stanislavski, the distinguished commander who has done so much for the cause of the Allied Nations in Eastern Europe. So sensible of his deeds and services were the people of Burbleton that they decided to confer upon him the Freedom of Burbleton. Accordingly, in a moving ceremony this year, the young Marshal was made an honorary Freeman of the Borough. There was a banquet; there were noble speeches; there was a procession, during which the excited citizens swarmed affectionately about the Marshal's car.

These emotions had scarcely subsided when, to the surprise and delight of the citizens, it was announced that the Marshal proposed to take up his residence in the first city to make him a freeman. Burbleton is by the sea, the Marshal is fond of swimming and boating; and in his own country, it appears, even a Marshal is subject to so many restraints and restrictions that the status of a freeman (unknown in his own land) made a very practical appeal to him. The grateful citizens purchased and presented to the Marshal a fine freehold mansion beside the sea; and there he resides.

Unfortunately, at no stage was it made clear to anyone or by anyone exactly what the privileges of a freeman are, which is indeed the question the Court has now to answer. Some light, but not much, emerges from a study of the Honorary Freedom of Boroughs Act, 1885. It is there laid down that persons of eminence may be made Honorary

Freemen of a Borough, with a proviso that the persons so distinguished shall not be entitled to a share in the produce or the proceeds of a sale of any property or stocks belonging to the Corporation.

This purely negative information does not lead us very far. Counsel for the plaintiffs has urged persuasively that the word 'honorary' is equivalent to 'formal', that the whole affair is no more than a symbolic courtesy and that no substantial privileges are in fact or law conferred by it. The Court rejects this view. We are satisfied that the word 'honorary' is used in distinction from the old, and now forbidden, practice by which it was possible to purchase the status of a freeman. Further, putting the best construction, as we feel bound to do, on the acts of a municipal corporation, we decline to assume that this and other bodies can have performed with so much pomp and circumstance an act that was practically meaningless.

Sir Roger Wheedle, K.C. (*for the Corporation*): Milord, if I may—with great respect—I think my clients might reasonably take exception to the expression 'meaningless'. The public display of goodwill, the generous refreshment, the illuminated address, the casket——

The Judge: Yes, yes, Sir Roger. But what I said was 'practically' meaningless. That, at all events, was the view taken by the Marshal, who argued simply that a freeman must be more free than one who was not a freeman, especially if he was made free with so much ceremony and emotion.

On the first Wednesday after his arrival he drove out in his car to stop in the narrow High Street of the city. On that day, by the bye-laws, it was the turn for motor-cars to park on the west side of the street. The Marshal, however, left his car, unattended, on the east side, while he conducted with considerable gaiety, and even familiarity, a long conversation with a comely shop-assistant. A big and intractable traffic-jam resulted. The Marshal emerged at last to find a curious crowd, two stern policemen, and a long line of vehicles, all hooting indignantly. When the identity of the delinquent was recognized, however, the scowls of the citizens gave way to smiles. The policeman, in simple terms, explained the bye-law; the Marshal said charmingly, 'I have understand—but I am Freeman—is it not?' and the incident passed off with good-humour.

The next day the Marshal was seen driving very fast along the sea-front, on the wrong side of the road, ignoring the lights, singing a wild old cavalry song, and with a young lady on his knee. When stopped at last and chided by a constable, he said again, with his delightful smile: 'But I am Freeman of Borough—yes?' The officer, with singular tact and intelligence, remarked that the Marshal was a Freeman of Burbleton, but not of Great Britain, and that neither the Corporation nor anyone else could give him licence to violate the general traffic-laws of the kingdom. The Marshal, according to the evidence, took the point at once; and has not since offended in this manner.

The distinction made by the constable, however, may well have fortified the Marshal's evident belief that within the bounds of the Borough he was entitled to ignore the obligations of a citizen of the Borough. There followed, at brief intervals, a series of incidents which have caused disquiet. The first was the great soldier's resolute refusal to pay any rates. A Freeman, he said, must surely enjoy the public services of the Borough—the police, the gas, the water, and so on, free of charge. There seems to be some reason in this contention, and the Corporation at length assented.[1] Similarly, with success, the Marshal declined to make any payment for entry on to the Victory Pier, or for the use of a deck-chair on the Esplanade.

Next came the Rocket Episode. On the fifteenth anniversary of the foundation of the Revolutionary State in his own land the Marshal gathered a number of his compatriots in the evening on the Esplanade. A great many

[1] Before the Municipal Corporations Act, 1935, which respected existing usages, a Freeman was exempt from all 'tolls and dues'.

toasts were drunk; a small but active balalaika band played stirring folk-songs, in which the chorus joined, interfering no little with the efforts of the municipal band to please the citizens not far away; and there was a fine display of that acrobatic form of dancing described by one witness as 'dancing sitting down'.

Rockets and other fireworks were then produced and discharged: and finally the Marshal fired one hundred and one live rounds into the air from his revolver in honour of the Revolution. There is, it appears, a very strict bye-law against the use of fireworks on the Esplanade; and one of the rockets discharged at a low angle set fire to the head of the Pier. The fire was quickly extinguished, and for this part of the evening's work the Marshal charmingly expressed regret; but, as to the rest, he again genially reminded the authorities that he was a Freeman.

The Marshal has a large steam yacht which he has berthed in the Harbour, refusing to shift his berth when desired, or to pay any harbour-dues. The Corporation is rightly proud of the various bye-laws and regulations which it has established to keep the practice of sea-bathing within decent and orderly limits. No undressing on the beach, not even 'macintosh-bathing', is permitted: and all must enter the sea from Corporation huts, within well-defined limits and in standard costumes. The Marshal and his friends have consistently ignored these arrangements. Hilarious parties of young men and women have emerged from his house and noisily entered the sea at all hours of the day and night, in costumes variously described as bizarre, scanty, and Continental, and, on at least one occasion, it is rumoured, in no costumes at all. And the mischief is, say the Corporation, that some of their own citizens are inclining towards indiscipline too.

These assaults upon public order and the decent name of Burbleton at last provoked the Council to firmer action than they had cared to contemplate before. With admirable tact they caused to be conveyed to the Marshal a private intimation that unless he could find it convenient to comply with the local bye-laws, customs and charges his presence in the Borough would be no longer welcome. The Marshal replied laughingly 'But I am Freeman. The people love me.' Which appears to be true.

What are the Corporation to do? They cannot eject him, for he is a freeholder. It would be odious to prosecute the great man whom they have delighted to honour for what many would think to be small offences. Moreover, they are not sure of their position at law: and they have come to this Court for a declaration.

The Court holds, with some reluctance, that they have brought this trouble on themselves. By the way, does the Marshal get a vote?

Mr. Mould (for the Marshal): The rights and privileges of a Freeman, milord, in the old days, generally included the right to vote at a Parliamentary election of the borough. Whether a Freeman of foreign birth——

The Judge: Well, there you are. There must be some substantial significance in the appellation 'Freeman', or it would not have been made the subject of an Act of Parliament. That significance can only be a degree of freedom within the Borough not enjoyed by the citizen who is not a freeman. Discretion and taste will, no doubt, in most cases suggest the limits within which such a privilege shall be enforced; but, so long as he does not infringe the law of the land, we hold that in Burbleton the Marshal can do what he likes.

4 July, 1945

(10) THE KING *v.* BROADWICK

The Dodged Deposit

A JUDGMENT which must have profound political effect, and may even, it is considered, lead to a General Election, was delivered by Mr. Justice Twigg to-day.

These proceedings, said his Lordship, arise from an application by the good Mr. Haddock, whose interventions in the forensic field have caused so much happy and fruitful deliberation.

The nature of the case can be briefly indicated. Mr. Haddock asks that there should be issued to the Returning Officer of Burbleton (West), the prerogative writ of *Quare benevolentiæ causa*, or (in English), 'Why, for goodness' sake——?' to show cause why he did not, according to law, 'deem' Mr. Q. Smith, M.P., to be 'withdrawn' from the Parliamentary election for Burbleton (West) in the circumstances now to be related.

By Section 26 of the Representation of the People Act, 1918, the celebrated measure of reform which has brought us to the pretty pass in which we find ourselves to-day, it is provided that: 'A candidate at a Parliamentary election, or someone on his behalf, shall deposit or cause to be deposited with the Returning Officer during the time appointed for the election the sum of £150 ... and if he fails to do so he shall be deemed to be withdrawn within the provisions of the Ballot Act 1872....'

Why exactly, his Lordship proceeded, the Legislature thought fit to place this additional obstacle in the path of citizens offering to serve their country in Parliament is not at all clear. The old and useful custom of the 'preamble' has been abandoned. By the preamble, beginning always with the obscure but pleasant 'Whereas', before a Bill, or even before a Section, the Legislature used to announce to the people—and, more important, perhaps, to the judges—the general purpose of the enactments, and so assisted the people—and the judges—to interpret, later, the particular words in which it endeavoured to express its purpose, and its decrees.

In the present case, wanting a preamble, the Court is officially unable to say exactly why a candidate for Parliament must stake £150 before he is permitted to expose himself to the rude ordeal of universal suffrage. It is true that if the Court were to peep, unofficially, into the Official Reports of the speeches in Parliament delivered during the passing of the Act the Court might possibly determine what was intended and desired.[1] But this is by no means certain; for a man can read a great many lively and persuasive speeches in those Reports, all tending in the same direction, only to find at the end that the majority voted for a policy opposed to that of the speakers. For this, among other reasons, the Courts have always declined to use such aids in interpreting the Statutes, and we have to rely on the ingenious theories of leading counsel, assisted by such modest suggestions as the judges may feel themselves qualified to offer.

This is a democratic age, and the Act in question is without doubt a democratic Act. As amended by subsequent Acts it provides that any man or woman of the age of twenty-one may vote and, with some exceptions, be nominated at a Parliamentary election. The humblest hind, the poorest wage-slave, the unemployed, the illiterate, may 'serve'—mark the word—in that high place if they can persuade a majority to send them there. All property qualifications have been swept away: and only at the old-fashioned universities does the elector have to pass an intelligence test before he is permitted to vote.[2] It is somewhat surprising therefore that any citizen who offers to 'serve' in this way is required to put down £150, and highly

[1] See Note, p. 56.
[2] And this last survival has now been abolished by the Representation of the People Act, 1948.

surprising that the poor candidate should be confronted at the outset with what may well be regarded as a property qualification or 'means test' under another name.

I should add, by the way, that if the candidate is elected, or if, though not elected, he obtains more than one-eighth of the votes polled, the deposit is restored to him: but if he does not obtain the magic proportion of one-eighth his money is forfeit to the State. In effect, he makes a bet of £150 that he will obtain one-eighth of the votes. One learned counsel, indeed, has suggested plausibly that, the whole thing being in the nature of a gaming transaction, no Court would assist a successful candidate to recover his money if wrongfully withheld by a Returning Officer.

Now, counsel for the Crown has urged with force an explanation of these bizarre provisions which the Court is inclined to accept. In his view, the purpose is to deter the frivolous or 'freak' candidate, the man of straw—politically speaking—from crowding the electoral lists, confusing the electors' minds, and adding without good cause to the national expense. He is therefore required, himself, to risk £150 and to lose it if he cannot satisfy the electors that he is a serious aspirant; and in that sentence, says counsel, the accent should be on *himself*, since a risk which does not fall on a man cannot act as a deterrent.

What happened in this case? Mr. Smith, who gave his evidence with engaging frankness, has told us that he did not risk a penny, nor did any friend of his. A certain bank, it appears, advanced the sum of £150, on condition that he paid £10 to the Party to which he belongs. The same was done by the same bank for all the candidates of his Party, who numbered many hundreds. Mr. Smith himself says that he did not even pay the £10, having taken the firm line that he would not pay a penny to anyone for permission to serve his country.

Now, I asked Mr. Smith what were his relations with the bank. Was he interviewed or examined by the bank? Did any representative of the bank visit the constituency and

THE DODGED DEPOSIT

inquire into his personal qualifications and prospects of success? The answer was No. He had no dealings with the bank whatever.

Still more important was his answer to Question 5,081: Did you yourself expect to succeed?

Answer: No. I was astounded. I did not think I had a chance. In fact, I was not too pleased about it, for I am a poor man.

Question 5,082: If you had had to find £150 out of your own pocket would you have stood for Parliament, Mr. Smith?

Answer: Not on your life, my lord.

A candidate who does not expect to succeed, who thinks that he has no chance, who is not even eager to succeed, and would not have thought of standing if he had had to risk his own money—what is this but a freak or frivolous candidate, the very type of candidate whom, if our interpretation of the Section be correct, it was designed to deter and keep away?

Through the operations of the bank and others Mr. Smith was not deterred; and, for all the Court knows, there were many hundreds of candidates in like case. It may well be that in other proceedings, after fuller inquiry, there may be disclosed a criminal conspiracy to evade and defeat the purpose of a Statute. The fact that Mr. Smith, or others, were in the event elected has no relevance, except perhaps as an aggravating circumstance. Counsel has defended the transaction as a kind of insurance by the bank: but insurance transactions must not be against public policy, and to insure the return to Parliament of frivolous candidates in large numbers must be against public policy. The more successful it is, the more repellent to the law.

Into these wider and attractive fields of thought I must not stray farther to-day. It is enough to say that in this case the writ must issue, as desired, to the Returning Officer, Mr. Broadwick. It was his duty to satisfy himself that Mr. Smith, 'or someone on his behalf' (by which words may be intended his agent, but not a bank of which he had never heard), had deposited, at his own peril, £150: and since it appears that Mr. Smith did no such thing the Returning Officer should have deemed him to be withdrawn. He is to attend this Court to show cause why he did not do so. I am told that my decision may ultimately affect the position of many hundreds of Members of Parliament. I cannot help that. They should observe the law.

3 October, 1945

NOTE—The Returning Officer duly attended. He said that he knew nothing of any bank. The money was handed in by Mr. Smith's agent and he had no reason to suppose there was anything wrong.

The Judge: But you should have made sure. You should have put to him the simple question: 'Do you assure me that if you fail to gain one-eighth of the votes you will yourself be poorer by the sum of £150?' A man is not likely to begin his political career—or end it—by lying to the Returning Officer.

Mr. Broadwick undertook to put that question to all candidates in the future, and the Judge reluctantly discharged him.

If his Lordship had 'peeped into the Official Report' he would have found much to fortify his opinions. See *Hansard*, 22 May, 1917, Vol. 93, Col. 2,141: 'We further propose that a candidate shall make a deposit, which will be returnable to him if he has not less than one-eighth of the votes. That is intended to prevent mere freak candidates' (Sir George Cave, Home Secretary, moving the Second Reading of the Representation of the People Bill). Colonel Sanders said (Col. 2,153): 'Extraordinary people are returned to the House of Commons. I do not know, if I may use a sporting term, whether my right hon. Friend has carefully weighed the odds in this case. You are giving £150 to get £400 a year for five years—that is, £2,150. It is about 100 per cent. It is a good outside price that a good many sporting men might be ready to take, and I think you want to make that Clause rather stronger in order to stop these *speculative candidatures*.' In Committee (15 August, 1917) Sir Frederick Banbury moved to make the deposit £250, 'to prevent large numbers of bogus candidates coming forward' (Vol. 97, Col. 1,253). Mr. A. Williams said: 'It seems to me that if a man can get one voter he is justified in testing the opinions of the constituency, and that no one has the right to call him a freak' (Col. 1,255). Sir George Younger (Col. 1,257) moved to make it one-sixth instead of one-eighth of the votes. Sir George Cave said: 'I think one-eighth is enough. If a freak candidate gets one-eighth of the votes polled he will be a fairly successful freak.' That amendment was withdrawn also (Col. 1,259).

Earlier (Col. 1,251), there is an illuminating passage. The original clause 19 read:

'A candidate at a Parliamentary election ... shall deposit with the returning officer, during the time appointed for the election, the sum of one hundred and fifty pounds. ...'

Colonel Sanders moved to insert after 'election' the words 'or some person on his behalf'. He did this to cover cases in which 'a candidate cannot possibly be present at the nomination. For instance, a candidate is sometimes put up while he is on service abroad. ...'

Sir George Cave: 'I am advised that these words are really not necessary. If the candidate cannot make the deposit anyone can make it on his behalf, and that comes to exactly the same thing. It is better not to insert the words unless they are necessary, *because I do not in the least want to encourage the idea that candidates may be financed by someone else.* It is far better that the actual deposit should be made by the candidate himself wherever it is possible.' After some argument he agreed to accept, instead, the insertion of the words 'or cause to be deposited' and these words were accordingly inserted.

On the Report Stage (26 November, 1917, Vol. 99, Col. 1,749) it was again moved, this time by Mr. Nield, that the words 'or someone on his behalf,' be added, purely on the ground that 'a candidate may not be in England at the time of the election if the election takes place before the conclusion of hostilities.' Sir George Cave again thought the words 'unnecessary', but this time did not resist, and they passed into the Bill. But it is quite clear that they were inserted only to safeguard 'these men who are serving abroad', and that the sense of the House was with Sir George—that is, against deposits 'financed' by others.

The evils that may arise from the 'insuring' of candidates against 'loss of deposit' were vividly illustrated at the General Election of 1950, at which 460 candidates forfeited their deposits. *Quaere*—is not this practice also contrary to the clear intention of Parliament?

See Lord Mildew in *Lord Havers* v. *The Imprudential Assurance Society* (1951). 'In this case,' he said, 'it was like insuring the life of a conscientious suicide.'

(11) HADDOCK v. OUNDLE; HADDOCK v. SMITH; HADDOCK v. THE GENERAL PRESS; HADDOCK v. BUZZINGS AND THE BILIOUS WEEKLY; HADDOCK v. COOPER

THE WHALE CASE

MR. JUSTICE RATCHET, giving judgment to-day in the '*De mortuis*' case, said:

In this unusual series of actions, which for the general convenience have been heard together, the plaintiff, Mr. Albert Haddock, is suing a number of persons and papers for libel. Mr. Haddock, while a passenger in a small sailing-vessel which was proceeding southward along the coast of Labrador, had the misfortune to fall overboard. What is now known as 'fog conditions', but the Court still prefers to describe simply as fog, prevailed. The crew did what they could, but were unable to pick up the plaintiff. On that coast at that time of the year are many large icebergs, and in the sub-Arctic water no swimmer could be expected to survive for long.

Accordingly, on the return of the vessel to Newfoundland, the captain sorrowfully reported that the plaintiff must be presumed to have perished in the icy sea. The distressing news was telegraphed to London: obituary notices of the plaintiff's life and professional career appeared in many organs of opinion; and there was a fairly well-attended memorial service at St. Luke's, Brunswick Square.

But a few days later news came to this country that the plaintiff was still alive. Besides icebergs, there are numerous whales in those waters: and, according to the plaintiff's story which he has repeated in the box with a wealth of plausible detail, he was, like the prophet Jonah, swallowed by a whale. He contrasted vividly the warm interior of the mammal with the freezing grip of the ocean. He repelled,

under cross-examination, the suggestion that the whale,
being fitted with a trellis-like or 'gridiron' structure in its
mouth for the purpose of catching small fish, is quite incapable of swallowing a man—or perhaps I should now say,
adult male personnel. Not all whales, the plaintiff assured
the court, are thus constructed,[1] and, if they were, what
would become of the story of the prophet Jonah, which has
never yet been doubted—except, maybe, by the prophet's
wife on his return. We do not know what she said. We do
not know what was said by the wife of Sir Isaac Newton
when he informed her that after observing the fall of an
apple he had solved the riddle of the spheres. We do not
know what comment was made by the wife of William
Shakespeare when he announced that he proposed to
establish the family fortunes by writing a stage-play called
Henry VI, Part One. Fortunately, the Court is not required
to arrive at a finding of fact upon these points: but it is
useful to recall that many stories as unlikely as the plaintiff's have been accepted without a murmur for many
centuries. He said, by the way, that the whale was a white
whale; and he asserted that in those regions more white
whales were encountered than black.[2] When asked if that
did not make nonsense of *Moby Dick*, that masterpiece of
literature, he answered that that was no affair of his.

Next day, the narrative continued, the whale in question
was harpooned by the whaling-ship *Terra Nova* and towed
into the whaling-station at Hawkes Bay, Labrador. The
carcass was at once cut up, and—fortunately, before the
boiling process—the plaintiff was extracted, not much the
worse.

Whatever may be thought of this story, which received
keen attention throughout the world, there is no doubt that

---

[1] See *Physeter catodon* (sperm whale: 'size gigantic ... head immense ... snout
enormous' (*Encyclopaedia Britannica*, Vol. 5, p. 171*b*).
[2] See *Independent Member*, by A. P. Herbert (Methuen & Co.), 21*s*. (absurdly
cheap), p. 284: 'I asked the Norwegian (manager) if they ever saw a white whale.
He said that they catch many white whales.'

the plaintiff is alive, and indeed is present in court. The defendants' counsel, unwilling to accept the episode of the whale, have suggested that in fact he was picked up by the fishing schooner *Heart of Grace*, which brought him to Newfoundland: and this contention, right or wrong, has more relevance than may at first appear to the issue joined before the Court. On his return to England the plaintiff took exception to certain expressions in some of his 'obituary notices'. Death comes unexpected to most men still: and insufficient praise is given to those great newspapers which produce so readily the following morning a careful account and assessment of the careers of public men; though the thought that in so many offices the record is being ghoulishly brought up to date each year in readiness for the last event must be disturbing to anyone in the public eye. The ancient motto *De mortuis* still seems to prevail in these accounts. The plaintiff does not claim that any of his 'obituaries' was deliberately offensive, though he was disappointed by them all. They were not even likely to aggravate the grief of his relatives if he had been dead. But they are, he says, of a character to damage him in his profession now that he is, in fact, alive. In particular, he objected to the suggestion that, though a careful observer and recorder, he was lacking in imagination. Two writers, he complains, hinted that he was a seeker of publicity, though in fact he is the shyest man alive and suffers a sharp physical revulsion when he sees his name in the papers. Why such a charge should be pressed or resented in the case of a writer is not clear to the Court; for if his name is not known to many how can many be expected to buy his books? It would be as reasonable to blame a nun for her retiring ways. But to say that a romantic author has no imagination may well be damaging, all must agree: and the same, perhaps, applies to Mr. Oundle's observation that the plaintiff was deficient in a sense of the sublime.

Now, it is established law that a libel suit cannot be entertained which arises out of anything written concerning a dead person. Other remedies must be sought by the aggrieved family where the dead are defamed. The defendants say that in good faith and upon proper information they presumed the plaintiff to be dead; that what they published was published only on that assumption and would not have been published had they known him to be alive; that any reasonable man would have thought him to be dead; that at the time of publication he was constructively dead; that the libel, if any, was a libel, to all intents and purposes, on a dead man, and therefore cannot be a cause of action.

This argument, though it was pressed with much ingenuity and force by Sir Ambrose Wett, the Court is unable to accept. We find that the plaintiff was in fact alive when the words complained of were published; and the fact that he was in the belly of a whale at the time, if that is true, or swimming in the sea off Labrador, cannot deprive him of his rights at law. Indeed there is something to be said for Sir Roger Wheedle's contention that for a journalist comfortably placed in London to vilify the character of a public man who is in the belly of a whale off the coast of Labrador might well be a circumstance to be thrown into the scale in any assessment of damages.

Equally we must reject the somewhat unworthy suggestion of defendants' counsel that the entire affair was a 'publicity stunt'—or, alternatively, a plot to obtain damages from trusting newspapers. We cannot imagine a man so eager to secure mention, or money, from the newspapers that he will voluntarily step into sub-Arctic waters in foggy weather off the coast of Labrador. On the other hand, as we have indicated already, we cannot find it defamatory to say that a writer seeks publicity. The mere publication of a book is a request for public attention. Smith, therefore, and the General Press are dismissed from the action; though, since they have been rather a nuisance, they will pay the plaintiff's costs.

There remain the other defendants, and the other

charges. These they have tediously attempted to justify by reference to the plaintiff's works, seeking to show that for this reason or that he is not worthy of regard as a composer of romantic fiction. Fortunately, I am relieved of any duty to go into all that by the defendants themselves, who have made so much of the story of the whale. After a strong attempt, and indeed inclination, to achieve credulity, I find myself unable to accept the story of the whale. But the manner in which the tale was told, and the doubts which I have felt concerning it, have persuaded me that the plaintiff is richly endowed with the qualities necessary for the writing of fiction, romantic or other—with imagination, with the capacity to assemble corroborative detail, and that indefinable power called plausibility. In short, it is clear to me that all the remaining defendants have libelled the plaintiff in his professional capacity, and they must pay damages, between them, of *about* £10,000—or more, if the plaintiff wishes. What is the next case, please?

19 March, 1947

(12) REX *v.* BOPPLE

'Avoid Litigation'

(Before Mr. Justice Codd)

This extraordinary case came to a sensational end to-day. Throughout the trial the behaviour of the prisoner has astonished all beholders. Slight, white-haired, mild, respectable and even refined of feature, he does not suggest to the student of psychology the type of man who could violently attack, with a hammer, a Minister of the Crown in the public street, or would glory in such a deed if he were driven to it by some unusual circumstance. Yet at no time, as the net of evidence closed around him, has he shown any sense of guilt, of discomfort, or even apprehension. Indeed, it was noticed by many that as the trial drew near its end he became more cheerful, nodding and smiling to acquaintances in the body of the court.

To-day, at the conclusion of counsels' addresses, the judge summed-up to the jury. He said:

Members of the Jury—Andrew Bopple, the little old gentleman in that dock, stands before you charged with felonious homicide, or murder: and it is for you to say whether he be guilty or no. I do not envy you the task. Your eyes behold the face and form of the prisoner; your ears have heard the evidence concerning him: and your minds may find it difficult to reconcile the two. He does not look like a murderer. One would have said that he lacked both the strength and the spirit of the assassin. Yet the evidence which you have heard is clear and copious; and in the ordinary course I should not have thought it necessary to address you for long. You will, you must, most patiently examine and measure the smallest wisp of doubt that seems to blow his way. But you may well find it impossible to resist the conclusion that the prisoner did in fact, on April 16th—mark the date—at about 11.0 p.m., in Parliament Street, attack with a hammer the Right Honourable Mervyn Jarrow, so that he died.

The defence have remarked that there appears to be no motive for this murder by this man (they did not, by the way, assist the Court and jury to discover one by putting him in the box). The prisoner has been a Civil Servant all his life: but it is uncertain whether he had ever worked in the same office as the late Minister for Drains, and for all we know they had never met before the fatal night. It is not essential, as the deceived husband said, to prove a motive where the facts are plain; but it often helps: and though, of course, you will pay no attention to anything I say, I must tell you that I have formed a theory about motive in this case which I think is rather good.

A few months ago the prisoner, being sixty-five years of age, as you have heard, retired, or rather was retired, reluctantly, from the Civil Service. He has a small pension, but has saved nothing, being the father of seven; and he can no longer live as comfortably as he did. His wife is dead, and, being unwilling to thrust himself into the homes of any of his married children, he lives in a single small room in a dismal neighbourhood. He has a tendency to rheumatism, and probably finds travel about the Metropolis difficult, as in these days the elderly do, even if they are not rheumaticky. Travel abroad to sunny climes is almost impossible. As the taxes and the prices rise, his pension dwindles: and not even the statesmen are predicting an early 'turn' of that particular 'tide'. It would not be surprising, then, if like so many elderly people to-day he felt little enjoyment in the autumn of his life and less hope for the winter.

'Still,' you may say, as men of the world 'this is a common tale; and there is nothing in it which should lead such a man to take his own life, much less another's. "Life is sweet—however disgusting," as the poet Haddock remarked long ago; and it is still the law of the land that for

murder a man must suffer the extreme penalty, to be destroyed by hanging.' That is so; but at the present time that
law is in suspense. As I enjoined you before, observe the
date. The alleged murder was committed on April 16th.
On April 14th the House of Commons, by a small majority,
had added a new clause to the Criminal Justice Bill, the
effect of which, if it becomes law, will be to suspend for five
years the imposition of the death penalty for murder. It is
not law yet: it may never become law. For the House of
Lords, it appears, is likely to reject the clause when it is
considered in Committee, and the House of Commons, in
that case, may still agree with them, a month or two from
now. But meanwhile it has become law, most strangely, in
effect: for it was announced, after the decision in the
Commons, that reprieve and imprisonment 'for life' would
become the rule at once. The logical reasoning is not easy
to follow, for the Commons House is only one of the two
Houses of Parliament, and only three-eighths of its
Members declared themselves in favour of the change.
Logically, if the Lords rejected the Clause in Committee,
the citizens concerned would all at once be placed on the
hanging list again: but that is not likely to happen in this
humane land.

All this is highly relevant to the task which has been laid
upon you. If you find the prisoner guilty, it will be my duty
formally to pass sentence of death upon him according to
law. But it is as certain as anything can be that that
sentence will not be carried out, that he will go to gaol for
the rest of his life, but not to the gallows. Never before in
the history of this island has a man been able to take the
life of another with that certitude in his mind; and in two
months, perhaps, it may be impossible again.[1] You may
think it a lucky chance for the prisoner that after a lifetime
of peaceable behaviour he was impelled to commit his
murder (if he did) when he did.

Or you may think that it was something more than

[1] It was.

chance. The prisoner, it may be, has not many years to live. It is likely that, in many ways, he would live those years more comfortably in prison than he would outside. He would be housed, fed, clothed and doctored by the State, with none of the troubles of rent, repairs, rates and taxes, ration-books and coupons and insurance-payments which beset the free man. I have ascertained that he does not smoke or drink, and will not suffer the same deprivations as other men. An old Civil Servant, he will still enjoy the congenial atmosphere of the State. An educated man, he is sure to be placed in charge of the Library, very soon: and, when he is not there, he will probably be comfortably in bed in the hospital. Many a lonely old man might envy him.

Now, however enlightened may be our theories of punishment, it is clearly undesirable that lonely old men should be encouraged to go about murdering people in order to escape the troubles of ordinary life and to enjoy the security and quiet of prison till they die. I shall in a few years retire myself: but no such comfortable refuge awaits me. Our prisons are about to be reformed: and the better they are the better should it be understood that people cannot get into them without good cause. There should be sincerity in crime, as in everything. A spurious murder is abhorrent to British juridical notions. It is a kind of contempt of Court. But perhaps I have said enough. You had better retire.

The jury, after a few minutes' deliberation, found the prisoner 'Not Guilty'. The prisoner scowled angrily.

The Judge: Andrew Bopple, you are a free man. You will go back into the big world. And serve you right.

Bopple: That was a dirty trick, my lord. I thought I had everything in the bag.

The Judge: Tell me, why did you pick on the Minister for Drains?

Bopple: I had nothing against him, my lord. I never saw him. But somehow I never could stand what he said in the papers.

The Judge: You should apologize to his family.

Bopple: I will, my lord. It had to be someone.

The Judge: And, in future, avoid litigation. You never know where you are.

12 May, 1948

NOTE—And see *Tough* v. *Twigg* (1949), 2 A.C., where a habitual criminal, under the Poor Persons' Rules, asked for a writ of *mandamus* to be issued to a judge who had put him on probation instead of sending him to prison again.

(13) HOUSE OF COMMONS (KITCHEN COMMITTEE) v. HADDOCK

THE EGG OF EXCHANGE

(Before Mr. Justice Codd)

SIR RONALD RUTT, K.C.,[1] opening the case for the plaintiffs to-day, said:

May it please your Lordship, I appear for the Kitchen Committee of the House of Commons. As defendant, the Court, no doubt, will be glad to see that veteran litigant, Mr. Albert Haddock, who is always welcome, however erroneous. His present appearance arises out of a gathering of dramatists at the House of Commons, some of whom were Members and some, more fortunate, were not. Mr. Haddock had made himself responsible for the cost of the refreshments provided, which, considering the eminence in their profession of many of the guests, could hardly be described as 'lavish'. Nowadays, if two citizens occupy a dwelling-place consisting of two small rooms and a bath-room where some of the appliances work it is described as a 'luxury' flat. But that word, I am satisfied, is not here appropriate.

At the close of the proceedings, when the bill was presented to him, Mr. Haddock drew a cheque for Ten Pounds (£10) on an egg.

The Court: An egg?

Sir Ronald: If your Lordship pleases—an egg.

The Court: A turkey's egg?

Sir Ronald: No, milord, a hen's egg. Milord, it appears that the defendant, no doubt legitimately, had acquired three eggs, and brought them to the dinner at the House of Commons.

---

[1] Son of Sir Ethelred (now Lord Justice) Rutt.

The Court: And the Kitchen Committee are insulted? I do not wonder. But is this a libel action?

Sir Ronald: No, milord. The eggs, it appears, were intended as a tribute to the distinguished dramatist who presided over the gathering.[1] On two of them those present wrote their 'autographs', and these two were duly presented to the President. On the third——

The Court: What a party!

Sir Ronald: Your Lordship will realize that the company included a good many bright and imaginative spirits. On the third egg, then, in small but legible characters, the defendant drew a cheque in the ordinary form of words: a stamp was duly attached and cancelled, according to the Stamp Act, and the whole document, if it can be so described, was presented to the Manager, Major Sidwell, in discharge of the debt. The Manager presented the cheque at the bank having charge of the Kitchen Committee's account, and asked that bank (which I will call Bank B) to collect the money in the usual manner from the defendant's bank (which I will call Bank A). The manager of Bank B, however, demurred to handling the cheque at all, and especially to making himself responsible for forwarding it through the usual channels. It would require, he said, the employment of special receptacles and messengers——

The Court: Was the cheque hard-boiled?

Sir Ronald: No, milord, it was a fresh cheque. Indeed, there is some evidence that it was a new-laid cheque.

The Court: What a waste!

Sir Ronald: That, milord, was one of the considerations which affected the minds of my clients. 'No man,' as Lord Mildew said in a recent case, 'can pretend to full cognisance and understanding of all the rules and regulations concerning the feeding of the King's subjects at the present time.' But it would be unlikely, my clients thought, if there were not some Statutory Rule or Order against the use of a fresh egg as a Bill of Exchange.

[1] Major Ian Hay Beith.

The Court: Yes, Sir Ronald, but I thought that in these affairs the House of Commons could do what it liked? Surely, that was all settled by the singular but satisfactory case of *Rex* v. *Sir R. F. Graham-Campbell and others. Ex parte Herbert (1935) 1 K.B.*

Sir Ronald: That is the best opinion, milord: but the House has never cared to abuse its privileges, or to set an unworthy example to the people. If it were to get about, they thought, that Members of the House of Commons were in the habit of using fresh eggs as cheques, promissory notes, I.O.Us. or—who knows?—for the transfer of shares or securities, an unfavourable impression might be made upon a people still bravely suffering under the reign of Austerity.

The Court: But stop a moment, Sir Ronald. I think, perhaps, I was a little hasty. Let us see what would happen to the egg. It was, I take it, the defendant's property? There is no suggestion that it was a pilfered or unrationed egg?

Sir Ronald: No, milord. Indeed, in these days the relevant eggs might even have been what are described officially as 'surplus eggs', though they have still, for most of us, a merely notional existence.

The Court: Pretty notional, I agree, Sir Ronald. Very well. The egg, I suppose, passes from your client's bank, through the Bankers' Clearing House, or whatever it is, to the defendant's bank. They read and obey the instructions on the cheque: and, their duty discharged, return the cheque, as usual, to the defendant. If it were a paper-cheque he could use it to light his pipe: if it is an egg-cheque, he can eat, or, I suppose I should say, consume it. I do not really see what objections can be raised by the Ministry of Food to such a transaction.

Sir Ronald: As your Lordship pleases. But there remains the question of the difficulties of transit——

The Court: Why didn't your bank have the cheque hard-boiled?

Sir Ronald: Milord, that was considered by the bank. But it was thought that the stamp would become detached in the process of boiling, and perhaps the writing be extinguished.

The Court: The stamp, Sir Ronald, could surely have been attached again: and there is nothing, I think, to prevent the holder from attaching and cancelling a new stamp, if necessary. As for the writing, if I know anything of Mr. Haddock, he uses one of those queer new pens which write under water.

Sir Ronald: As to that, milord, I am not instructed.

The Court: Extraordinary. Go on, Sir Ronald.

Sir Ronald: My clients, milord, declined to accept the cheque in payment and presented their account again. The defendant——

The Court: The defendant, I suppose, took umbrage? He said that he was not accustomed to having his cheques scorned and rejected—and you could take it or leave it?

Sir Ronald: That was roughly his position, milord. And he has obstinately refused to discharge the debt.

The Court: Sir Ronald, before you proceed any farther you may care to consult with your clients, and with learned counsel on the other side. It is true that your clients are not bound to accept a cheque of any kind. But in practice, without doubt, many of your debts are collected in this way; and, having regard to the general custom and his own position, the defendant is naturally reluctant to get the name of one who passes worthless cheques. Your clients, or rather your clients' bank, are not in fact objecting to payment by cheque, but to payment by this particular cheque: and the defendant may well have expected to hear some stronger objections than those which you have, so far, exposed. There is nothing magical or mystical about a cheque. It is simply a written instruction by one person to a second person to pay money to a third—to which, of course, a rapacious State insists upon the addition of a stamp. It does not matter where it is written, provided the intention is clear. It can be written on a bill of fare, upon a napkin, or, if no other paper be available, the label of a brandy-bottle, and such cheques have, in fact, passed safely through the banking channels and been duly honoured and met. It could, I suppose, be written on an out-house or the side of a balloon, provided that it was brought effectively to the notice of the bank addressed and the necessary stamp was attached before presentation. Between a brandy-bottle, an outhouse and an egg there can clearly be no great distinction of principle. Nor am I much impressed by the practical difficulties to which you have referred. It is the duty of a bank to keep the stream of commerce flowing and navigable, and to destroy, not to create, new obstacles in the fair-way. You tell me, Sir Ronald, that your bank, because of the brittle and breakable quality of the cheque in question, was reluctant to undertake the responsibility of transporting it to the proper quarter, though all that was necessary, after all, was to place the cheque in the hand of a trustworthy boy (or even girl) and hire a motor-cab. On the other hand, it shrank, I understand, from making the simple experiment of boiling the cheque—and boiling it hard. This, Sir Ronald, was not the spirit of those old merchant venturers who made the name of commercial England famous and admired. Of course, if it became a general practice for men of commerce and industry to employ the egg for such purposes, a state of affairs might arise in which Parliament would feel itself compelled to intervene. But it is always a great mistake to treat the individual on the chance that he may become a crowd. And meanwhile, I, at least, have to deal with the law as it stands to-day. Call Mr. Haddock.

Sir Ronald: But, milord——!

The Court: I am well aware that this procedure is unusual, Sir Ronald. So is the case.

Mr. Albert Haddock was sworn and said: Yesterday I wrote in ordinary ink upon an egg the same form of words as were on the egg in this case. I boiled the egg for nine minutes, and the writing was as clear as ever.

The Court: You see, Sir Ronald? The Court will adjourn.

16 February, 1949

NOTE—The later history of this cheque is recorded in Mabane on *Bills of Exchange.* The cheque was hard-boiled by Major Sidwell, conveyed to the defendant's bank, Messrs. Grindlay's Bank Limited, and duly honoured. It is now in the Museum of Queer Cheques at that establishment, cheques drawn on napkins, the labels of brandy-bottles, bills of fare, etc., cheques drawn in verse and uncomplimentary language, cheques illustrated with sketches for the better identification of the drawer and drawee, etc. 'They are all my property,' said Mr. Haddock laughingly in a recent interview, 'and should have been returned to me. But my good Bank has impounded them. Never mind. They have my overdraft too.'

(14) *IN RE* EARL OF MUNSEY: STEWER *v.* COBLEY

The Missing Day Case

Mr. Justice Plush said: In this difficult case I have to decide the destination of some enviable property. The deceased testator, the revered Lord Munsey, left all his property (excepting Munsey Castle and Park) to his great-nephew George Stewer '*if he has attained the age of 21 before the date of my death*': and, if not, to his own brother the Hon. Thomas Cobley. Cobley was the heir to the title and Stewer, it seems, to the Earl's affection. So far, so good.

George Stewer celebrated his twenty-first birthday in London on Monday, May 2, 1949, with his widowed mother, Amanda Stewer, who impressed me favourably. A cable of congratulation, dated May 1st, was received from the Earl, who, enjoying a voyage round the world, was then on passage from Honolulu to Sydney in the S.S. *Asthma*.

But a few days later there came a cable from the captain of the vessel:

DEEPLY REGRET REPORT LORD MUNSEY PASSED AWAY TUESDAY MAY 3 BURIED AT SEA IN 10 S 176 E[1] LETTER FOLLOWS COOPER MASTER S.S. ASTHMA.

The late Earl, it seems, was very fond of port-wine, which, after a certain age, should be avoided near the Equator. Thomas Cobley, of whom the Court thought very little, succeeded to the title and the Castle; and the grief of the Stewers was allayed by the reflection that, just in time, young George had qualified for his inheritance.

But it had been a near thing, so near that interested parties were naturally anxious, or hopeful, about the possibility of error: and, when the *Asthma* arrived at Sydney the Captain was interviewed by lawyers acting both for the Stewers and Thomas Cobley. At these interviews a com-

[1] Latitude 10° South, Longitude 176° East.

plex question emerged which it is now my duty to elucidate
if I can.

It was revealed by Captain Cooper that the Earl, by an
unhappy chance, had perished very near to what is known
by mariners as the Date Line. As a ship goes round the
world in a westerly direction she adjusts her clocks to the
sun each day, so that the time is 12 noon and lunch is
present in the mind when the sun, as the merry sailors say,
is 'over the yard-arm' or reasonably near it. ('Lunch follows the sun,' said Lord Mildew in *Hawaii Harbour Board* v.
Pacific Navigation Company (1901), or, as some poet has
it—probably the man Haddock—'The farther east, the
sooner feast!' for the sun comes, or seems to come, from the
east.) But, in so doing, the farther the *Asthma* goes from the
meridian of Greenwich the more she falls behind Greenwich Time. Can you explain why, Sir Ambrose?

Sir Ambrose Wett, K.C.: Because every day, milord, as she
goes west, away from the sun, the sun rises later, and she
must put her clocks back to keep pace with it. Otherwise,
in New York, say, where the difference is 5 hours, she would
go to bed at 3.0 or 4.0 in the morning.

The Judge: They often do, I believe.

Sir Ambrose: And have lunch at 6.0 p.m.

The Judge: I hope you're right, Sir Ambrose. I'm sure
you are. So, when the ship is on the other side of the earth
and is approaching the meridian of 180° she will be nearly
twelve hours 'slow' on Greenwich, and must add nearly
twelve hours to find her 'Greenwich Date'.[1] In practice, of
course, it would be tiresome to change the clocks continu-
ally, and the ocean is divided into 'zones', in each of which

[1]'Consider the hypothetical experience of an aeroplane going round the world
in latitude 60° at 450 knots, the Sun's speed in longitude in that latitude. If the
pilot starts at noon on a Monday, when the Sun is on his meridian, and flies West,
the Sun will remain on his meridian. He will thus experience no day at all.
Wherever he is it will be noon and people will be thinking about their midday
meal. But when he arrives back on his starting point, the people he left there will
be thinking about Tuesday's meal. Somewhere during his journey, therefore,
Monday has suddenly become Tuesday. That somewhere is the Date Line, on one
side of which people are calling the time noon on Monday, and on the other noon
on Tuesday.' *Admiralty Navigation Manual*, Vol. II.

for general purposes an exact number of hours is added or subtracted.

Now, a ship—let us call her *Pneumonia*—a few miles on the other side of the meridian of 180°, steaming east, is in the opposite condition. All the way from the meridian of Greenwich she has been gaining on Greenwich: and she is now nearly twelve hours *fast* on Greenwich. Is that right, Sir Ambrose?

Sir Ambrose: Yes, milord.

The Judge: So, in that zone, to find the correct day and hour at Greenwich she must *subtract* twelve hours from the time shown by her clocks. How damn confusing the whole thing is!

But let us return to the *Asthma*. Captain Cooper, who gave his testimony with the refreshing simplicity of the sea, told us that she crossed the meridian of 180° at 1345, by Ship's Time, on Sunday, May 1st, having had lunch earlier every day. The moment before crossing, to find his Greenwich Date, he would have to add twelve hours, which would bring him to 0145 on Monday, May 2nd. But, the moment after crossing, he is in a zone (Zone – 12) where the Captain of the *Pneumonia* must subtract twelve hours to find his Greenwich Date. But if the Captain of the *Asthma* subtracts twelve hours from 1345, on Sunday, May 1st, he is back at 0145 on Sunday, May 1st. He will then be a whole day behind Greenwich Time. To avoid this unfortunate situation it is the custom of the sea to drop or miss one day and so catch up with Greenwich: and accordingly, the Captain told us, at midnight at the end of Sunday, May 1, ship's time, he declared the next day to be Tuesday, May 3. And it was so. Almost at the same moment—'just after the ship's bell', said the valet—the Earl died: and at eleven on the same day his remains were committed to the deep.

The *Pneumonia*, on the other hand, must make a similar adjustment, or she will be a day *ahead* of Greenwich. She, I am informed, would repeat a day: she would have two Sundays, May 1, or, better perhaps, two Mondays, May 2.

In passing, I hope a mere sedentary judge may be permitted to envy the active life of a sea-captain who is able by his lone decree to create or erase a whole day in the lives of his passengers and crew.

It seems that in a sense, unscientific perhaps, the late Earl had the misfortune to leave this world on the missing day. One rather junior advocate did seem to query whether juridically he was dead at all. But the Captain truthfully reported that he died on May 3. The fact is duly recorded in the log, and upon that fact Sir Roger Wheedle claims that Mr. Stewer should succeed.

On the other hand, it was forcibly argued by Sir Ambrose Wett, for Cobley, that in scientific and physical fact Lord Munsey died on Monday, May 2, and was buried at 2300 that night. He was in vain reminded that there is no reference to May 2 in the ship's log, and no evidence that anything happened on that day in the *Asthma*. Sir Roger mildly remarked that it was going rather far to suggest that an English peer had died on a day of which there is no record, and was buried near midnight an hour before he died, according to the Captain. Sir Ambrose said angrily that he was thinking of Greenwich; Sir Roger said that the Earl did not die at Greenwich or anywhere near it; and the Court had to intervene.

Whatever tricks may have been played with the ship's clocks, Sir Ambrose continued, the Earl died at a point in time which could easily be identified and related to the time of George Stewer's majority by reference to the time at Greenwich. He died, according to the evidence, in Zone − 12, at 0000^h, by Ship's Time, on Tuesday, May 3, and therefore the date of his death was Monday, May 2, the same day as George Stewer's birthday. That being so, said Sir Ambrose, Mr. Cobley was entitled to succeed: for George Stewer had not, according to the terms of the will, 'attained the age of twenty-one *before* the date of the testator's death'.

This somewhat unworthy contention raised the question

of the meaning of 'date', about which learned counsel argued for two or three days. Sir Ambrose said that in ordinary parlance 'date' meant a particular, specified, numbered day. Sir Roger maintained that 'date', among mariners, and especially 'Greenwich Date', included the hour as well as the day and the month: that by Sir Ambrose's own showing the Earl had died at about 12 noon G.M.T. on May 2, but young Stewer had come of age, in law, at midnight the day before.

At length, I ruled that about the meaning of 'date' Sir Roger was right: but I called for evidence about the time of George Stewer's birth. No hour is mentioned in the birth certificate.

Sir Roger called Amanda Stewer, who gave her evidence quite charmingly, I thought. She said it was 'before lunch' because of the smell of hot boiled bacon, a favourite dish of her husband's. Sir Ambrose called an aged nurse, who had been in attendance on the occasion. She was sure that the time was one o'clock, because, at the dramatic moment, she heard Big Ben strike the hour. (They lived at Westminster.) That looked, at first, as if Sir Ambrose had prevailed: but in cross-examination it emerged that British Summer Time was then in use. Therefore the time of the majority was 1200 G.M.T., the same time precisely as, according to Sir Ambrose, the Earl passed away. Even then Sir Ambrose submitted that, if the time were the same, George Stewer could not have become twenty-one 'before' the Earl died.

I then caused Captain Cooper to be recalled, in the hope of more precise information. The Captain said, very readily, that it took five and a half seconds to sound eight bells, and so, having regard to the evidence of the valet, he would put the time of the Earl's death six seconds after midnight on the 3rd by Zone, or Ship's Time, and so at six seconds after noon on the 2nd by Greenwich Mean Time— six seconds later, that is, than the birthday hour.

The Court confesses that it is as nearly confused as it has

ever been. My difficulty might have been less, perhaps, if the Earl had been a passenger in the S.S. *Pneumonia*, and the Captain had elected to have two Sundays, May 1, for then by some time or other the Earl might have died on the second Sunday before the birthday on the Monday. But the Court is far from sure: and, fortunately, it is not necessary to decide the point. The Court (it thinks) has learned a great deal, and is filled with wonder at the arrangements of the sea, by which men can fix and relate exactly to a single standard the deeds and movements not only of men and ships but the heavenly bodies in any corner of the earth or sky. And—oh, Sir Ambrose—how moving it must be to any Briton to think that all this world-wide calculation is done by reference to an imaginary line drawn through a suburb of London called Greenwich!

Moved by these thoughts, by the reasoning of learned counsel, and the beauty of Amanda Stewer, the Court declares that, as a matter of law, by Greenwich Mean Time, the Earl of Munsey died at 12^h 00^m 06^s on Monday, May 2, and so George Stewer succeeds under the will by the small but sufficient margin of about six seconds.

But still some practical doubts remain. The Court is loath, for example, to dispute Captain Cooper's log and say that there must, after all, have been a Monday, May 2, in his well-found ship. If I did that I might lay the whole record of his voyage, upon which so much depends, open to question. And with what trepidation would every master of a vessel approach the Date Line in future! Further, I ask myself, what is to be inscribed upon the memorial stone or tablet—perhaps in Westminster Abbey—which salutes the life, and deplores the death, of the late Earl of Munsey? Certainly it cannot say 'DIED MONDAY MAY 2 IN S.S. ASTHMA': for that would be a lie, an affront to the customs and the records of the sea. I therefore declare that, as a matter of fact, the Earl died, as the Captain says, early on Tuesday, May 3, 1949. This makes no difference to George and his delicious mother: but, for all the Court knows, it

may cause all sorts of trouble elsewhere. Leave to appeal
will eagerly be granted: and the Court looks forward with
respect to reading the judgments of their Lordships in the
House of Lords.

7 December, 1949

EDITOR'S NOTE

Fractions of a Day

There was no appeal: but there has been some interested comment in legal circles,
and some too hasty criticism, on the judgment of Plush J. in the recent case of
In re Earl of Munsey: Stewer v. *Cobley* (December 7, 1949). The Earl, it will be
remembered, left property to George Stewer 'if he has attained the age of twenty-
one before the date of my death'. Stewer 'celebrated his twenty-first birthday' in
London on Monday, May 2, 1949: the Earl died at sea on the other side of the
world, at a few seconds after midnight May 2–3 (Ship's Time), which, reduced
to Greenwich Mean Time, was 12^h 0^m 6^s, on May 2. The Court was at
great pains to discover the precise moment of George Stewer's birth, which, by
a happy chance, was established at 12 noon exactly, and the learned judge
declared that George Stewer succeeded under the will 'by the small but sufficient
margin of six seconds'.

Surprise has been expressed that the learned judge did not avail himself of the
old common law doctrine concerning Fractions of a Day, which would have put
the young man's majority much earlier and saved the Court much troublesome
work; and it is thought by some that the case cannot have been fully or accurately
reported. Sir Roger Wheedle (for Stewer), it is said, did claim that his client 'had
come of age, in law, at midnight the day before': but the learned judge, without
further argument, it appears, insisted on determining the exact hour of the young
man's birth and basing his decision on that. His Lordship was unquestionably
right. It is not to be supposed that he was unfamiliar with the doctrine or the
precedents. Some of our correspondents, therefore, have suggested that he may
have thought it proper, in the special circumstances of the case, to ignore without
mention a doctrine which has been pushed to absurd extremes. But, of course,
there was ample authority for ignoring the doctrine: and it is a pity that the cases
which, without doubt, guided him were not cited in the report.

The main common law rule, though crazy, is clear enough. Halsbury's *Laws
of England* (2nd Edition, Vol. XVII. pp. 582–3) asserts:

'Full age is attained at the close of the day preceding the twenty-first
anniversary of birth, but in so much as the law does not take cognizance of
fractions of a day, a person is *deemed* to have attained the age of twenty-one
years at *the first moment* of the day preceding the twenty-first anniversary of his
birth, and is therefore capable of acting as a person of full age at any time on
that day.'

Sir Roger Wheedle, then (above), must surely have said 'the last midnight *but
one*'. Lord Mildew's famous ejaculation in *Travers* v. *Travers*: 'There is too much
of this damned deeming,' will be in the minds of many. As recently as 1918 (*In
re Shurey, Savory and Shurey* (1 Ch. 263)) the ancient doctrine was affirmed, with
evident reluctance, by Sargant J. The testator left his residuary estate upon trust
for such of his three sons, C.S. and two others, 'as shall attain the age of twenty-

five years'. The eldest son, C.S., was born on July 22, 1891, and died on July 21, 1916—namely, on the day preceding the twenty-fifth anniversary of the date of his birth. It was *held* that C.S. had attained the age of twenty-five years at the time of his death. Sargant J. said that 'the anomaly' began with an Anonymous Case of some antiquity. 'If one were actually to look at the clock for the purpose of determining the age of the deceased in that case, it would appear that he was *one day and twenty-two hours* short of attaining the age of twenty-one years: but the law does not take cognizance of part of a day, and the consequence is that a person attains the age of twenty-one years, or of twenty-five years, or any specified age, on the day preceding the anniversary of his twenty-first or twenty-fifth birthday, or other birthday, as the case may be.'

Mr. Justice Sargant used the expression 'anomaly'. Those less highly placed may prefer the word 'nonsense'. There is something to be said for disregarding a fraction of a day in many fields of life. An Act of Parliament, for example, becomes law, sensibly enough, at the first moment (0000 hours) of the day on which it is passed (an interesting exception was the King's Abdication Act, which, by express provision and for obvious reasons, became law at the midnight (2400 hours) after the Royal Assent). And where a man is born at, say, 11.0 a.m. on May 1, it is sensible enough, in general, to disregard the eleven hours and say that he becomes twenty-one at midnight (0000 hours) May 1. But then the law goes mad and disregards 'as a fraction' the *whole* of the *preceding* day.

The twisted logic of this affair, we understand, runs as follows:

'The Law disregards part of a day: *de minimis non curat lex*. A child must therefore be regarded as born at the *first* moment of its natal day: so it completes the first year of its life at the *last* moment of the day before the "first birthday". But, again *the Law disregards part of a day*: so a child completes the first year of its life at the first moment of the day before its "first birthday". It therefore completes the first twenty-one years of its life, and comes of age, at the *first* moment of the day before its twenty-first birthday.'

The fallacy, as a learned reader points out, lies in regarding the period between the first and last moments of a day as a *part* of a day. The law should surely correspond to the facts and customs of life, and say that a man comes of age on his twenty-first birthday—meaning the twenty-first anniversary of his birth.

That this is the commonsense view is shown by Section 79 of the National Health Insurance Act, 1911[1] in which our wise Parliament prescribed as follows:

'A person shall be deemed (for the purposes of Part I of the Act) according to the law in England, Wales, and Ireland, as well as according to the law in Scotland, not to have attained the age of seventeen until *the commencement of the seventeenth anniversary of the day of his birth*, and similarly with respect to other ages.'

This section was referred to by counsel in the Shurey case as an indication that the common law was as we have stated it: for otherwise the section would not have been necessary.

Presumably, then (but *quaere*), a man born on Jan. 3 could become twenty-one at midnight Jan. 1–2 for general purposes, but not till midnight Jan. 2–3 for the purposes of the Act.

A correspondent with a morbid turn of mind puts the problem of 'twins, one of which is heir to an earldom. It is an established fact that A was born an hour before B on May 2. But the doctrine of Disregarding Fractions must surely mean that for the purposes of inheritance they were born simultaneously two midnights earlier, at 0000 hours on May 1?'

Another correspondent suggests that the common law doctrine of Disregarding

---

[1] Re-enacted in the National Health Insurance Act, 1946.

Fractions is inconsistently applied to births and deaths. In *Lester* v. *Garland* (1808), 15 Vos. at 257 (English Reports Vol. 33), a testator bequeathed the residue of his estate to X on condition (*inter alia*) that X gave to the trustees of the will such security as they might approve within six calendar months from his decease. The Testator died on January 12, 1805, and the security was given on July 12, 1805.

Held per Sir William Grant, M.R., that the six months began to run at the commencement of the day *after* the testator's death.

In other words, in this case the law, still disregarding fractions, worked forward instead of backward. If Plush J., therefore, had followed the precedents on both sides he would have had to find:

(*a*) that George Stewer attained his majority thirty-six hours *before* the twenty-first anniversary of his birth: and

(*b*) that the Earl was alive throughout Monday, May 2, and did not die legally till twelve hours (less six seconds) *after* his actual death.

Fortunately, there is a good answer to such conundrums. It was laid down long ago by Lord Mansfield in *Combe* v. *Pitt* (1763), 3 Burr. 1423, that 'Though the law does not, in general, allow of the fraction of a day, yet it admits it in cases where it is necessary to distinguish.' So 'Where the defendant died between eleven and twelve in the morning and a writ of *fieri facias* was sued out against him between two and three in the afternoon of the same day, the Court will set aside the writ as irregular. *When it is necessary to show which was the first of two acts*, the Court is at liberty to consider fractions of a day.' (*Chick* v. *Smith* (1840) 8 Dowl. 337).

In a later case (*Campbell* v. *Strangeways*, 3 C.P.D. 105) Grove J. said: '*Chick* v. *Smith* and other cases explain where the law will distinguish the fractions of a day, viz. *where it is necessary* ... for the purpose of a decision *to show which of two events first happened.*' *Clarke* v. *Bradlaugh* (1881), 8 Q.B.D. 63 (Court of Appeal), is a decision to the same effect.

These authorities clearly cover the misleading case of *In re Munsey*, and, though not mentioned in the report, were, without doubt, in the mind of Plush J. Enough has been said, at least, to show that much of the adverse comment on his judgment was hasty and ill-informed. Good, however, may result. It is to be hoped that Parliament may now come to the rescue of the courts, abolish the monster they have created, and make the rule provided by the National Health Insurance Act general, retaining of course the special exceptions required by such cases as *Chick* v. *Smith* and *In re Munsey*—and applying the same rule to death.

If not, the old doctrine may well be extended to other fields. If the law indeed 'disregards fractions of a day' a publican may have a good answer to a prosecution for selling liquor half an hour after the end of 'permitted hours'. The *Laws of Cricket* may require attention. A batsman who is out at ninety-nine should surely be 'deemed' to have scored 100. *De minimis non curat lex.*

The exhibit below may perhaps make the problem clearer to the practitioner and student.

X. is born at 11.0 a.m. on 1 May 1900
He dies at 11.0 a.m. on 1 May 1950

Becomes 21 at Common Law	0000 hours April, 30 1921	Halsbury
Becomes 21 by National Health Insurance Act	0000 hours May 1, 1921	
Dies—at Common Law	2400 hours May 1, 1950	*Lester* v. *Garland*
Comes of age— by proposed law	0000 hours May 1, 1921	Unless necessary to decide priority between two events. (Lord Mansfield)
Dies—by proposed law	0000 hours May 1, 1950	

(15) MORTIMER *v.* THE BRITISH BROAD-CASTING CORPORATION AND OTHERS

SUNDAY ON THE AIR

AT Bow Street to-day the Chief Metropolitan Magistrate announced his decision in this important case. Mr. Mortimer, a common informer, laid an information against the B.B.C. and some of their servants for an offence against the Sunday Observance Act 1677. The Attorney-General appeared for the defendants.

Though I took time to consider my decision, said the magistrate, the case seems clear enough. On Sunday, May 21, between 9.15 and 10.45 p.m. the defendants caused to be performed on their premises at Alexandra Palace 'a comedy by Arnold Bennett' called *The Title*: and by a process called television the performance was made visible and audible in the homes of the many thousand subscribers or licensees. The laws concerning private labour and public entertainment on the Lord's Day are in this country severe; and, in particular, the presentation of stage-plays at a play-house has been prohibited, under heavy penalties, since the reign of George III (Sunday Observance Act, 1781). 'If a house, room or place be opened for any public entertainment, or for debating upon any subject, on Sunday, to which persons are admitted only by payment, the keepers thereof shall forfeit £200, the manager or president £100, the receiver of money or tickets £50, and every person printing an advertisement of such meeting £50.' Even when by Act of Parliament, in 1932, the exhibition of moving-pictures, for money, on Sundays, was made lawful, performances by living actors were carefully excluded.

So far as it is possible, or proper, to interpret the mind of the Legislature, it seems to consider the actor in two ways: (1) as a person whose lewd and worldly performances should not be allowed to corrupt and distract the citizens from religious contemplation on the evening of the Lord's Day, and (2) as a worthy and God-fearing person who should not be compelled, or even permitted, to labour on the Lord's Day for the selfish enjoyment of others. Whether the main purpose was the protection of the citizen or the protection of the actor, it has not prevented actors from using their gifts and experience on Sundays in the service of the B.B.C. and in programmes which it would often be difficult to describe as unworldly. The invention of television took the thing a long way farther, for now the actors are using all the apparatus of a stage-play. They paint their faces, they wear costumes, are surrounded by scenery and artfully illuminated. Mr. Mortimer—a deeply religious man, he assured the Court—is persuaded that such performances are contrary to the intentions of the authors of the Act of George III, and, in a sense, are more harmful than the production of a stage-play in a play-house. Few, he says, but the lewd and worldly might be attracted to such a place on a Sunday: but by television the unwholesome influences of the theatre are brought into the homes of the people and assail the young and innocent by their own hearths, even, it may be, at their mothers' knees.

His difficulty lies in the wording of the Act. Though it is evident that the defendants are providing a 'public entertainment' no one is admitted to any house or place 'only by payment' in order to enjoy it. If he had relied upon the Act of George III, I should have been compelled to dismiss the case at once.

But he has drawn the Court's attention to the wording of the Act of Charles II, which provides that:

'No tradesmen, artificers, workmen, labourers, or other persons whatsoever shall do or exercise any worldly labour, business, or work of their ordinary callings upon the Lord's Day, or any part thereof (works of necessity and charity only excepted).'

There are, in fact, other exceptions. Barbers are excluded: and farmers, attorneys, and surgeons do not come within the classes mentioned in the statute. It would be an abuse of language, perhaps, to describe an actor as a tradesman, workman or labourer. But many of those who attend and are necessary to his performance fall clearly into one or other of those categories; the man, for example, who places the scenery and the arc-lights, the carpenter, the property-man, the man who acts as his dresser or guards the door of the building. Then there are the 'artificers'. These are defined in *Wharton's Law Lexicon* as 'persons who are masters of their art and whose employment consists chiefly in manual labour'. Here, I have no doubt, should be included all the higher grades of theatrical labour of this kind: the electrician who regulates the flow of light, the man who directs the camera or the sound-recording, the lady who assists the actress in her make-up, adjusts her wig and fits her dresses.

The *Oxford English Dictionary*, I need hardly say, gives six different meanings, three of which I think are richly relevant to our purpose: (1) 'One who makes by art or skill', (4) 'Contriver, inventor, deviser' and (5) 'One who practises any art, or applied science'. These, between them, seem to me to cover almost all those who contribute actively to a theatrical production on the Lord's Day. The producer and stage-manager are, without doubt, contrivers and devisers, 'making' something by their art and skill. No actor would be heard to say that he is not 'one who practises an art': indeed, that is the whole of his somewhat flimsy claim to consideration. Only the author, I think, escapes. It must be assumed, in the absence of evidence to the contrary, that he is a God-fearing man and wrote his play on a week-day: and, unless he actively assists at a Sunday rehearsal, he should be blameless. All the other individuals concerned in this performance I find guilty of an offence, and they will forfeit five shillings.

There remains the question of the principal defendants, the British Broadcasting Corporation. I should be reluctant, indeed, to punish the small man under orders and let the responsible employer go free. Such injustices cannot always be avoided: but here I am in no doubt. The Corporation is clearly an 'artificer' within the meaning of the Act. If the defendants think themselves too high and mighty for such a title, I can but remind them that the Creator has been described as the Artificer of the Universe. The Corporation will pay five shillings too. I am aware that this decision, though concerned with television and stage-plays only, must raise some anxious doubts about the legality of all the Corporation's activities on Sunday. I cannot help that: but I should be willing to state a case for the opinion of a higher Court.

14 June, 1950

NOTE—And see a sparkling speech in the House of Commons, April 1, 1941: 'Let us look at what happened last Sunday. According to the *Radio Times*, there were no fewer than seven theatrical entertainments put forward by the B.B.C. last Sunday.

'The entertainments, which were performed by professional actors, would be unlawful in the theatre outside. At 4.30 in the Home Service programme, at the time when in Victorian days the children were massing about their mothers' knees, there was a performance, with elaborate music and dialogue, of the degrading stage play called *Peter Pan*. It lasted one and a quarter hours. At 9.25 there was a play by the alien writer Euripides. The position was far more serious on the Forces programme, where there were at least five such performances. At 12.30 there was "Services Variety", at 1.15 "Music Hall", and at 2.15 "Sunday Matinée", and at 6.30 something called "Hi-Gang". All these performances were given by well-known actors and actresses. At 8 o'clock an entertainment with the horrible name of "Happidrome" was given, and at 10.8 there was Bobbie Pagan at the theatre organ.

'Meanwhile, as my hon. Friend has already pointed out, on Sunday in Fleet Street and in every other big town there were hundreds of thousands of men preparing Monday's *Times* and *Express* and all the papers which my hon. Friend reads in bed on a Monday without a protest or a qualm. Let me put it in another way. Take it from the point of view of a well-known actor, like John Gielgud. On Sunday, if the B.B.C. like, he can act *Hamlet* or *Henry V* all day long. He can appear on the films as Hamlet or Henry V. He can give a long lecture on *Hamlet* or *Henry V*. He can appear—this is remarkable—at a concert or cinema and act passages from *Henry V* so long as he does not make up, put on costume, and do the job properly. In other words, I think we are trying to keep the horse in the stable long after it is far away.' (*Petty Officer Alan Herbert, Oxford University.*)

(16) CANTER AND OTHERS v. HOWARD

THE CANTER POLL

(Before the Lord Chief Justice)

HIS Lordship, giving judgment, said: In this important case a writ of *habeas corpus* was issued to the defendant Howard on behalf of three persons, Dr. Canter, Mr. Knocknee and Miss Gambier-Truce, who were said to be held in custody without due cause or legal process. This great prerogative writ is one of the finest props, foundation-stones, keystones, bulwarks, sheet-anchors and so forth of liberty in this fair land: and black will be the day when it loses power or respect. But in this case the defendant Howard is none other than Sir Charles Howard, Serjeant-at-Arms to the House of Commons, and it was in obedience to an Order of that honourable House that he confined the three complainants in the Clock Tower at Westminster.

Now, it is well established that either House of Parliament can do almost anything it will (short, perhaps, of execution) to any person who offends it. Certainly, it can, for breaches of privilege or contempt, commit any person to custody: and, in general, the causes of the commitment cannot be inquired into by any court of law, though it is the practice for the Serjeant-at-Arms to make a return to a writ of *habeas corpus*. There is, however, one exception to this healthy doctrine. When the warrant for arrest or commitment goes beyond the general assertion of contempt and breach of privilege and states particular causes for the infringement of liberty complained of, the Court (*per* Lord Ellenborough in *Burdett* v. *Abbot*) may inquire whether the causes disclosed are sufficient and within the jurisdiction of the House. In this case particular causes were set out in the warrant: and this Court gaily accepts the challenge—or, it may be, the invitation—of the High Court of Parliament.

The charge is that Dr. Canter and his friends 'did falsely purport to take a poll of the people in relation to the constitution of Parliament and did publish the same contrary to the Representation of the People Acts and in derogation of the rights and dignities of the Commons House of Parliament'.

The complainants frankly confess that they are responsible for an institution called the Canter Poll which from time to time announces that the popularity of the Prime Minister has risen from 51·3 to 52·6 per cent., while the chances of his Party at the next Election have fallen from 37·5 to 33·8 per cent.

The 'poll' is an essential part of British democratic practice, whether the scene be great or small. There may be a poll of a parish, a city, a county, a private society, a limited liability company, a House of Parliament, the nation. But what is a 'poll'? Literally a poll is a 'head'. Socially, and politically, it means a counting of heads, whether at a census, an election, or similar occasion. It is an exact and mathematical process, opposed, for example, to such uncertain guides to opinion as the 'show of hands'. This distinction is familiar to the Courts; for, whenever a person has to be chosen, or a thing may be ordered to be done, by a majority of the persons entitled to vote, there is a Common Law right to demand a *poll*, so that *all* entitled to vote may have a second and fairer opportunity of voting (*Reg.* v. *Wimbledon Local Board* (1881), 8 Q.B.D.—459— C.A.). And, whatever the scene or scale of affairs, the meaning of 'poll' is plain enough to the ordinary citizen of 'reasonable' intelligence.

But in this affair, it is clear, the word has no such meaning. There are about fifty million inhabitants of the United Kingdom, and about thirty-four million Parliamentary voters. Dr. Canter admitted in the box that the questions upon which his 'poll' is founded are addressed to about two thousand only. There is no secret, it appears, about the figure two thousand: but it is not published with the 'results' of the 'poll', and so, for any misunderstanding that may arise, the promoters must be held responsible. The announcement of a "poll-tax" which was to be levied upon one in every twenty-five thousand citizens would be greeted with public derision: and no more respect, it is clear, is due to the 'poll' in 'Canter Poll'. Whatever it is the Doctor does, he does not count *all* the heads.

So much, under cross-examination, he conceded. But he said that his two thousand were a 'cross-section' of the people, so cleverly, so 'scientifically', selected, that their opinions 'represented a poll'. A contradiction in terms: but let that pass, for the moment. Further, he claimed with pride that upon certain important occasions the predictions, or premonitions, founded upon his 'Poll' had been confirmed, or nearly confirmed, by events, that is, by the voting of the people at a subsequent election. I must say at once that all this boasting did not impress the Court. Not only the method, but the matter must be considered. It may be innocent, and useful, to ask one in every twenty-five thousand of the people how often they wash, what they think about the South Bank, or whether, when cleaning brass or silver, they use Bozo or Shinit, and to found upon their answers certain general conclusions. But when the questions are: 'Do you like the Prime Minister?' or 'How will you vote at the next Election?' (which is as much as to say 'Do you think the House of Commons is properly constituted at the present time?') we must halt for reflection. Here, it seems to me, the more right the complainants claim to have been in fact, the more wrong they are in law.

'Two rights,' as Lord Mildew said in a famous case,[1] 'may well make a wrong.' For our ancient Constitution has provided means by which these questions can be put and answered; and Dr. Canter, so far as this Court is aware, has no place in the Constitution. Speaking as a citizen, and not

[1] *The Queen* v. *Merino* (*1901*), A.C. 1, where a crystal-gazer told two clients, both married, that they would meet a dark woman and a tall fair man respectively. They did: and, according to the newspaper-report, 'became involved in a suicide pact'.

as a Judge, I feel an inexpressible repugnance when I read that the Prime Minister has declined in popularity from 48·9 to 47·3 per cent., however little I may agree with him politically. What an impertinence! Speaking as a Judge, I am sure that it is against public policy and constitutionally improper. Any statesman, it is true, any journalist, is free to say that in his opinion the Prime Minister, or the Party in power, have lost the confidence of the country, and should 'go to' it. It is quite another thing to pretend that by 'scientific' means you have discovered the opinion of thirty-four million people. For this must be untrue, and if it were true, would make elections unnecessary and the Constitution nonsense.

So far, then, as this Court has any say in the matter, I find that the complainants were incarcerated for good cause: and they will return to their noisy quarters in the Clock Tower. In time, no doubt, the House of Commons will mercifully discharge them. The question will then arise whether they should be dealt with as rogues and vaga- bonds, pretending to tell fortunes 'by palmistry or other- wise', or as the authors of seditious libels 'tending to bring into hatred and contempt' the Constitution as by law established, and the House of Commons, in particular. Upon that, at the moment, I express no opinion.

6 June, 1951

(17) REX v. HADDOCK AND VINE

Bookmakers All

'One of the most shameless frauds on the Revenue ever conceived,' said the Attorney-General, Sir Anthony Slatt, in his final address to the jury at the Old Bailey to-day. 'You will know what to do,' he concluded grimly.

Mr. Justice Codd, summing-up to the jury, said:

The learned Attorney-General has allowed himself to become more excited than is customary in counsel prosecuting for the Crown. That, in the circumstances of this case, is understandable: but you must not allow his emotion to affect you. Nor should you be swayed by the almost universal loathing for the prisoner Haddock. Address your minds to the facts, and to so much of the law as I am able to explain.

No excitement was caused, a year or two ago, when the ancient and respected firm of Lotwood put the words 'Bookmakers and' before the word 'Publishers' on their fine building and elegant notepaper. After all, it is part of their business, and the Memorandum of Association says, to 'prepare, devise, make and manufacture' books: and the addition was thought, by the few who noticed it, to be an unnecessary but pardonable essay in precision.

But one of Lotwood's authors is the notorious Albert Haddock who stands before you in that dock to-day. This man is chiefly known for his unreasoning and unrelenting objection to the rates of income tax and the methods of the selfless officers whose duty it is to assess and collect it. But again, members of the jury, though, as good citizens yourselves, you may delight and glory in the income tax, I must adjure you to put aside such odious sentiments as may naturally arise in you towards weak, eccentric characters who do not think as you do.

In February this year the officers of the Inland Revenue

Department were placidly planning, according to law, to take away from Albert Haddock two-thirds or more of the money he had earned by his brains and labour in the two preceding years. During their kindly researches into his banking account—which, to do the prisoner full justice, was offered for their inspection—they came upon a 'credit' entry of £1,000, a cheque signed for that amount by Mr. Stanley Vine, the general manager of Lotwoods. 'This,' they said, 'is, we presume, part of your professional earnings, an "advance on royalties" for one of your books, perhaps?' 'No, no,' said the prisoner; 'that was my winnings on a successful bet—and, therefore, is not subject to income tax.' 'What was the bet?' said the officer. 'That,' said the prisoner, 'has nothing to do with you. I do a good deal of betting with Mr. Vine,' he added, and he indicated in the bank-book several small payments to Mr. Vine. These, he said, were for unsuccessful bets on horses and dogs. You snorted at that, didn't you, Sir Anthony?

The Attorney-General: Milord?

The Judge: Never mind. The Inland Revenue then visited the Lotwood office, where the prisoner Vine, it appears, was as frank and open as he has been in the box. The Memorandum of Association says that the company may conduct 'any other business whatsoever which can be advantageously carried on by the company': and side by side with the ordinary business of producing and marketing books in the literary sense his firm are now conducting the business of a credit 'bookmaker', in the sporting sense. So far as the Court knows, there is no objection to this in law. Many citizens, including the prisoner Haddock, and at least two Royal Commissions, have recommended that all 'bookmakers' should be registered and licensed. But the Legislature has never thought fit to provide for this. Indeed, in these days, it is about the only thing that can be done without a licence. Anyone, therefore, can set himself up as a bookmaker, if he so desire, and, provided he sticks to credit-betting, and does not allow persons to resort to his office for the purpose of betting, nobody can interfere with him. Of course, he will have to produce his accounts to the Inland Revenue and pay tax upon his profits, if any.

Further, as counsel for the defence have suggested, you may think that there is a special affinity between these two types of business. As the prisoner Vine told the Court, 'Nothing could be more like a gamble than the production and sale of works of art.' Some of Vine's bets, it seems, have been directly connected with the other branch of the business. Authors, he told us, are sometimes idle, sometimes temperamental, always uncertain. He may sign with them a generous contract for the production of a novel in time for the spring season, with an advance on royalties to be paid on delivery of the manuscript. Paper is bought: the printers stand ready. Years pass; no novel appears: and there is nothing he can do about it. But such febrile characters, he says (and, after all, he should know the psychology of his business best), are often stimulated by the challenge of a bet. Accordingly, sometimes, he will bet Author A £500 that he will *not* deliver his new book by April 30. Author A, as a rule, he says, roars into action, toils day and night, produces the book on time, and wins the bet—to the advantage of all concerned.

The £1,000 payment to the prisoner Haddock, it was revealed in evidence, was the result of what you may think to have been a singularly 'sporting' wager. Haddock bet Vine £1,000 that his book *Forty Years of Fun* would sell five thousand copies. In fact, it sold many more than that. Vine paid up like a man, and the payment, of course, being a betting payment, was free of income tax.

It does not appear that the bookmaking side of Lotwood's business is very successful. The cheques paid out by Vine are generally large: the bets he wins are often small. But that may happen to anyone in the gambling business. At the end of the last financial year the business showed a loss: but that loss of course he is entitled to set off against the profits of the publishing business as any man who runs two businesses may do. Vine, it is said, hopes for better things in the current year, and, meanwhile, is borrowing money from the publishing side, with whom he is on good terms.

So far, you may think, the story does not disclose anything that calls for the attention of a criminal court. The Crown, however, say that here is a criminal conspiracy between Vine and Haddock, and Vine and other authors, to avoid payment of income tax. Let it be said, at once, that the avoidance of tax is not necessarily an offence or even wrong. The prisoner Haddock could avoid tax by ceasing to write at all: and so harsh is the treatment of authors that it would not be surprising if he did. But it would be no crime. And, if a man chooses to acquire money by betting (untaxed) rather than by hard work (taxed), that, again, is his own affair. Haddock, in the box, shyly admitted that, elated by winning a bet of £1,000 from Mr. Vine, he waived his royalties on the first five thousand copies of *Forty Years of Fun*. The Attorney-General found something fishy in that. You may think, as the Court thinks, that it was a very generous gesture. At all events, Mr. Haddock is not bound to accept the royalties due to him. If he chooses, he can write for fun and give his books away.

The Attorney-General: But, milord——

The Judge: I know, I know, Sir Anthony. To the Treasury, of course, any transaction that does not yield them a fat harvest is tainted: but that is not the law.

The Attorney-General painted a lurid picture of what may happen if the prisoners are acquitted. All sorts of firms, he said, film companies, theatrical managers, banks, will set up ancillary bookmakers' businesses and millions of pounds will go free of tax as winning bets. That may be. But it does not mean that the transactions we are considering are illegal. It may mean that the law requires amendment. That is the business of Parliament. It is our business—yours and mine—to administer the law as it stands. Consider your verdict.

The jury found the prisoners *Not Guilty*, and recommended a complimentary grant to them from the public funds.

13 June, 1951

NOTE—See also *Board of Inland Revenue* v. *the Dean of Alnwich* (1952), H.L., where the defendant made a successful wager of £5,000 with the Ecclesiastical Commissioners that a certain number of persons would attend divine service at the Cathedral within a certain period. *Held* (Lord Moon dissenting) that the payment was not liable to tax, though it was proved that the defendant had waived certain emoluments.

(18) THOMAS v. LOWDER; LOWDER v. THOMAS

THE LAW OF THE BAR

Mr. JUSTICE PLUSH, giving judgment, said: These two actions, which for convenience have been heard together, concern an incident which is happily rare in the life of our land, the forcible ejection of a police-officer from a public house. Mr. Thomas is a constable, a good officer, according to his superiors, but young and inexperienced. Mr. Lowder is the licensee of the Blue Moon at Burbleton.

'Permitted hours' in the Borough of Burbleton end at 10.30 p.m. At 10.42 p.m. (B.S.T.) on the night in question Constable Thomas heard voices 'proceeding', as he put it, from the saloon bar. He opened the door and entered, as any constable may do, without warning or warrant, if he has reasonable cause to suspect a breach of the law. There had been, that evening, a skittles match between the Blue Moon Club and the Lord Nelson Club (of Lower Wallop) and in the bar, besides the landlord, were about a dozen men discussing the affairs of the skittle world in general and the victory of the Blue Moon that evening in particular.[1] Is it 'skittles' or 'skittle', Sir Eliot?

Sir Eliot Ember, K.C.: They speak milord, of playing 'skittles'. But the governing body is called the Amateur Skittle Association.

The Judge: Very singular. Ha! But the evidence is clear that at 10.30 all drinking had stopped and that none of the men had even glasses in their hands. Mr. Lowder, it appears (a teetotaller, by the way), is almost pedantic in his observance of the law. At 10.30 he rings an old ship's bell and cries, 'Last orders, please.' At 10.25 he rings the bell twice and calls 'Finish your refreshments, please.' At 10.29

---

[1] In the 1950–1 season members of the Blue Moon Skittles Club (President, Mr. Albert Haddock) won eight out of the sixteen trophies presented by the Amateur Skittle Association.

the bell is rung for the last time and all glasses are collected or handed over the bar. This precise ritual had been observed that evening.

But Constable Thomas, standing at the door, said suspiciously, and, according to one witness, offensively, '*Rather late, aren't you?*'

'Late?' said the wounded licensee, indignantly. 'What's it got to do with you? There's no one drinking. Have a look.'

The constable 'had a look'.

'Satisfied?' said Mr. Lowder.

'Yes,' said the officer.

'Good,' said the licensed victualler. 'And now get out. I've private business with my friends here.'

'Don't talk to me like that,' said the officer. 'I'm doing my duty.'

'You've done your duty,' said Mr. Lowder. 'Out you go, please. What's more, I'll be glad if you withdraw the remark you passed. This is a respectable house.'

'Remark? What remark?' said the officer.

'About being late. It's no business of yours what time we go to bed.'

'I meant you were late shutting up.'

'That ain't your business, either,' was the reply. 'If you don't apologize, you go.'

'I'll go when I'm ready,' said the officer: and he added, unworthily: 'How do I know you won't start boozing when I've gone?'

'Because I tell you,' said the indignant victualler. 'I'm a liar now, am I? Here, out you go!'

With these words, he put a hand on the officer's shoulder and quietly but firmly conducted him out, to the astonishment and awe of his companions. The constable brought an action for assault, and Mr. Lowder issued a writ for slander.

It is now necessary to explore the legal significance of this spirited and unusual encounter. Loathsome though the provisions of the Licensing Act, 1921, must appear to any thinking citizen, that measure had one point of merit. It abolished what was known as 'closing-time'. The sale and consumption of 'alcohol', as it is called, can only take place within certain 'permitted hours': but the inn need never be 'closed'. It is lawful to enter or stay upon licensed premises at any hour of the day or night, if the landlord is agreeable. A man could sit in the public bar all day, playing back-gammon, or chess, without breaking the law, though, if the landlord desired him to go and he refused, he would become a trespasser.[1] The landlord, on the other hand, can converse with friends in the public bar all day, if he will, as freely as in his private parlour. This beneficent distinc-tion should be more widely known than it is: and I hope that it will be impressed upon all young policemen. For it does something to correct, on the one hand, the notion that the inn or public house is a place for 'boozing' only, and, on the other, the sense of regimentation which must come from punctual expulsion at fixed hours. It is a pity, perhaps, that so many licensees bring back the atmosphere of 'closing-time' by churlishly bustling their customers out as soon as 'permitted hours' are over: but they are under no obligation, one way or the other.

Now, as has been said, Constable Thomas, if he had reasonable cause to suspect that an offence was being com-mitted, had a right, a duty, to enter the bar. Having satis-fied himself, as he admitted, that there was no offence, his duty was to depart at a reasonable pace: for, in the absence of an invitation from the landlord, he was intruding on a private gathering. He had no right to remain there on the vague suspicion that an offence *might* be committed in the future: for, if he could do that, he could sit in the bar all day; and Parliament has expressly provided against such behaviour. When he was requested to go and refused, he

[1] See *Rex* v. *Lambert* (1945) where 'for a record' a man sat 12 hours in the public bar of the *Black Lion* drinking soda-water, as a result of which he swelled up and died. It was *held* that no offence against the Licensing Laws had been disclosed: but the court issued a warning against the excessive consumption of soda-water.

became a trespasser: and as a contumacious trespasser Mr. Lowder was entitled to use reasonable force to eject him. The charge of assault, then, falls to the ground.

There remains the question of slander. The innuendo complained of in the words *'Rather late, aren't you?'* is said to be that the plaintiff had been late—illegally late—in terminating the sale of intoxicating liquor. This being a criminal offence it is not necessary for the plaintiff to prove special damage, if the words can be thought to carry a defamatory meaning. I rule that they can, that they were defamatory, and, in fact, untrue. Then there was the remark about 'starting to booze when I've gone'. The plaintiff is rightly jealous for his reputation. In his business he has to be. Lord Mildew said, in *Lott* v. *The Great Western Railway*, 'It is easier to become a priest than a publican.' A licensed victualler must be able to show a blameless record for seven years, and every year his licence must be renewed by the justices. A whisper of wrong-doing may cost him his position. The plaintiff says that the defendant, by his remarks, suggested to those present, many of them men from another borough, that his was a house where the law was habitually and shamelessly broken. Again, since such an accusation affects him in his way of business, no proof of special damage is required. Mr. Lowder's action must succeed, and I award damages of £1,000. The constable will pay all the costs in both cases. I am glad they came before me. Things have come to a pretty pass if police officers can go up to innocent citizens and tell them they are 'late', especially if, by Greenwich Mean Time, it is only twenty-to-ten. As Lord Mildew said in *Stannaway* v. *Miles*, 'There is not yet a law about going to bed.'

20 June, 1951

(19) THE MERCHANTS' CASE

DOES MAGNA CARTA MATTER?

THE Judicial Committee of the Privy Council on June 1 gave their decision in the Merchants' Case.

The Lord Chancellor said:

In this important case we have to answer an unusual question. Under Section 4 of the Statute of 1833 it is open to His Majesty to refer to us any matter which he thinks fit, whether that matter has been the subject of litigation or not. It is a rare power, but on occasions has proved its usefulness: and this, I think, may be another.

The question is whether certain provisions of the Finance Bill, 1951, are in conflict with Chapter 30 of Magna Carta. An academic question, admittedly—indeed, in a sense, a hypothetical question—for the Finance Bill has not yet become law: and no man can tell exactly in what form it will be presented for the Royal Assent.

On the other hand—and this consideration, I am sure, was in the mind of His Majesty, and the Attorney-General, who advised him—the last chapter of Magna Carta is very clear about the nature and effects of a conflict such as has been posited in argument before us. The Great Charter, that chapter relates, 'was bought from the Crown with a fifteenth of our movable property' ... in consideration of which the King grants 'for us and our heirs, that neither we nor our heirs shall *attempt*'—note the word—'to do anything whereby the liberties contained in this charter may be infringed or broken. And if anything should be done to the contrary, it shall be held of no force and effect.'

'It shall be held of no force and effect,' the Lord Chancellor repeated gravely. That, no doubt, was a too optimistic assertion: for no British Parliament can be bound by those who came before, as His Majesty's Ministers showed very firmly two years ago concerning the pledges made to the Dominion of Newfoundland by their predecessors in 1933. But no loyal citizen can contemplate without dismay the possibility of the Finance Act, or anything in it, after due consideration by Parliament, receiving the Royal Assent, if it is evidently inconsistent with an important chapter, not repealed, of the Great Charter. Better far, upon an authoritative warning of such a conflict, for the King's Ministers to withdraw their proposals, to abandon the 'attempt', before they, and Parliament, are irrevocably committed. That I take to be sufficient justification for these unusual proceedings.

Now Chapter 30 of the Great Charter says, wisely and generously, as follows:

> All merchants (if they were not openly prohibited before) shall have their safe and sure conduct to depart out of England, to come into England, to tarry in and go through England, as well by land as by water, to buy and sell without any manner of evil tolls (that is, extortions) except in time of war.

The passage which follows deals with the treatment of foreign merchants in time of war: but it is clear that the words I have read cover 'all' merchants, English or foreign. Not only their freedom of movement, but their freedom from 'evil tolls' is guaranteed, as a recognition of the importance of their activities and their advantage to the realm.

The importance of those who 'buy and sell' is hardly less to-day. Indeed, without them starvation would descend upon this island in quick time. Nor is it any less desirable that foreign merchants should be free to bring their merchandise or their money into the country and take it away if they are so inclined. But in the Finance Bill new restrictions upon the free movement of 'merchants', in the wide sense which ought to be given to the word, are proposed. By Clause 32 it is made unlawful for 'a body corporate resident in the United Kingdom to cease to be so resident' and 'for the trade or business, or any part of the trade or business of a body corporate so resident to be transferred from that body corporate to a person not so resident'. Any person concerned in such an offence may be savagely punished by two years' imprisonment or a fine of ten thousand pounds, or both.

Now, it was powerfully argued before us, by Mr. Albert Haddock among others, that these provisions are an infringement—so far only 'attempted', it is true—of the 'liberties contained in this Charter': and in my opinion that argument ought to prevail. The Attorney-General told us that by going abroad some 'merchants' may pay fewer taxes. But they may also, I suppose, enjoy better food, more beautiful scenery, more attractive music. It does not seem to me to be relevant to the principles in issue. If that is the trouble the remedy is not to reduce the liberties but to reduce the taxes. And what of the foreigner? What inducement will remain to invest his capital and brains and enterprise in this country if, once in, he can never get out? I hold, without doubt, that the penalties named in Clause 32 are 'evil tolls' of the character which the authors of the Great Charter had in mind and, if that clause be forced on to the Statute Book, the Great Charter should be *pro tanto* amended.

While we are considering the Great Charter, I wish to refer to another chapter, Number 14, which is directed against excessive fines:

A freeman shall not be amerced (that is, fined) for a small fault, but after the manner of the fault; and for a great fault after the greatness thereof, saving to him his contenement; and a merchant likewise saving to him his merchandise. . . .

A man's contenement has been defined as that which is absolutely necessary for his support and maintenance, as his tools and instruments of trade. I note in the minds of Ministers, legislators, and even judges, a shocking tendency to forget Chapter 14 of the Great Charter. In these days so many new and subtle offences are created, so many ordinary acts may not be done without a licence, a certificate or a form that the simple citizen may easily become bewildered. The restrictions on the flow of 'currency', as it is still laughably called, are a good example: the building regulations are another. A man may dimly understand why he must not take more than a few pounds in notes abroad, but not why he may not bring more than £10 of English money, lawfully acquired, back into his own country.[1] Too often, instead of improving the regulations, or making their purpose plain, the authorities impose increasingly savage fines, and those who inflict them, so far from preserving the wrongdoer's contenement, seem to care nothing if they ruin the man. A citizen can be punished more severely to-day for breaking a building or currency regulation than he would be for manslaughter or burglary. I wish to say that if any such sentences are brought before me in any of my numerous capacities I shall declare them null and void according to the provisions of the Great Charter.

There is an opinion, I am well aware, that so little of Magna Carta is left that none of it is left. Indeed, that was the decision of Mr. Justice Lugg in *Rex* v. *Haddock* [1927]. But I have always thought that that case was wrongly decided.

Lords Right and Left, Middle and Off concurred with the Lord Chancellor. The Cabinet, we understand, are considering the position, and drastic amendments may be made to the Finance Bill.

27 June, 1951

NOTE—No amendments were made; and the Section complained of is now the law of the land. Mr. H. G. Strauss (Norwich, South) put down an amendment to repeal cap. 30 of Magna Carta, but the amendment was not 'called'. On the Third Reading of the Finance Bill (*Hansard*, July 3 1951, Cols. 2,224–5) he said:
'Let us examine what Clause 33 does. First of all, at what companies is it

[1] See *Rex* v. *Haddock*, p. 111.

directed? ... The companies at which Clause 33 is directed are companies which, though resident in the United Kingdom, are trading abroad. That is the important thing to remember: they are trading abroad but they are resident in the United Kingdom. The object of the Clause is to prevent them from leaving the United Kingdom and going abroad, possibly to the country where they are carrying on their trade.

The first thing to realise is that those companies need never have been resident here at all. Why did they choose to be resident here? The answer is, for some of those advantages ... such as the banking facilities of the City of London, the insurance facilities, shipping and, I might add, the reputation of, and the possibility of access to, English law. All those things made it attractive for them to be resident in the United Kingdom. From that residence the United Kingdom drew immense advantages in invisible exports, which even today constitute one of the main things on which the Chancellor necessarily relies.

'This Clause, then, is directed at companies which are trading abroad and which need never have come here at all. What is the form of the prohibition? It says this:

> All transactions of the following classes ... shall be unlawful,

unless carried out with the consent of the Treasury. Now let me read the first of those classes of transaction:

> for a body corporate resident in the United Kingdom to cease to be so resident;

That is what the Socialist Government say ought to be prohibited in 1951. I ask hon. Members, with those words fresh in their minds, to remember these words:

> All merchants, if they were not openly prohibited before, shall have their safe and sure conduct to depart out of England, to come into England, to tarry in, and go through England, as well by land as by water, to buy and sell without any matter of evil tolles by the old and rightful customs, except in times of war;

'That is from Magna Carta, 1215. The text can be found in the first volume of the *Statutes Revised*, which any hon. Member can find in either of the Division Lobbies. They will find it in the Statute of Magna Carta of 1297, 25 Edward I, Chapter XXX. That shows the extent of the revolution that is here being enacted and the blindness of the nature of British greatness which the mere putting forward of this Clause involves.'

The Chancellor of the Exchequer said (Col. 2,237):

'In fact, under the Exchange Control Act, so far as the migration of companies is concerned, there has already been existing for the past four years control of the kind to which he objected so much. . . . I cannot therefore readily accept that all the sinister consequences that the hon. and learned Member seemed to indicate would follow, have any substance whatever, because they certainly have not been apparent in the last few years.'

But, in that case, Magna Carta should have been amended four years ago.

(20) REX *v.* GENTLE, GOOD AND HADDOCK

'Paying to Rule'

(Before a Divisional Court)

Mr. Justice Hornet, giving judgment in this enthralling case, said:

The defendants, Gentle, Good and Haddock, are charged with offences against Section One of the Finance (New Duties) Act, 1916. That Act, for the purpose of raising new revenue for the temporary[1] purposes of war, accepted the barbarous principle of a tax upon amusement. 'No persons', it said, 'shall be admitted to any entertainment except

'(*a*) with a ticket stamped with a stamp (not before used) denoting that the proper Entertainment Duty has been paid, or

'(*b*) in special cases, with the approval of the Commissioners, through a barrier which, or by means of a mechanical contrivance which, automatically registers the number of persons admitted.

Theatres, as a rule, do not employ turnstiles; the business of affixing stamps to tickets was tiresome; manpower was precious: so, in the circumstances of war, there was a third arrangement. Theatrical managers and other 'entertainers' were permitted to give security that they would keep an exact account of the numbers of persons admitted and hand over the appropriate tax at the end of the week. This was a great convenience for the Board of Customs and Excise. They did not have to provide stamps or (except for an occasional visit by an inspector) officials. The managers did the Crown's work for it. For them it was a great labour, and required very often an increase in staff. Moreover, since the

---

[1] Ha!—ED.

duty was included in the price of the tickets, the arrangement concealed from many of the public the extent of the tax, and the managers were blamed for high prices which were really the work of the Crown. Yet these toils and troubles were cheerfully endured by patriotic men. What is more surprising is that when the war was concluded, and the 'temporary' tax continued, they still sheepishly cooperated with the perfidious State, and have done so ever since.

In the present year, according to the evidence, there has been a change. One of those unpredictable gusts of spontaneous feeling familiar to the student of affairs has swept through the entertainment world as an April gale blows through the forest. Each brand of entertainment, it seems, has a different grievance. In the cinema, at a time of exceptional difficulty, the tax has been increased in the present year. In the theatre, objection is expressed to an arrangement by which some theatres pay no tax at all. Football and billiards pay at a lower rate because they are 'live' entertainments, but motor-bicycle racing is not so indulged. Circuses pay at one rate and horse-racing at another. The defendant Gentle, for the greyhound-racing world, expressed a particular grievance against the State. Dog-racing, with 'live' dogs, it seems, pays entertainments tax at the full rate, and in addition a betting tax is levied upon the dog-race course which is not levied upon the horse-race course, or anywhere else.

These complaints do not concern the Court except as an atmospherical background to the case. They all had one result. The defendant Good, we are told, wrote to the Board of Customs and Excise as follows: 'I am producing a play called *Hamlet* at the —— Theatre. The State, I understand, desires to levy a tax on the tickets of all those admitted to see it. Very well. The State is supreme. But I am a theatrical manager, not a tax-collector. Let the State collect its own —— taxes! From Thursday next pray send your officers to the Stalls, Dress Circle, Upper Circle, Pit and Gallery entrances of this theatre (at 6.45 Mon. to Sat., and 2.15 Wed. and Sat.), ready to affix the appropriate stamps to any tickets I may sell. This will be a nuisance to our public, but it cannot be helped. At least they will realize where their money is going, and the odium of the tax will fall where it should.'

Mr. Gentle wrote, not less robustly: 'Next Saturday we are having a greyhound race-meeting at the Stadium. We are loyal citizens doing our best to give pleasure to the people, pay our due taxes, and make an honest living. But the State has given us so little consideration that we see no reason why we should cosset the State. We are tired of doing sums for the State and we can no longer afford the extra staff. Let the State do its own dirty work. Pray send officials (with stamps) to the twenty-six entrances of the Stadium in good time on Saturday—also to the many other race-courses controlled by this Association, a list of which is appended. *L'État—ce n'est pas moi.*'

These two letters, by themselves, might have caused no great anxiety at the fine Customs House at Billingsgate: but, as I have said, a kind of contagious fever was abroad. Entertainers of every kind sent similar letters in the same week from every city and corner of the realm: and it may well be that the Board of Customs and Excise, in these days of full employment, was unable to furnish officials sufficient to meet the very numerous demands. Accordingly, by his own account, the defendant Haddock, having purchased an expensive stalls ticket for the play called *Hamlet*, waited in vain at the head of an eager queue for an Excise official to stamp his ticket. It never entered his mind, he told the Court, to enter the auditorium with an unstamped ticket, for he is, he says, an unusually law-abiding subject. But, when the orchestra was heard, the pressure of the impatient people behind him was too much for him, and he was swept unwillingly into the stalls. A similar misfortune befell him two days later when, through no fault of his own, he found himself watching the dog-races with an unstamped ticket.

Now, the Crown says that in both these cases he is 'liable to an Excise Penalty' of £50 as a 'person admitted' contrary to the Act, and that the defendants Good and Gentle are each liable to the same penalty as 'the proprietors' of the entertainments to which he was 'admitted'.

The answer of the defence is simple. They say that he was not 'admitted'; that both he and the proprietors did all that could reasonably be expected of them to prevent his 'admission'; that he was forced into the theatre, and into the dog arena, by the irresistible pressure of the crowd: and that for that pressure the Crown itself was responsible by its failure to provide sufficient officers to stamp the tickets lawfully sold and purchased.

The Crown says that it was the duty of the proprietors to stamp the tickets. But for that contention the Court has been unable to find any support in law. There is nothing in the original Act, or in the numerous regulations made under it, which commands the proprietor in every case to affix the stamp (there is an exception where tickets are issued in 'books or sheets' and the tickets pass out of the proprietors' control). It would be surprising if it were otherwise. Many Customs and Excise Duties are collected every day at our sea-ports. If the Customs officers failed to be present to collect what was due from the passengers of a home-coming ship, no one would expect the shipowner to do their duty for them, and no Court would condemn a passenger who, after searching vainly for a Customs officer, entered the waiting train and proceeded to his home with his dutiable goods. The parallel seems to me to be exact. The Crown is wrong.

Mr. Justice Codd said: I agree. But I wish to add a word or two. It may be that after this decision the Excise Commissioners will seek to escape from their difficulties by making a regulation requiring the proprietors to stamp the tickets in every case. I may say at once that in my opinion such a regulation would be *ultra vires* and of no effect. Tax-collection is the business of the Crown, and if Parliament desires these serious powers and duties to be handed over to private citizens it will, without doubt, clearly say so, as it has in some affairs, but not in this. For one thing, the tax-collector is worthy of his hire, and must be remunerated like the rest of us. The case is dismissed.

25 July, 1951

(21) REX *v.* HADDOCK; HADDOCK *v.* REX

The Lords Rebel

THE House of Lords to-day laid down a new principle of law in this important case.

The Lord Chancellor said:

This charming morsel of litigation would not, in the ordinary course, have reached your Lordships' table. It was sent up to us by the rough but sensible procedure first used in the misleading case of *Board of Inland Revenue* v. *Haddock*, 1931.[1] A succession of courts below, apprehending at a glance that being bound by previous decisions they were unable to determine the matter except in a manner repugnant to natural justice, declined to waste their time and talents on a full hearing but remitted the case *quam celerrime* to this, the highest tribunal in the land.

Not for the first time, a high question of law has sprung from the lowly, and sometimes squalid, affairs of Mr. Albert Haddock. In this case that tenacious litigant and friend of freedom, returning from Australia in the Orient Line steamer *Orchid*, was examined as usual at the port of landing in this country by the customs and immigration authorities. When asked how much English currency he had in his possession he answered frankly that he had about £80 in what are still amusingly known as British 'pound notes'. At this information, according to the evidence, one of the examining officers fainted. Another, with a white face, asked Mr. Haddock whether he was not aware of some regulation made under the Exchange Control Act, 1947, the exact title and number of which I confess I forget myself. It is—or was, at that time, it appears—ordained by this bizarre regulation that no British subject should leave these shores with more than £5 in British currency, and,

[1] See Note, p. 115.

stranger still, should not return with more than the same amount. (The figure, I have been informed, has since been graciously raised to £10.)[1] Mr. Haddock said that he was well aware of the regulation, but added rashly that he had never regarded it as worthy of serious consideration and in this case found it impossible to observe. 'So,' he added, in an idiom which is new to this House, 'what?'

The officers, shocked, it seems, as much by his *insouciance* as by his offence, confiscated 75 of his £80, and he was prosecuted and fined for a breach of the regulations. He has appealed. He also wants his money back.

In evidence, he painted a vivid picture of the last days in a great British liner returning to the mother country. The passengers, he said, have incurred various financial obligations; wine-bills, bar-bills, laundry-bills, radio-bills, besides the tips which will be expected by many obliging stewards. To meet these numerous calls they cash their Travellers' Cheques: but the calls are not always easy to assess exactly, and their minds are haunted by the fear of error. If they draw out too little money they may be confronted as they go ashore, when it is too late to draw any more, by the sad reproachful face of some steward they have forgotten or have insufficiently rewarded. If, on the other hand, they draw too much there is the menace of the regulation already mentioned. Those who through inadvertence, or faulty arithmetic, have more than £5 when all their obligations are discharged, must somehow get rid of the unlawful excess; and it appears that unnecessary and wasteful drinking is almost the only practical way out. Deplorable scenes, described by Mr. Haddock, are directly due, he says, to the regulation; and many a young person has been set on the downward path to drink through having a few pounds more than the law of Britain permits them to 'import'.

---

[1] 'There should be a new term for "currency". A current moves freely. Money, in these days, does not' (Lord Mildew in *Bank of England* v. *Thomas Cook* (1949), 2 A.C.).

During these last days an Australian friend expressed a desire to purchase a very fine and elaborate camera belonging to Mr. Haddock. That gentleman was uneasily aware of the unjust and merciless demands which would be made upon him by way of income and other taxes the moment he reached his native land: and he consented, with some reluctance, to the sale. The price fixed was £80. The Australian insisted—and Mr. Haddock agreed—that the price should be paid in English Treasury notes. How the Australian, a sheep-farmer, came to be in possession of so much United Kingdom currency is not clear. One suggestion is that he had betted heavily and successfully on the 'Ship's Run' throughout the long voyage. But that does not concern us. No doubt he heard about the regulation, and, as a stranger, was eager to conform with the law. Mr. Haddock, on the other hand, could not suppose, as he told us, that there could be any serious objection to a transaction so evidently advantageous to his own country. There may be good and obvious reasons for forbidding the citizen to take more than a fixed sum in English money out of the country: but who can condemn the man who goes forth into the world with £5 only, and by the exercise of legitimate commercial enterprise, comes back with £80? Great would have been the surprise of Drake, of Raleigh, and Cook, if after long voyages their Monarch had received them in such a manner. The learned Attorney-General, by the way, somewhat half-heartedly I thought, suggested that it was not a legitimate transaction, that Mr. Haddock should not have sold the camera without an Export Licence. Mr. Haddock replied that the article was sold in a British ship approaching British shores, and is in this island at the present time, so that it can hardly be said to have been exported. I think that he is right.

There, then, the ugly matter rests. The country is richer by £75. Mr. Haddock, the author of the increment, has been placed in the dock and fined, and his innocent gains have been taken from him. In the long history of State rapacity and harsh dealing I can recall few episodes like it. Counsel for the Crown, with the familiar Treasury shrug, say 'It is the law' and leave it at that. That, too, must be enough for lesser courts than this. But we, my Lords, guarding the supreme fount of justice, must be sure that the well is pure. We have endeavoured earnestly to ascertain the point and purpose of the regulation. Civil Servants of high character and advanced years were summoned from the gloomy dens of the Treasury. They mumbled through their beards the mystic formula 'Currency Control'. They whispered that the regulation had been first devised in time of war, when it must have had some purpose, but they could not remember what—'something', one muttered, 'about Black Market'. They admitted that if Mr. Haddock had sold the camera in Australia and sent the money home through a bank all would have been well: but they could not explain what important difference arose when the money came to London in notes. I suspect that the regulation has been allowed to survive in times of peace through sheer inertia or pure love of control. But, for your Lordships' House, I take it, there is no special magic in the words 'Currency Control'. Whether or not, in general, there is something to be said for the regulation we cannot discover. As applied and enforced in this particular case it appears to me to be nonsense. Your Lordships ought never to be asked to give their blessing and support to nonsensical regulations masquerading as law: and I hope they will never consent. If Parliament originates and carefully passes through all its stages an imbecile Act of Parliament, that is one thing. It is the law, and must be upheld. The whimsical edicts of Whitehall worthies deserve, and will receive, much less respect. To them, I suggest, we should apply a new maxim— '*Lex non stultitiam admittit*'. In the light of that maxim, Mr. Haddock's conviction should be quashed, he should get his money back, and I recommend that a sum of *about* £1,000 be paid to him out of the public funds by way of compensation for grievous injustice and loss of sleep.

Lords Right and Left, Lords Wool and Strawberry, agreed. Lord Strawberry thought that £2,000 would be more like it.

17 October, 1951

NOTE—In *Board of Inland Revenue* v. *Haddock* (1931) to which the Lord Chancellor referred, the Master of the Rolls delivered his celebrated judgment on the appellate system: 'The institution of one Court of Appeal may be considered a reasonable precaution; but two suggest panic. To take a fair parallel, our great doctors, I think, could not claim to be more respected or more advanced in their own science than our greatest jurists. But our surprise would be great if, after the removal of an appendix by a distinguished surgeon, we were taken before three other distinguished surgeons, who ordered our appendix to be replaced: and our surprise would give place to stupefaction if we were then referred to a tribunal of seven distinguished surgeons, who directed that our appendix should be extracted again. Yet such operations, or successions of operations, are an every-day experience in the practice of the law. . . . The people can be taught to believe in one Court of Appeal; but when there are two they cannot be blamed if they believe in neither. When a man keeps two clocks which tell the time differently, his fellows will receive with suspicion his weightiest pronouncements upon the hour of the day, even if one of them happens to be right. Moreover, the expense of successive appeals must make the acquisition of justice difficult for the rich and impossible for the poor. The unsuccessful litigant who cannot afford to go beyond the Court of Appeal must always be haunted by the thought that in the House of Lords he might have won; while the Inland Revenue, relying on the public purse, can pursue their unjust claims to the end and, if they lose, can send the bill to the taxpayer.

'For all these reasons we recommend that either this Court or the House of Lords (as a Court of Appeal) be abolished: or, in the alternative, that the House of Lords retain its appellate functions as a specialist body for the settlement of questions of exceptional difficulty, such cases to be referred to them upon the order of a High Court judge. As for the present case, we decline to discuss it. It will go to the House of Lords in any event, so let it go at once.'

(22) ALBERT AND GLORIA HADDOCK v. THE KING

Whose Passport is Yours?

The House of Lords to-day determined this appeal from a decision of the Court of Appeal reversing (Merry L. J. dissenting) a judgment of Dandrough J. in the King's Bench Division.

The Lord Chancellor said:

Your Lordships are well acquainted with one of the appellants, that patient apostle of liberty and good sense Mr. Albert Haddock. But this is the first time, I think, that his help-meet, Gloria, has come into Court with him. We bid her welcome and will do what we can for her.

This important appeal concerns the nature of a passport and the property in a passport; and the rights, if any, of the Crown to restrict the movements of the citizen in time of peace. Mr. Haddock's passport is of the fine old vintage of the late Mr. Ernest Bevin. It 'requests and requires in the name of His Majesty' that Mr. Haddock may be allowed 'to pass freely without let or hindrance'. It is stated to be 'valid' till a date five years from the date of issue. On the last page there is a wise cautionary note, reminding the holder that the passport is '*a valuable document*' and 'should not be allowed to pass into the possession of an unauthorized person'. But what, one wonders, is meant by 'an unauthorized person'?

Note, also, my Lords, in passing, the words 'valuable document'. It is certainly that, for, to obtain it, Mr. Haddock had to pay a sum of money to the State.

Now, in the present year, *consule* Morrison, Mrs. Haddock had occasion to acquire a new passport, in order to travel with her husband abroad. He assisted her in the prolonged formalities and paid the money demanded by the Passport Office. But Gloria's passport was 'new' in more senses than one. 'What' says Mr. Haddock (page 4375 in the transcript of evidence) 'was my astonishment to find (on the last page, before the usual caution about the "valuable document") the following entirely novel statement:

> ' "*This passport remains the property of His Majesty's Government and may be withdrawn at any time.*" '

There is nothing to that effect in Albert's passport: but it appears that the passport of Mr. Haddock's son, of an intermediate vintage, has a different formula. This one '*may be withdrawn if the holder ceases to be entitled to the protection of His Majesty's Government*'.

Now it is clear, as Mr. Haddock maintains, that in this land of equality a husband and wife can hardly hold two passports of different status or quality. If Gloria's passport belongs to the Crown, so does Albert's.

The appellants, therefore, have asked for a declaration (*a*) that their passports are their own property, duly acquired for value, or (*b*) in the alternative, that the Crown has obtained money from them by false pretences, and should restore it.

My Lords, if you please, I will discuss the second point first. The money-claim is small in amount (fifteen shillings) and by some may be considered squalid in character. But in my opinion it throws a powerful light on the constitutional point which is at the heart of this case. The Crown, with the citizens' assistance, prepares—and 'issues'—many official documents: the Birth Certificate, the Motor, Dog, Game or Radio Licence, the Ration Card, the Identity Card, the National Health Insurance Card. For some of these it charges a fee; for others not. Any citizen, I think, would be greatly surprised to hear that any of these documents were not his 'property', especially one for which he had paid a fee. On his Identity Card, for which no charge is made, he is told what to do if he finds a card 'not *belonging* to him'. There are legislative provisions for the suspension or cancellation by a court of law of a driving licence where offences have been committed. But no one, surely, would suggest that the Crown, that is, a Government Department, would be entitled to 'withdraw' a Birth Certificate (for which one penny is charged) or a Dog Licence 'at any time', that is, without showing cause in some process of law. That, though, is what the Crown claims in relation to the passport. They make it, on an early page, in prominent type, 'Valid for five years.' In small type, on the last page, they say that it is Government property, and can be taken away to-morrow. If the citizen's rights in the document are indeed so small and fleeting it is surprising, and possibly fraudulent, that he should be made to pay fifteen shillings for them.

But are his rights so small? At a day not very distant, but now almost forgotten, the passport was not required at all for travel in normal conditions in civilized lands. But it could be demanded as a right by any good citizen who proposed to travel in dangerous times and regions, and thought that a good word from His Majesty's Government might assist him whether with British or foreign officials. Wars came; the world was more difficult and dangerous; and the passport slowly grew into an instrument more for the restriction than the assistance of movement. But still the *prima facie right* to the passport remained: and the passport could only be 'withdrawn', as we have seen, where the holder 'ceased to be entitled to the protection of His Majesty's Government'—or, in other words, was guilty of some grave offence, to his own country, or perhaps another.

The new formula, on the latest breed of passport—and let it be noted that there are now three differently worded forms of passport in currency—goes very much farther. It can be 'withdrawn' (whatever that means) 'at any time', not because the holder 'has ceased to deserve His Majesty's protection', but because the Foreign Secretary does not like his face, or thinks that he should not waste his time and money on holidays abroad. But this is to turn a right into

a privilege; a security into a gamble; an open door into a
barricade. For though, so far as I know, there is still no law,
or even regulation, which ordains that a man may not pass
from England to France without a passport, in practice he
will not get far without one, unless he travels in a yacht. A
railway company might as well announce that, having sold
a ticket, it is entitled to take it away at once.

It is highly important, therefore, that your Lordships'
House should determine, once for all, the question of
property. If a private citizen took Mr. Haddock's passport,
he could without doubt proceed against him, as if the man
had taken his watch—or his Birth Certificate. Suppose that
the Crown asks Mr. Haddock to surrender his passport,
and Mr. Haddock refuses. Can the Crown send a policeman to take away his passport by force? I think not. For
there is nothing in any Act of Parliament, or, so far as I
know, any Statutory Regulation or Order that gives the
Crown that power. They have sold this document, for value
received, and it is now the personal property of Mr.
Haddock. After five years it may lose its 'validity' but,
unless he wants to acquire another, no-one can compel him
to hand it over.[1] If the State has any good reason for
wishing to stop him travelling, the State, no doubt, will find
some good way of doing so.

From this decision many small but valuable results may
follow. All over the world innumerable officials are making
a living by defacing Mr. Haddock's passport with what are
known as 'stamps'. These are often illegible, and their
purpose and justification is seldom plain. If, as I have
declared, the passport is Mr. Haddock's personal property,
all this stamping, it is clear, amounts to a trespass unless
Mr. Haddock agrees to it: and if all the Mr. Haddocks
united in objecting much time and trouble and money
would be saved. It follows too that the modern practice in

---

[1] The police or the Official Receiver may *ask* the citizen to surrender his
passport as a condition of the granting of bail or an earnest of good intentions,
but, *quaere*, they can do nothing if he refuses.

certain countries by which the traveller's passport is taken away from him for inspection by the police and others must be contrary to law. For no Government is entitled to take a Briton's property away from him.

I therefore find for Mr. Haddock and his lady. The appeal should be allowed, and a declaration made in the terms demanded.[1]

Lords Right, Wool, Strawberry and Bindweed concurred.

24 October, 1951

NOTE—See also a lively paper on 'Passportery' read at the 18th Congress of Indignant Travellers (*Sunday Times*, September 15, 1951):

The persecutions of passportery have increased, are increasing and ought to be diminished. It is about a quarter of a century since we observed that the passport, designed to allow us 'to pass freely, without let or hindrance' is, in fact, the cause of more lets and hindrances than anything else. Things are much worse now, and, here and there, they seem to gather new evil every year. The nerves of the globe are worse, it is true, and its future seems even less assured than in 1925. But the disturbing suspicion grows that passportery has very little practical purpose except the maintenance of full employment among the passport tribes.

A journey by train from Marseilles (France) to Barcelona (Spain) sounded fairly simple. But then we had not heard of Port Bou, the frontier station. (It is, we have since heard, a name of major ill-omen, even among frontier towns.)

At the station before it, at 0630, our passport was stamped by a Frenchman and a Spaniard, and we filled in the first form. This was a four-page affair about the money we possessed. We counted laboriously our own surviving cheques and our grubby packets of French and Spanish paper. We wrote the results down, in pencil, on the wrong page, and added, without resentment, for it was a fine warm morning, the number of our passport, where and by whom it was *expedido*, and so forth. We signed our declaration grandly, the train started, and we observed then that the whole thing should be *escrito en tinta*, the quaint old Spanish word for ink. We pitied the poor traveller who had no Spanish (or no fountain-pen) and hastily inked over our pencilled information. The train joggled, our fountain-pen spluttered and oozed, and the form looked fairly fishy when we had done. But we approached the Spanish frontier with a light heart. After all, we had His Majesty's passport, showing that Britain thought well of us: we had presented two

---

[1] See a letter to the *Sunday Times*, September 30, 1951:

'In 1945 many passports were issued free of charge to persons taking up posts on the Control Commission for Germany (of whom I was one).

'On returning to the U.K. I was informed by the Foreign Office that my passport was not my property but would become so on payment of 15*s*. As it is now once more the property of His Majesty's Government, I have asked the passport office to refund my 15*s*.

'J. W. NIXON.'

'*Geneva.*'

photographs and a mass of information to the Spaniards in London, and they had given us a *visa*. If these documents meant anything, there would be one swift glance and we should be through.

But we did not know Port Bou. Our fellow-travellers were nearly all Italian, French or Spanish. From time to time, in the loud and excitable talk so deplorably common on the Continent, we caught the word *maquis*, and once we heard '*mucha batalla!*' That seemed to be the mood of our companions. They had no queue-discipline. Indeed, there were no queues—only scrums: and there were some heavy-weight women who could have got a cap for almost any country. We think the British do passportery best. At least, you are clearly directed or ushered from one operation to another and herded into narrow tracks where shoving does no good. Here it was a pure fluke if you found yourself in the right scrum.

We have heard since of travellers being driven near to madness at Port Bou. The lady next to us at the Customs counter was not far off it. She had just heard about the *tinta* and had no fountain-pen (and why should travellers be compelled to carry fountain-pens?). We nobly lent her ours and waited a long time while she scribbled on the top of a squashy bag.

Done with the Customs, we noticed two large sweating and shouting scrums outside two tiny windows labelled Exchange of Money. We did not want to change any money, so we marched confidently on to the next door. 'Show the passport,' we thought, 'and we are through.' But they waved us back towards the scrums. '*Banco—banco!*' they said. By sheer brutality and rudeness we fought our way at last to the little window. The owl in the window gazed solemnly at the 'declaration' page of our money form and stamped it. He also stamped our passport. But since we had failed to put anything about money over our signature our 'declaration' declared nothing but our name and the number of our passport. In other words, the form was meaningless—but it did not matter. It was stamped, just the same.

We marched on to the gate and showed our passport. 'Through at last?' 'No.' The man simply handed us a form and indicated yet one more scrum. The form required us to state—*en tinta*—nearly all the information contained in our passport—when and where it was issued—date and place of *visa*—age—place of birth—nationality—domicile—profession—address—the whole box of tricks. The small room was full of luggage, porters, and yelling passengers, sharing fountain-pens. The near-mad lady was now practically raving, for her glasses had fallen off and broken in one of the scrums and she could not see the form. An interpreter took charge of her and we suppose she is now in a Home. Half-way through our own form our fountain-pen ran dry and we had to borrow. A porter cried that the train was due to leave *pronto*. We plunged into the scrum round a little window labelled *Pasaporte Controle*. When we touched down a scruffy little owl turned over a page or two of our passport, looked wise, and stamped it again—the fourth stamp that happy morning. We just caught the train, but there was no time for so much as a cup of coffee. It was a horrible little one-waggon train which rolled like a destroyer for three hours to Barcelona. But such are the fortunes of travel. At least we were in Spain—*Spain!*—and all passportery done. We admired the sunny hills and valleys of Catalonia. We almost admired the unshaven little man in the light-blue suit who rolled and sweated opposite to us. But presently he rose up and went round the waggon asking all passengers to show their passports. We did. He had no uniform. *Dios* knows who he was and what was his authority. Perhaps it was a joke. But our spirit was broken; and no one asked him.

We reached our hotel in Barcelona in very fair fettle, still one of the Friends of Spain, though we had not eaten or drunk for sixteen hours. The hotel at once (a) took away our passport, to send to the police, and (b) handed us a huge form, requiring, once more, *all the information contained in our passport*. At this point, we did begin to wonder what our passport was for.

On this short passage into Spain:

 (*a*) our passport had been stamped four times;
 (*b*) our passport had been presented seven times;
 (*c*) we had filled up two forms giving all the particulars already set out in our passport, and one giving a few of them: and at the end of all this
 (*d*) our passport was taken away and sent to the police—'for checking'.

Can all this be really necessary to the safety of any State—however nervous? True, our passport came back quickly: but why did it go at all? It should be part of the Law of Nations that an innocent traveller's passport must never be taken from him. While he is without it he may get into a row, or fall under a bus—and then he is lost. And why, if they take our passport, must they have the form as well? Both cannot be needed. What is checking what? Is it supposed that a villain holding a false passport would be so foolish as to copy out the particulars erroneously? And what happens to the form we filled up at the frontier? That perhaps is 'checked' at last with the form we filled up at the hotel. But, by that time, we may have left the country. And what, in any case, can the operation tell them except that we have said the same thing three times? This persecution is not even practical. We are told that by this system the Spanish authorities are supposed to know where all foreigners are: but when a Briton disappeared, a British Consul told us, the Spanish with all their forms were quite unable to trace him. In spite of all the forms a 'missing diplomat' cannot be caught. Crooks and criminals 'pass freely, without let or hindrance'. The innocent traveller is harried and robbed.

The Nations may not be able to agree about the big things: but could they not get together about the little ones? We suggest the following resolution for this great Conference:

 'Except in special circumstances of emergency or suspicion
 (1) Each State shall treat with respect the passport of another State—and its own *visas*.
 (2) The passport is the inviolable property of the individual.'

From this would follow a lot. All round the planet there are thousands of scrubby unshaven little men gazing with suspicion at our passports (and their own visas). They turn the pages and look profoundly wise. Then comes the condescending stamp. But they have seen nothing. We do not believe that a single thought is in their minds: except perhaps 'After this lot we shall have a good breakfast,' or 'This is a good job. I must keep it.' Accept our resolution, and most of these gentlemen could be removed to some more productive toil.

The passport is an excellent thing: but *Pasaporte Controle* has gone too far.

(23) TEMPER *v.* HUME AND HADDOCK

Slander at Sea

Sir Eliot Ember, K.C., to-day concluded his final speech for the plaintiff in this protracted case: and the aged Mr. Justice Codd, shortly to retire, began his summing-up to the jury:

This difficult case, he said, has, I think, no fellow in the history of litigation. For one thing, it is, so far as I know, the first action for defamation in which the words complained of were conveyed by flag-signals at sea. It was suggested, at one point, that the case should be transferred to the Admiralty Court: and, though I had to say No, I have regretted it more than once, so unfamiliar are the waters in which we find ourselves.

The plaintiff, Temper, is the owner and master of the motor-yacht *Perfume II*. The defendant Hume is owner and master of the motor-yacht *Iodine*. The defendant Haddock was a passenger, or rather a guest, in the *Iodine*. Both vessels were cruising in the Mediterranean. At their first encounter in a crowded Italian harbour (X——) there was, it seems, a childish, unseemly and unnecessary altercation between the plaintiff and the defendant Hume. The details do not greatly concern you: but you may well form the opinion, on the evidence you have heard, that the plaintiff was in the wrong, that he was angry and ill-mannered, without due cause: and it is common ground that when the dispute was over he went out of his way to send by boat an insulting message. Mr. Hume, it seems, a man of dignity and calm, thought the insult no more worthy of notice than the buzzing of an inflated blue-bottle, and throughout behaved with good humour and gentleness. But, his friend and guest, Mr. Haddock, less forgiving than the Owner, thought that the last word should not be left where it lay. Hence this action-at-law.

Mr. Haddock, as he told the Court, has long been an admiring student of the International Code of flag-signals. This great Code, begun in a small way by our own Captain Marryat, is one of the many fine marine affairs in which our country has led the way, got the nations together, and benefited the world. It is now so copious and well-planned that almost any thought that one ship can reasonably wish to express to another is provided for. It ranges from the short sharp one-flag signals such as the famous 'Blue Peter' (P), or K—'You should stop your vessel instantly'—to such complex queries as

> LVI 'Can you suggest any means whereby my radio apparatus could be made serviceable?'

Mr. Haddock thinks that the Code should be better known, and more commonly used, than it is, especially by small yachts on the high seas. Instead, for example, of fumbling vainly round the dial of a crackling 'wireless', seeking the weather-report in a foreign language, they should, he says, steer close to the nearest big steamer (whatever her nationality) and hoist the two flags:

> ZB 'What is the weather forecast for to-day?'

to which the steamer will reply:

> YV 'Heavy weather coming: take necessary precautions.'

or

> ATI 'There is no need for alarm.'

or whatever it may be.

Instead, he said, of laborious morsing with lamps which suddenly cease to work or cannot be clearly distinguished, two or three gaily coloured flags will often do what is wanted quicker and better—as, for example:

> OVG 'Thank-you.'

or

      WAY   'I wish you a pleasant, happy voyage.'

But, he said—and all this is more relevant to the case than you may at once perceive—practice makes perfect, and custom grows with use. Accordingly, he has often sent messages to other yachts and steamers which were not made absolutely necessary by any marine emergency. Not all these communications, it appears, were uniformly well-timed. On one occasion, he confessed, passing the *Queen Elizabeth* in mid-Channel, he hoisted with all solemnity the three groups:

    GSX   'Good'
    JMR   'Morning.'
    QUH   'Have you any women on board?'

On another occasion, in war-time, as assistant to the Commodore of a Convoy, he persuaded the Commodore to send to all the merchant ships, in 29 hoists, the whole of the famous peroration of Mr. Churchill which begins 'Let us therefore brace ourselves to our duties' and ends 'This was their finest hour.' How these communications were received by the masters of the vessels addressed we do not know; but you may think that Mr. Temper was not the first mariner to complain of Mr. Haddock's fondness for the International Code.

I pass now to the facts of the case. The yachts *Perfume II* and *Iodine* met again frequently, sometimes at sea, sometimes in the many harbours which all yachts seem to visit, sooner or later, in the Western Mediterranean. While passing the *Perfume*, a much slower vessel, Mr. Haddock got permission from Mr. Hume to 'practise with the flags': and he hoisted the first signal complained of:

    IBQ   'Do you know'
    RLO   'Rules of the Road at Sea?'

The plaintiff regarded this as an offensive reference to the former encounter, but could think of no adequate reply in flags. That signal was followed by:

LWV   'Have dead rats been found on board?'

The plaintiff, as you have heard, angrily seized an Aldis lamp and began a strongly-worded reply in morse. The defendant Haddock sent up two hoists:

WX   'I cannot stop to communicate with you.'
LVE   'You should use radio.'

And the *Iodine* steamed ahead.

When the *Perfume* arrived in the crowded little harbour of Y—— the *Iodine* was flying, as if by way of welcome, the distinguishing flags of the *Perfume*, and the signal:

LWV   'Have dead rats been found on board?'

The plaintiff called on the *Iodine* and expostulated with Mr. Hume. Mr. Hume said mildly that Mr. Haddock was only 'practising with the flags as usual'. Mr. Haddock, on the other hand, said that he had noticed a dead rat on the quay-side at Port X——, and, when passing the *Perfume* (who was upwind), he had fancied perhaps, a similar smell. Naturally, he had wondered anxiously whether both vessels were threatened by the same infection. But if the flags offended, they should come down at once. And they did.

But in the next port, Z——, there was more trouble. The Code is rich in medical signals. These are designed to assist one ship to describe to another the condition of a sufferer for whom the first ship requires medical aid. The *Perfume II* was greeted, as usual, with LWV, but, this time, paid no attention. On the second night there was a little party in the *Perfume*, rather noisy, rather late. The next morning there appeared at the yard-arm of the *Iodine*, addressed to *Perfume II*, the following signals which, I must say, look jolly gay and satisfactory to me:

AGW   'Group which follows is a question.'
HGQ   'Headache is very severe.'

PCP   'Tongue is coated.'
VGF   'Belly wall is tender.'

The plaintiff again complained.

Mr. Albert Haddock's reply to the complaint was simple. He said that that was how he felt that morning, and, as one mariner to another, he was asking a sympathetic question. This time, the flats were not taken down.

At Port W——, after the routine LWV ('Have dead rats been found on board?'), there was a new and singular set of signals:

AGW   'Group which follows is a question.'
VGI   'Breathing is noisy or snorting.'
VGQ   'Have night sweats.'
VGO   'Eyeball burst.'

At Port V——, it was:

AGW   'Group which follows is a question.'
PCP   'Tongue is coated.'
HGQ   'Headache is very severe.'
PJP   'Troubled.'
CPT   'By.'
ATL   'Alcohol.'

And so on.

Now, gentlemen, it is for you and me to analyse and assess the legal significance of this unusual story of the sea. The plaintiff complains of various *innuendoes* or suggestions in the signals, to wit, that he was unseamanlike, that his ship was plague-ridden or otherwise unhealthy, that he was given to excessive drinking; and he says that he has been held up to hatred, ridicule and contempt in the yachting world. He says that in more than one harbour he was greeted by acquaintances with remarks about 'vermin-vessels' or 'deratization'. I have ruled that certain of the flags might bear a defamatory meaning, and you will have to decide whether in all the circumstances they were defamatory or not.

The next question is: By whom were the statements, if defamatory, made? You will probably find that Mr. Haddock in each case selected and hoisted the flags: but that he did so with the general permission of Mr. Hume, the owner and master of the vessel. In the case of a newspaper the proprietor, the editor and the writer of libellous matter may each and all be sued. But a motor-yacht is not a newspaper (see *The Queen* v. *Robinson* (1891), 2 Q.B.). The nautical experts who testified before us were unanimous that a signal flown at the ship's yard-arm is a signal from the ship, and that, in the absence of fraud or mutiny, the master is alone responsible. It may be, then, that whatever you find in fact, I shall have to strike Mr. Haddock out of the action as a matter of law. A further difficulty will then present itself, concerning damages. Whatever you may think about the mind of Mr. Haddock, you are not likely to find any evidence of malice in the mind of Mr. Hume, who showed gentlemanly forbearance under great provocation. There need, it is true, be no evidence of express malice where a libel is proved, unless the occasion be privileged, which this is not: but you may well think it right to assess different damages for the two defendants, unjust though that may seem. Dear me, what a case!

There remains, for me, at least, perhaps the most delicate question of all. Is this a case of libel or slander? Though the plaintiff complains that his reputation has suffered, he has been able to offer no evidence of any actual damage such as must support, in most cases, an action for slander. He has not suffered professionally or been turned out of a club. Now, the historical but crazy distinction between libel and slander is thus expressed by the good Mr. Salmond (I quote the textbook because if I began to quote the judges I should be at it for many days):

In *libel* the defamatory statement is made in some permanent and visible form, such as writing, printing, or effigies. In *slander* it is made in spoken words or in some other transitory form, whether visible or audible, such as gestures, hissing, or other inarticulate but significant sounds.[1]

Very well. Where are we now? What are flags? They are 'visible', like writing, printing, or effigies, but unlike words, whispers, or hisses. So, *prima facie*, they must be libel. But are they 'permanent'? Surely not. At sea, the flags remain at the yard-arm till the receiving ship has hoisted the Answering Pendant to the peak, signifying that the signal is understood. Then the flags come down. Gone like the wind. A 'transitory' defamation, surely. But then the plaintiff has sworn that in some ports the flags complained of remained on view *all day*. Should such an exhibition be regarded as transitory or permanent—or, to put the thing fairly—non-transitory? Gentlemen, you now perhaps begin to apprehend the kind of difficulties which confront me in this case. But I do not know why I am troubling you with all this: for these are things that I have to decide alone. The truth is, I am thinking aloud. And, I tell you what, I am going to make you help me as much as I can. After all, this may be the last case I try. Get your pencils, gentlemen: and do try, his Lordship added testily, to keep awake. We shan't get lunch for another hour and a half.

The Judge left the following questions to the jury:

(*a*) Were any of the signals complained of defamatory?
(*b*) Which?
(*c*) Why?
(*d*) Were there, in fact, any dead rats in M/Y *Perfume II*?
(*e*) If so, does it matter?
(*f*) Do you believe a single word that Mr. Haddock says?
(*g*) If 'yes', give examples.
(*h*) Between ourselves, don't you think the plaintiff is a fairly unsympathetic character?
(*i*) Have you the faintest idea, after all my laborious discourse:

[1] *Law of Torts* (Stevens and Haynes).

    (i) What is the difference between libel and slander?
    (ii) Why?

(j) If 'yes', would you say that flag-signals were:
    (i) Transitory?
    (ii) Non-transitory?

(k) And, if you were in my place, though, mind you, this is my job, not yours, would you say that this was a case of libel or slander?

(l)   (i) Why?
    (ii) Why not?

(m) What damages:
    (i) Against Mr. Hume?
    (ii) Against Mr. Haddock?

(n) You may have to find for the plaintiff: but, honestly, if you were me, would you give him any costs?

(o) By the way, I forgot to ask you—do you think that the plaintiff's reputation has suffered?

(p) If 'yes', does this upset you?

(q) Now will you retire, please? And come back soon.

The jury retired, for seventeen hours. On their return, the Foreman said: My Lord, we are a little confused. We disagree on almost every particular.

His Lordship: Well done. I think you are quite right.

Sir Eliot Ember, for the plaintiff, asked for costs.

The Judge: Well, no. You see, I have decided to strike Mr. Haddock out of the action as he was not the master of the ship. And Mr. Hume has behaved very decently throughout. So I am afraid the plaintiff will have to pay all the costs.

Sir Eliot: If your Lordship pleases.

Sir Ronald Rutt: Shall we have a new trial?

The Judge: Not before me. Why don't you appeal? Your father would love this case.[1]

3 October, 1951

---

[1] Sir Ethelred Rutt, K.C., was recently appointed a Lord Justice of Appeal.

Note—Lovers of the law of libel, that unique English heritage, must regret that yet one more problem has, after all, failed to find a solution, as it were, at the post. The celebrated case of *Chicken* v. *Ham* [2 H.L. 1926] will be in the minds of many students. There the question was whether defamatory words spoken deliberately through a gramophone record were in the nature of libel or slander. There were two trials of the action, and two appeals to the Court of Appeal, which arrived, unhappily, at two contradictory conclusions. Finally, in the House of Lords, two Lords of Appeal were for 'libel', and two were for 'slander': Lord Goat was about to deliver what would have been the fifth, and (presumably) decisive, opinion when, most unfortunately, he perished of a heart-attack. So the point remains *in dubio*. Now we have the signal-flags. Lord Lick in the gramophone case (above) mentioned *Silvertop* v. *the Stepney Guardians* where (he said) a man trained a parrot to say three times after meals, '*Councillor Wart has not washed to-day.*' 'It was held', his Lordship asserted, 'that this was a libel.' With the greatest respect to a most distinguished judge and public servant, it must now be said that prolonged researches have failed to disclose any authentic report of *Silvertop* v. *the Stepney Guardians*. This is a pity. For a parrot trained to utter the same insult at regular intervals would seem, *prima facie*, to provide such an element of continuity as might serve to convert the spoken slander into libel: and from the intermittent, recurring parrot-cry to the intermittent, recurring signal-flag might have been an easy step.

Some passage across a border-line too strictly drawn is evidently desirable. There is now the 'loud-hailer', an instrument by which the spoken word can be carried over very wide spaces and, in urban districts, to the ears of many thousands. A hearer, however much he may resent what is said through this machine, is quite incapable of replying to the speaker—or, at the same range of sound, to anyone else; and, what is more, though the utterance may damage him in the minds of millions, he is still restricted to the remedies for 'word-of-mouth' slander. The case of *Taylor* v. *Twerp* is worthy of note, although—or indeed, because—it never came into court. Taylor was an 'official' Conservative candidate for Burbleton at a General Election. He had been the Member for Burbleton, and lived in Burbleton, for many years. Twerp, a London journalist, who was a candidate too, went round the town in a van with a loud-hailer through which he, or his assistants, cried, hour after hour, and day after day: 'GEORGE TAYLOR IS A LIAR—L-I-A-R—LIAR!' There was nothing at all behind this accusation: and Taylor was willing to ignore it. But his friends persuaded him that, in his own 'home-town', he would be expected to take notice of an assault upon his honour so powerful and so persistent. He issued a writ. Considerable costs were incurred in the preparation of the case. But at the election Taylor was triumphantly returned and Twerp lost his deposit. Taylor's lawyer then had to explain to him (*a*) that the insults, since they were spoken, not written, were slander, not libel; (*b*) that therefore he would have to prove 'actual damage'; and (*c*) that, since he had been elected, he could do no such thing. The writ was withdrawn, which, the ignorant said, showed that there was something in the accusations.

In my Law of Libel Bill of July, 1938—and also in my second Bill, introduced by Sir Stanley Reed on 3 February, 1939—I proposed to assimilate the law of slander to the law of libel. In evidence before the very distinguished Porter Committee I urged the same course, and I told the learned gentlemen the story of *Taylor* v. *Twerp*. With two dissentients, they rejected my proposal. They did say, 'We consider that all defamatory broadcast statements should be treated as libels': but they meant only 'statements or images broadcast by radiotransmission', so they would not help poor Mr. Taylor at all. Mr. Richard O'Sullivan, K.C., and Professor E. C. S. Wade (bless them!) were on my side: 'They consider that no adequate reason now exists for perpetuating a distinction which

originated by an accident of English legal history, finds no place in Scots law, and
has led to a confusing volume of case-law.'

Concerning the 'accident of legal history', see a speech by one of the burgesses
for Oxford University (*Hansard*, February 3, 1939, Col. 585):

'It often happens that such distinctions arise from historical causes, and
because we are too lazy to remove them or amend them we create an elaborate
philosophical defence of them which we pretend has been there all the time.
... Slander was dealt with in the beginning by the feudal courts, and then by
ecclesiastical courts. Then printing came in and the Star Chamber leapt upon
printing, and an action for libel has retained some of the criminal character of
that court's proceedings and no proof of damage is required. Now we say that
because a written wrong is a solid, enduring, fundamental thing therefore it
must be made more easy for the victim to pursue it. I should submit that the
contrary was the case; the whispered slander is far more difficult to catch, and
therefore the distinction, if any, should perhaps be the other way round. At all
events, it is surely absurd to say that what is written on a postcard is more
dangerous than what is shouted at a mass meeting, perhaps through a loud-
speaker. However, that is the law as it stands to-day.'

To-day, likewise.

On 1 February, 1952, Mr. Harold Lever (Labour), a 'private' Member,
introduced a Bill founded on the excellent Porter Committee's Report. It
obtained a Second Reading, and, when these reports left the editor's hands,
looked like becoming law. The Porter Committee was the direct result of the
editor's 1938 Bills, and he applauds their labours and Mr. Lever's efforts with a
grandfatherly interest and pride.

(24) REX *v.* RUNGLE

Codd's Last Case

At the Old Bailey to-day, after counsel's closing speeches in the Burbleton Burglar case, the aged Mr. Justice Codd summed up to the jury. He said:

Gentlemen of the jury, this is a trial for murder—or maybe manslaughter. A man's life hangs—pardon—depends upon your decision: and you will, I know, approach your task with due solemnity. So do I. But this is the last case that I shall ever try. Once I'm back in the old flannel bags in the garden that old Chief will never coax me into a court again, whatever epidemics may decimate the Bench. You, gentlemen, have spent two or three days in a court of law, and already you are longing to get back to civilization. I have been here for fifty years. Imagine it! Fifty years of quarrelling and crime, quibbles and costs, adulteries, assaults, burglaries and motor-accidents. 'Running-down cases' we call them. Remember the story about old Hewart, when he was Lord Chief Justice? Some-one asked him how he enjoyed his life on the Bench. 'It's all right', he said, 'when any legal business crops up. But I seem to spend most of my time adjudicating on disputes between insurance companies arising out of collisions between two stationary motor-cars, each on the right side of the road, and blowing its horn.' Ha! Yes, I thought you'd like that. Don't look so shocked, Sir Roger. Mind you, gentlemen, I'm not complaining. We like the life, of course: and we live a long time, I can't think why. But fifty years, you may decide, is just about enough. You may think, having heard all the evidence—pardon me, I was forgetting—you want to hear about this case.

Well, there is the prisoner, George Rungle. He's killed a burglar, there's no doubt about that. But he looks a good chap, you must agree. I believe he is a good chap: and ‧

I may as well tell you at once that I'm on his side——

Sir Roger Wheedle (for the Crown): Milord! The jury can hardly——

The Judge: Of course, Sir Roger doesn't like that. I didn't expect he would. By the way, gentlemen, that's another big thing about my future. I shan't have to listen to any more speeches by my dear old colleague, Sir Roger Wheedle. You've heard one or two. I don't say they're not *good* speeches—they are: but you know what I mean. Going up now, aren't you, Sir Roger? Treasury briefs and all! The next thing, you'll be Solicitor-General. Which are you going to be, Conservative or Labour? Difficult to say just now, I suppose. Anyhow, you'll go far. You'll never sink to the Bench, like me. £5,000 a year, less 2. Well, about this case. As I have said, there's no doubt that Mr. Rungle killed this burglar.

Sir Ronald Rutt (for the defence): Milord, with great respect, that *is* one of the points on which——

The Judge: Now, what's the matter with you, Sir Ronald? By the way, how's your father? Dear Old Ethelred! The battles we used to have! And how your dear father used to bristle! 'Bristle!' Yes, that's the word. And now he's up in the Court of Appeal. 'Lord Justice Rutt.' Soon to be Lord of Appeal, I shouldn't wonder. 'Baron Rutt.' I shall laugh, rather. Old Wool's there already. Can't be a day less than 103. But there he is; blowing off like a juvenile grampus. You've done well, too, young Ronald. I can see you President of the Board of Trade. And I'm still a miserable *puisne* in the King's Bench Division. To-morrow I'll be plain Sir Humphrey Codd again. Never mind. About this case:

The prisoner killed the burglar. And what a good thing! If I have a chance, I'll kill a burglar too. What's more, it ought to be a capital offence. I never know why they make so much fuss about blackmail. After all, there couldn't be any blackmail if there wasn't something black to go upon. But these little squits of burglars—they creep into strange houses, poor houses too, frighten innocent old women and steal their wedding-rings. That's what this beast-boy had been doing for months! House after house. The police have got any number of——

Sir Roger Wheedle: With the greatest respect, milord——

The Judge: I know exactly what you're going to say, Sir Roger. So don't bother. That's what I think about burglars. You may say what you like about 'our barbarous ancestors', but in this department they knew a thing or two. In the eighteenth century—time of the *Beggar's Opera*—they were pretty harsh about stealing. They had to be. No police—no street-lamps—nothing. But they distinguished. If you stole property valued at five shillings you were hanged. If you stole from a person to the value of 1s., or from a dwelling-house to the value of 40s., you were hanged. But the juries were merciful, and scaled things down, if they liked your face. One Catherine Delavan, I remember, stole nine guineas and 11s.: but the jury found her guilty to the value of 4s. 10d. only. You see the point, Sir Roger? She was transported, not hanged.

Sir Roger Wheedle: The point is taken, milord.

The Judge: But there were two cases where no jury could save your neck. If you put people 'in Fear on the Highway', or if you burgled—that is, broke into a house *by night*—values didn't matter, and you were hanged, however little you stole. The same principle, no doubt—'putting people in *fear*'—whether it was the highway or the house. When the deceased beast-boy had been at it for a month or two not a woman in the neighbourhood could sleep peacefully in her bed. At the smallest sound, the creak of a stair, the bang of a shutter, everyone in the house sat up sweating with alarm. That's why they hanged them in the eighteenth century, and that's why we ought to hang them now. The prisoner, of course, popped ahead and killed the burglar himself: and I must say that I'm delighted.

Sir Ronald Rutt: Milord——

Sir Roger Wheedle: Milord, with great respect, the laws of the eighteenth century are hardly on all fours with——

The Judge: All right, Sir Roger, let's come to the nine-teenth century. Are you familiar with *Purcell's Case*?

Sir Roger Wheedle: No, milord.

The Judge: Well, Mr. Purcell was a septuagenarian, of County Cork. And in 1811 he was knighted—*knighted*, Sir Roger—for killing four burglars with a carving-knife. Pretty good, eh?

Sir Roger Wheedle: That, no doubt, was in self-defence, milord. In the present case, the deceased was offering no violence and in fact was leaving the premises.

The Judge: But he had offered violence, he had com-mitted a violent felony, and he was escaping. You see what it is, members of the jury? They're trying to whittle down our ancient rights. It's all part of this namby-pamby stuff about crime. I expect Sir Roger Wheedle's heart is bleed-ing for the deceased, the little pest. What was the burglar's name, Sir Roger?

Sir Roger: Moss, milord. And may I add, milord, that I am only trying to seek the truth and to do my duty according to law.

The Judge: Of course, Sir Roger, of course! Don't excite yourself. But you know Moss's record as well as I do. Left a good home and joined a gang. Began coshing at the age of twelve. Brought up in luxury at remand schools and approved schools and Lord knows what. Had every chance. Never done a day's work. Doesn't mind prison because it's all so cosy now. Keeps a whole neighbourhood in terror for weeks. And when he catches it at last we're told an unkind charwoman shut him in a cupboard when he was a child, and he's never been the same since. He's a pathological case or a psychological misfit.[1] Ha! Stuff and nonsense! Suffers from 'frustration'. Frustration, indeed! I

---

[1] See *Rex* v. *Lout* (1951), where a youth was charged with robbery with violence and other offences. His father said: 'At the age of fourteen he fell out of a tree. Since then he's been a different boy.'

wonder how they'd like to be a judge in these days, drawing the same pay for the last 100 years and more!

Sir Roger: Milord, with great respect, the character of the deceased is not strictly——

The Judge: I know. I know. I'm wandering, Sir Roger. But you provoked me. What I mean is that no one seems to bother about the psychology of the poor old men and women who lie shivering in their beds when a beast-boy's about. And when he gets his deserts——

Sir Roger: Milord!

The Judge: Don't interrupt, Sir Roger. We must get on. Now, jurymen all, recall what happened. Mr. Rungle, having no firearms, kept an ordinary garden-fork by his bed, as we all ought to do. That, or a hat-pin. At two o'clock in the morning he hears noises below; he takes his garden-fork, slips downstairs, and finds Moss, in a mask, filling a bag with the Rungle goods and belongings. Moss held a pistol at him (it wasn't loaded, but Rungle was not to know that), and in the childish language of his kind, said: 'Stick 'em up. This is a stick-up.' Rungle bravely, and rather wittily, replied, raising his garden-fork: 'Oh, is it? And this is a stick-*in*!' Ha!

When the bold burglar saw the garden-fork, he uttered a yell of terror, turned and made for the window. Mr. Rungle cried, 'Stop!' meaning to arrest him; but Moss did not stop. As he was passing through the window the prisoner threw the garden-fork after him, harpoon-fashion: it pierced the burglar's heart and he died.

Now, the Crown, rather mildly, it is true, suggest to you that this was Murder. The defence say that it was Justifiable Homicide.

Sir Roger, I know, does not think that I know any law: though in fifty years one does pick up some scraps of information. So I have been looking up the authorities, and, in these soft days, it does appear that there is some doubt. In one tremendous tome (under *Burglary*) I read:

The question whether and how far it is justifiable to kill a burglar is by no means clear. If violence on the part of the burglar is reasonably apprehended, it is not murder to shoot him dead with intent to kill him, but whether it is justifiable to kill merely in defence of property is doubtful.

But in another page of the same tome I find two of the categories of Justifiable Homicide set out as follows:

(*d*) Where an officer or his assistant, in the due execution of his office, arrests or attempts to arrest a person for *felony*, or a dangerous wound given, and he having notice thereof flies and is killed by such officer or assistant in pursuit.

(*e*) Where upon such offence as last described *a private person* in whose sight it has been committed arrests or endeavours to arrest the offender, and kills him in resistance or flight, in similar circumstances.

Note, gentlemen, that burglary is a felony, and a violent felony.

I turned then to Mr. Kenny's admirable *Outlines of Criminal Law*.[1] Here again I wandered, as one wanders in a wood, now in sunlight, now in the shade. First I was told, with some discouragement, that:

When the wrongdoer is not going so far as to assault a human being, but is only *interfering unlawfully with property*, whether real or personal, the possessor of that property (though he is permitted by the law to use a moderate degree of force in defence of his possessions) will usually not be justified in carrying this force to the point of killing the trespasser. . . .

But then I passed into the light:

Such a justification will not arise unless the trespasser's

[1] Cambridge University Press.

interference or resistance amounts to a felony, and moreover to a felony of some kind that is violent, such for example, as robbery, arson or *burglary*.

One more step and I was in the shade again:

Even these extremely violent felonies should not be resisted by extreme violence unless it is actually necessary; thus, fire-arms should not be used unless there seems to be no other mode ('Mode!' I like 'mode', don't you?) available for defeating the intruder *and securing his arrest*.

Sir Roger Wheedle: Your Lordship, no doubt, remembers the case of *Rex* v. *Cooper*?

The Judge: You mean that case in 1641? At the Surrey Assizes?

Sir Roger: Yes, milord.

The Judge: Of course. But I don't see that it helps you much. That was another window case. Cooper struck a burglar in the eye with a spit. And was acquitted.

Sir Roger: Yes, milord. But, milord, I should be prepared to distinguish.

The Judge: You can't distinguish any more. Well gentlemen, there you are. The Crown's case, I gather—and, by the way, I'm not sure that they believe in it very strongly, but they think, in these days, they have to be as soft as they can—where was I? Oh, yes, the Crown's case is that Rungle was not being attacked, and was in no danger himself; that the deceased beast-boy was merely interfering, or had merely interfered, with property (and property, of course, is very unpopular nowadays), therefore the prisoner was entitled only to use *reasonable* force: to stick a man through the heart with a garden-fork was more than reasonable in the circumstances, and therefore the killing was murder. Is that a fair statement of your case, Sir Roger?

Sir Roger: Yes, milord. I might add, of course——

The Judge: But you mayn't. Now, gentlemen of the jury, I must not, of course, attempt to influence you unduly (what an idea!). But let me tell you the story as I see it in the light of the law, as I understand it.

The deceased Moss committed a burglary. At Common Law this crime is committed when a dwelling-house or a church is broken and entered at night with the intention of committing some felony therein. Section 51 of the Larceny Act, 1861, extended the definition:

> Whosoever shall enter the dwelling-house of another with intent to commit any felony therein, or being in the said dwelling-house shall commit any felony therein, and shall in either case break out of the said dwelling-house in the night, shall be deemed guilty of burglary.

Now, burglary, I say again, is a felony and a 'violent' felony. It is a continuing offence. A man is a burglar from the time he breaks in till the time he breaks out. He does not cease to be a burglar if, having robbed the house, he sits down in an armchair and peaceably recites the poems of Keats. In this case he made a feeble threat of violence to the householder: but I am willing to forget that, if it pleases Sir Roger; for it is not necessary to my argument. The big point is that the householder finds the felon at work; that not only his instinct, and his interest, but his public duty instruct and oblige him to arrest the felon, if he can, and to hand him over to justice. There have been numerous burglaries in the neighbourhood which have gone unpunished (few indeed are the arrested burglars anywhere, and sadly few the stolen goods recovered). A householder is in the position of an unofficial police officer: if he lets the felon go he will be letting loose a menace to who knows how many other defenceless homes. Accordingly he orders the felon to 'Stop!' But the felon ('he having notice thereof') makes off. What is the householder to do? He can only use the nearest weapon to his hand. If Mr. Rungle had had a fire-arm he would have been well entitled to shoot the burglar in the leg, at least. As it was, he had only a garden-fork. He did not, I am sure, intend to kill the burglar. The one thought, the proper thought, in his mind, was 'I must stop him' (and let us not forget that the word 'arrest' means 'stop'). It is regrettable perhaps (though not, I think, very much) that his only weapon had the result it did: but for that there is nobody to blame but the burglar. As the harsh but wholesome saying goes, 'He should have thought of that before'—before, that is, he entered upon a crime which has rightly earned especial detestation from the State.

Now, gentlemen, I have done. I should not like my last judicial utterance to be quoted as something exceptional, relevant only to the circumstances of a special case. No, Sir Roger, since there appears to be some doubt in this important corner of life and law, I declare the law to be as follows:

'It is the right and duty of any householder, or any other honest citizen, who finds an undoubted burglar in a dwelling-house, to arrest him. He may, and should, order the burglar to stay quietly on the premises till any necessary arrangements have been made. If the burglar disobeys this order and attempts to make off, the honest citizen may use any force he considers necessary and any weapon that is at hand to stop him: and if the result is death it is justifiable homicide; not murder, or even manslaughter.'

But, of course, gentlemen, you are the jury: and you are well entitled to say that I am talking nonsense. Pray consider your verdict.

The Foreman stood up and called for three cheers for his Lordship. Then, without leaving the box, they found the prisoner Not Guilty.

The Judge: Discharge the prisoner. Goodbye, Mr. Rungle. Kill all the burglars you can. But don't forget to say 'Stop!'

Sir Roger Wheedle: Milord, if you can stand one more speech from me, I should like, on behalf of the Bar, to wish you a long and happy retirement.

Sir Ronald Rutt: I too, milord.

The Judge: Well that's very handsome of you both. I must say I've enjoyed my last case considerably. If you aren't careful, I shall come back after all.

7 September, 1951

NOTE—Since this case, the police inform us, the burglary rate has shown a marked decline.

(25) *IN RE* THE GOODS OF TRAMPLE, C. M., DECEASED: TRAMPLE F. *v.* COMMISSIONERS OF INLAND REVENUE

'I Thee Endow ...'

Sitting in the Chancery Division, Mr. Justice Puce to-day began to deliver a considered judgment in the 'Endowed Widow' case. Crowds gathered outside the Royal Courts of Justice from an early hour, and the magnetic plaintiff received an ovation when she arrived in a pale-blue toque and a primrose limousine.

His Lordship said:

The plaintiff in this case impressed me very favourably, which is more than I can say for the defendants. Fay, if I may call her Fay, after a brief career on the stage, married Cyrus Trample, a man about forty years her senior. Mr. Trample had acquired a large fortune in various ways, ranging from the conduct of a betting business to the financial support of those American musical plays which are now a permanent feature of the British way of life. It was during the rehearsals for one of these entertainments that he met, and was instantly—and, may I add, very naturally—bowled over by the plaintiff. He suffered, it seems, from high blood-pressure, and an overworked heart; and three years after the wedding, to Mrs. Trample's great distress, he suddenly died.

The plaintiff was also upset by the will, in which she was named as sole executrix. The dead man left some £750,000, on which, after payment of sundry small debts, the Estate or 'Death' Duties have been reckoned at the cruel figure of £525,000. There was also a long list of substantial legacies, some to institutions such as the British Bloodstock Society, the Bookmakers' Benevolent Fund, the Licensed Victuallers' Protection Association, and others to numerous individuals in the sporting and theatrical world, old servants, and, it has been suggested, flames. The residue of the estate was to go to the widow: but, what with Death Duties and the legacies, that residue looked like being much less than the plaintiff expected and, according to her evidence, deserved. Further, for reasons to which I shall come presently, she declined to have anything to do with the will: she therefore took no steps to obtain a grant of Probate, and indeed formally renounced her right to do so.

The defendants, that repugnant body the Commissioners of Inland Revenue, as eager and as prompt as vultures to get at the dead, thereupon flew down upon the Court of Probate and secured authority to administer the estate, to abstract their ghastly duties, to discharge the sundry small debts and pay the legacies. The plaintiff now appears before the Court as the principal creditor of the estate and asks that the Commissioners be ordered to pay to her the sum of £700,000.

Mrs. Trample's case is delightfully simple. The couple were married at St. Peter's Church, Lump Street, in 1949: and the evidence is that during the ceremony, the deceased man, addressing the plaintiff, solemnly used these words:

'*With all my worldly goods I thee endow.*'

Nothing could be plainer. The word 'endow' is an absolute word, descended from the Latin word *dotare*—'to *give*'. One of the secondary interpretations in the great *Oxford English Dictionary* is 'to provide (by bequest or gift) a permanent income ...' 'Endow', in short, is something quite different from 'lend' or 'share'. It denotes a complete, an enduring, transference of property.

Now, in lovers' talk, or romantic poetry, such strong plain words may be used in unreal, exaggerated fashion. In an old song one of the parties—I believe both—says 'I will give thee the Keys of Heaven'. No Court would listen to any suit that was founded upon such an undertaking. But the present case is very different. The Marriage Service— or, to give it its due title, 'The Form of Solemnization of Matrimony'—may be regarded as a religious ceremony having the force of a civil contract, or as a civil contract adorned and glorified by the blessing of the Church. Whichever way it is regarded, the central fact remains, that it is a binding contract, creating legal rights, obligations and penalties. Accordingly, says Mrs. Trample, all Mr. Trample's 'worldly goods' were made over to her, in due form, absolutely and finally, on the day of the wedding. It follows from that, first, that the will, with all its legacies, inasmuch as it purports to dispose of money which Mr. Trample no longer possessed, cannot be effective save in respect of any after-acquired property, and secondly, that no Death Duties can properly be levied upon 'estate' which did not, in fact, belong to the deceased. (A gift 'in consideration of marriage', by the way, is exempt from the wicked law that gifts made less than five years before death are subject to Death Duties.)[1]

To this straightforward claim the Attorney-General, for the Crown, made some replies which, upon reflection, I am sure he will agree, were hardly worthy of his high office.

Sir Anthony Slatt: My lord, with great respect, I said nothing that——

The Court: Don't splutter, Sir Anthony. First of all, you made the absurd complaint that the alleged contract was not in writing. You quoted a wearisome list of cases on Section 4 of the Statute of Frauds which says, among other things, that no one can be 'charged' 'upon any agreement made in consideration' of marriage, unless the agreement 'or some memorandum or note thereof' shall be in writing and signed by the party to be charged. I decline to flounder in your morass of cases, Sir Anthony. The evidence is clear that immediately after the ceremony both parties to the contract signed a certificate showing that they had just been married 'according to the rites and ceremonies of the Church of England'. Those rites and ceremonies invariably include the words upon which the plaintiff relies. Those

[1] Finance (1909–10) Act 1910, Section 59(2).

words are read from a book authorized by Act of Parliament: and I hold, without doubt, that, coupled with those words, the certificate, a copy of which is treasured by every proud and loving wife, is a sufficient 'memorandum or note in writing'. Consider, Sir Anthony, the case of *Ridgway* v. *Wharton* (1857), where Lord Cranworth said: 'The statute is not complied with unless the whole contract is either embodied in some writing signed by the party, or in some paper referred to in a signed document, and capable of being identified by means of the description of it contained in the signed paper ... *The two writings in the case I have put become one writing.*'

Indeed, if it were not so, where should we be? What would become of the holy estate of matrimony? Each party to this strange contract undertakes to 'keep herself (or himself) only unto the other'. Any failure to do that may have important legal consequences. A husband who fails may be sued in the divorce court: or you yourself, Sir Anthony, may prosecute him for bigamy in a criminal court. *Intra contractu non distinguendum*: or, in other words, neither the Crown nor the subject can be permitted to pick and choose among the clauses of a contract, accepting only those which advantage it.

But the Crown has impudently suggested that there was no true 'mutuality' or consent, or, shortly, that the husband did not mean what he said. The Attorney-General took us back to the ancient days, in which the words of the marriage contract were first devised. In those days the property of a woman passed absolutely, and automatically, to her husband, on marriage. The words about 'endowing', Sir Anthony suggests, were a mere rhetorical acknowledgment of a husband's duty to maintain his wife. That duty still remains: but now that, by statute, a married woman's property remains her own, it would be a preposterous reversal of history and equity, says the Attorney, to give any literal force to the husband's promise to 'endow'. The words, he said, must be regarded as an archaic and meaningless survival.

Such thoughts may well have been in the minds of the leaders of the Church of England when, in 1928, they put forward a revised version of the Prayer Book, now known as the 'Deposited Book'. If their numerous amendments had been allowed to prevail, Mr. Trample would have said:

'All my worldly goods with thee I share.'

But Parliament, after long debate, refused to permit that alteration. The present words, therefore, are much more than an archaic and insignificant relic. They may be said to have modern Parliamentary sanction: and Parliament, which gives such close attention to the marriage ceremony and its civil consequences, must be assumed to intend that every word in it having civil or secular consequences shall be strictly interpreted.

Even if I were wrong in this conclusion, which is most unlikely, it would be of no assistance to the defendants in this case. It was laid down long ago by better judges than I am, that a man is bound by an agreement to which he has expressed a clear assent, uninfluenced by falsehood, violence or oppression. The Courts, for example, will not permit one who has entered into a contract to avoid its operation on the ground that he did not attend to the terms of it; that he did not read the document or supposed it to be a mere form.

The present case is stronger still. At a pre-marital cocktail-party the plaintiff was heard by two or three of the witnesses to say that she was reluctant to promise publicly that she would 'obey' her husband. The deceased replied (Q. 1978) 'You jolly well will say "obey": and you jolly well *will* "obey". *Ha, ha.*' 'O.K.,' responded the plaintiff, in the modern argot, 'and *you* will jolly well "endow" me.' The deceased, then, received an express reminder of this particular term in the contract before it was made: and the plaintiff, it seems, did not allow him to forget it thereafter.

The Attorney-General made some play with the suggestion that the deceased did not acknowledge by his behaviour the alleged 'endowment', that he managed his affairs, and his money, as if he were master of both. 'Too right,' the plaintiff testified, in her charming, unaffected fashion. Mr. Trample, it seems, like other wealthy men, made no high name for generosity. Indeed, she said simply, he was 'a mean old——'. He gave her a monthly allowance ('From my own money!' the plaintiff exclaimed in the box) which fell far below the level of her merits, her needs, and her rights. 'Time and again' (Q. 2003) 'I said Hey! What about "endow"? Hand over my stocks and shares. But Cyrus only grinned and said, "Wait a while, honey. You eat well, don't you?"' (Q. 2224). When he died, I was on my way to a solicitor.' The Attorney-General will agree, I am sure, that a contract does not cease to exist because one of the parties ignores its existence. Don't mutter, Sir Anthony.

It was then contended, most unworthily, I thought, for the Crown, that this term in the contract was governed by the words of the marriage service 'till death us do part', and therefore lapsed on the death of Mr. Trample. That argument, no doubt, applies to the undertakings about future behaviour—'I *will* cherish'—'I *will* obey, love, serve, and so on' 'till death us do part'—for the State, unlike the Church, does not insist upon impossibilities. But the words about 'endowing' are in another section of the service, one of three positive assertions of present fact—with no reference to death whatever: 'I (now) thee wed . . . I (now) thee worship . . . and, with all my worldly goods I (now) thee endow.' The Court may listen to a man long-married who says that he no longer 'worships' his wife and is no longer willing to give her money, but not to one who says that that was the situation at the time of the marriage. The Crown's case must fail here too.

I find, then, that at this wedding the deceased man, in consideration of his wife's promise to love, honour, obey, serve and so forth, did in fact, once and for all time, endow her with 'all his worldly goods'—that is, with the worldly goods that he possessed *on that day*, which, by reference to

income-tax returns and other records have been assessed at
£700,000. He seems to have made some more money during his married life, and from that excess the Commissioners may extract what is lawful, and the legatees what
they can. But gifts, as I said before, made in consideration
of marriage are exempt from the wicked five-years' rule
relating to Estate Duty, and £700,000, no less, must be
paid to the plaintiff. Many brides, it is said, decline to utter
the word 'obey'. Some husbands, it may be, would be wise
to shy away from the word 'endow'. But Mr. Trample,
though well warned, did not: and he, or rather his estate,
must accept the consequences. Costs against the Crown. I
should like all present to give three hearty cheers for Fay.

This was done.

'Fair' Comment?

At the Old Bailey today Mr. Justice Ploon, the latest addition to the Queen's Bench, summing up to the jury, said:

This is the first time I have seen a dramatic critic in the dock—though it may not, I fancy, be the last. I asked the prosecuting counsel, Sir Adrian Floss, why the aggrieved persons had not taken the ordinary course of a civil action for damages for defamation. He replied, as you heard: 'My lord, the newspaper in which the words complained of occurred is, without doubt, insured against the results of suits for defamation, and the man Quirk would not be allowed to suffer. The author and manager of the play in question feel that he ought to suffer. It is not possible to insure against the consequences of crime; and, to be frank, we hope that he will be found guilty and sent to jail. Moreover, the words and circumstances of the libel in this case are exceptionally likely to provoke a breach of the peace, which is the main justification for criminal proceedings.' This, I must say, seems reasonable to me.

Now, it is common ground that the play *Queen Rat* was not a shining success. Few critics praised it, and many were hostile, as they are entitled to be. Most, however, expressed their disapproval in moderate and careful language. None ventured to say, as one critic did not long ago: 'If this play is still being performed next Monday I shall return and abuse it again.' But Mr. Quirk wrote:

> '*An onset of nausea prevented me from seeing more than the first half of "Queen Rat"* ...'

and after the first act, as he has admitted, he left the theatre.

I have already held that these words are capable of a

defamatory meaning, for, according to the dictionary, 'nausea' means '*a feeling of sickness, with loathing of food, and an inclination to vomit*'. The accused does not claim that his condition was due to any stomachic or abdominal disturbance: indeed he could hardly do that, for the evidence is that, having left the theatre, he ate a very good dinner. No, the 'onset of nausea' was caused, metaphorically, by his seeing and hearing the first act of this play. Few more damaging things could be said about a dramatic work.

I must now inform you that in criminal proceedings for libel, where a statement of fact is in question, it is not enough to show that the statement was true: it must be proved that the publication was 'for the public benefit'. Here, as we have seen, the assertion of nausea was not true, in substance and in fact: nor, you may think, if it had been true would it have contributed much to the public benefit. According to the evidence a new but small class of critics has appeared who, somewhat exaggerating their own importance, like to make a parade of their personal sensations: 'I wanted to scream,' says one; 'I felt like sleep,' says another; 'I gnashed my teeth,' 'I could hardly sit still,' 'I closed my eyes,' 'I suffered from indigestion.' You may well think, as I do, that the physical state of a critic, unless put forward as an excuse for folly or rudeness, is not a matter of the slightest public interest.

I pass to the main, and famous, defence of 'fair comment': and I shall begin with the most difficult of the many questions which I see sparkling in those innocent eyes— 'What exactly is meant by *fair* comment?' This has been the subject of engaging and profitable dispute among jurists, judges, and members of the Bar for at least one hundred years. 'Fair comment,' said Lord Mildew in *Platt* v. *Honeydew*, 'is a grand ingredient of our justly boasted political freedom.' It is not the privilege of a few but the right of all to comment loudly on 'matters of public interest,' meaning the affairs of Parliament, the public conduct of Ministers and Councillors and public servants, and even, within limits, the administration of justice, and so on. But this original freedom was extended to cover comment upon works of art or literature or music, exposed to the public and thus, it is said, 'submitted to criticism'. These, it is true, are 'matters of public interest', but not to the same extent as the conduct of the nation's rulers. A work of art, however disappointing, can seldom do so much damage as the foolish speech or wrong decision of a Minister. Moreover, the production of a satisfactory play is an enterprise much more difficult and dubious than the formulation of political policy. Unhappily, many distinguished jurists, misled by a false equation, have spoken as if 'fair comment', in both departments of life, meant exactly the same. Respected judges have said that 'fair' does not mean what the ordinary citizen would consider to be 'fair'. Words which to you or me would appear to be unreasonably or unnecessarily offensive, violent, extravagant, exaggerated, not far from mere invective or abuse, may still, according to these authorities, be 'fair comment' if the opinions, however expressed, are 'honest', that is, not inspired or swollen by 'malice'. Such a doctrine may well be accepted in certain forms of political comment. A simple, angry, but honest citizen who cries 'Murderer!' from the back of the hall when the Prime Minister defends the nuclear deterrent will probably be excused in the unlikely event of an action for slander. But a dramatic critic, writing in cold blood and, by the way, for money, must surely be judged by different standards. It seems to me to be nonsense to say that any insult he cares to use is 'fair', provided that it is 'honest'. 'Fairness' and 'honesty' are different qualities and do not necessarily travel together. I might most 'honestly' dislike Mr. Quirk and regard him as a public pest. But if I walked across the court and punched him on the nose the blow would hardly be considered 'fair'. I should, if necessary, be willing to defy the authorities of the past, risk the rebukes of the Court of Appeal or House of Lords, and say that in relation to a work of art 'fair comment' means comment that a jury would consider fair, whether honestly conceived or not: and I could pursue this line of thought for many days.

But in this case, I believe, I may be able to spare you from tiresome mental toil by shifting your attention from the words of the defendant to his deeds. He left the theatre after the first act, dined enjoyably while the second act was being performed and thereafter wrote and published more than a hundred words in terse but cruel condemnation of the whole. Nor, according to one witness, was it the first time that this particular critic has behaved in this manner, and publicly, even arrogantly, confessed it. Such conduct may be forgiven in the critic of an egg, where the lower half is unlikely to amend substantially an unfavourable verdict pronounced upon the upper. But a play is a very different affair. The first act may deliberately create an unpleasant effect or atmosphere which is to be cunningly corrected or dispersed in the second and third; just as a musical composer may resolve a whole series of hideous dissonances into a final noble, soul-satisfying chord. For all he knew, for all we know now, his inclination to vomit would have been abated by the final curtain. How, when Quirk left the building, can he have been sure that this was not the purpose of the dramatist? Even if he did impute to himself such supernatural powers, what right had he to abandon his place of duty? No man is compelled to be a professional dramatic critic; but, having accepted the office, he enjoys certain privileges and, you may feel he has certain obligations. He is paid by his newspaper to write just and careful accounts of the new plays. Accepting him, on his credentials from the newspaper, as a fit and proper person, the theatre provides him with a free seat—sometimes two— which might otherwise have been sold. He is not bound thereby to praise the piece, but he may be expected to behave with reasonable courtesy. If through an onset of nausea, neuralgia, headache, stomachache, or sheer intellectual distaste he finds it impossible to return to his place after the first interval, his proper course, you may think, is to make no comment on the piece at all, for in the circumstances no comment can be 'fair'. No judge, no jury, may go out in the middle. What, I wonder, would the defendant have said if after the case for the prosecution was closed you and I had said, 'So far, this case seems dreary and disgusting. Let us go out and have a drink. And then, without hearing the case for the defence, we will find the prisoner guilty.' He would hardly, I think, have agreed that that was a 'fair' trial. Pray consider your verdict.

The jury found the prisoner guilty, and Quirk was sent to prison for twelve months.

(27) REGINA *v.* RAKE, SMOOT *and* SHEPLEY

WHO DECEIVES WHOM?

PRESIDING over the Court of Criminal Appeal, the Lord Chief Justice gave judgment in the Soho counterfeiting case. He said:

This is an appeal upon a novel point of law. The appellants were convicted at the Old Bailey, and sentenced to terms of imprisonment, for counterfeiting banknotes, of the value of one pound, and for uttering the notes they made. The facts are not in dispute, and the appellants pleaded guilty. The notes were not numerous, and the appellants said that their main purpose was a worthy one, to show with what dangerous ease 'money' can now be made: but no one paid much attention to that. After the trial, belatedly, he admits, there moved in the mind of Sir Godfrey Lawn a new and ingenious defence. He has submitted to the Court that in law no felony was here committed.

Now, in the common forgery the essence of the offence is an intent to defraud: but in this affair it is sufficient for the Crown to prove that there was intent to deceive. It is the prerogative of the Crown to create and manage the currency of the realm, and counterfeiting or defacing it has always been punished with especial severity. But Sir Godfrey has asked the court to distinguish between metal and paper currency. In the days of my youth, when golden sovereigns and silver crowns were common in the pockets of the citizens, it was certainly an odious crime 'to make or counterfeit any coin resembling or apparently intended to resemble or pass for any current gold or silver coin of the realm.' Indeed, it was once High Treason. The recipient, for value, of a spurious sovereign was not only deceived but defrauded, for when he took it to the bank the watchful officials would detect the deceit and refuse to place a pound to his credit.

But the appellants made no false coins. They have confined their manufacture to paper. They are skilled craftsmen, and the work, arduous, they said, and trying to the eyes, was well done. In appearance, in printing style and pictorial design, their notes were precisely similar to the Crown's. Many of those to whom they were 'passed' presented them without question at shops and hotels, and received full value for them. Those establishments passed them to their servants by way of wages, and many were happily accepted by banks. Indeed, says Sir Godfrey, until the Crown began to make a fuss, no one was damaged or defrauded, and very many were made content, so far as true content can be attained through material possessions.

Now, on these notes were printed the words:

> BANK OF ENGLAND I promise to pay the Bearer on demand the sum of ONE POUND London. For the Governor and Company of the BANK OF ENGLAND L. K. O'Brien Chief Cashier

In these words, according to the Crown, reside the intent to deceive and defraud: for the appellants knew very well that if one of their notes were taken to the Bank of England the bearer would be sent away poundless. This, at first, seems an unanswerable accusation. But Sir Godfrey informed the Court, to our astonishment, that the same result would follow if a genuine pound note were presented at the Bank of England.

At our request O'Brien was called and gave evidence. His testimony was frank, but, I must say, shocking.

Q. 23. *The Court:* You have brought with you a genuine pound note? Thank you. Did you in fact put your name to these words—'I promise to pay', and so on?

Witness: Yes, my lord, under orders. I was by no means the first.

Court: Very well. Does the promise mean what it says? If I bear a note to you tomorrow, will you give me a pound?

Witness: Not a gold pound, my lord. I shall give you

value—twenty shillings or two hundred and forty pennies.

Court: But I can get them anywhere. And that is not what you say. This is the Bank of England, 'promising' me 'One Pound'.

Witness: No, my lord, the *sum* of one pound.

Court: Certainly—as you might say 'the sum of one penny', in which case I should expect a penny coin, not a penny stamp.

Witness: My lord, originally 'a pound' meant a pound weight of silver.

Court: That, again, is not what you say on this document. You do not even say 'the sum of twenty shillings', in the style of a ten shilling note. The words 'the sum of' are small: the words 'One Pound' are large. When I was born 'One Pound' meant a golden sovereign.

Witness: Not recently, my lord.

Court: Then the Bank of England should amend its vocabulary. Do you know the old election story?

Witness: No, my lord.

Court: A sound, but pompous, candidate was complaining about the fall in the value of money. Finally, he took out one of your pound notes and said: 'Look at this! What is it worth today? Seven and sixpence.' And a genial voice at the back said: 'I'll give you ten bob for it, guvnor.'

Witness: Ha!

Court: Showing the importance of precision in the use of language. We agree, then, that this note does not mean what—to me, at least—it seems to say?

Witness: My lord, I think everyone knows what we mean. It is only the occasional joker who comes in and demands a pound.

Court: Is this Court being compared with the occasional joker?

Witness: No, my lord.

Court: Have we got it right? 'Everyone knows' that a Bank of England note is a lie?

Witness: I did not say that, my lord.

Court: You are aware that the appellants in that dock have been convicted of a fraudulent offence?

Witness: Yes, my lord.

Court: And their offence is that they made faithful copies of a Bank of England note?

Witness: Yes, my lord.

These, we think, were damaging admissions: and there were more. It is an old and honoured tradition of British law that he who comes to the Courts for assistance must come 'with clean hands'. The Crown asks the Court to punish these three men for putting 'false' currency into circulation in competition with what the Crown is pleased to call 'genuine' notes. The charge, it seems to me, can only be sustained if it is shown that citizens who took these notes were deceived into supposing that they were getting something of a higher quality than they were in fact. But for the main purpose expressed on both kinds of note, the acquisition of 'one pound', the 'false' and the 'genuine' are equally worthless: and for ordinary purposes, as we have seen, both were equally useful, until, that is, the interference of the Crown. Moreover, as O'Brien rashly admitted, 'everyone knows' that the 'promise' on the genuine notes does not mean what it says, and the people have ceased to rely upon it. Where, then, was the deception? Who was deceived? In the old days, when paper money was solidly and scrupulously backed by gold, it was, without doubt, harmful to the realm to increase without authority the amount of paper money in circulation, for this, in emergency, might make the nation's gold resources insufficient. But now that the Crown, it seems, can issue notes at will, without much reference, if any, to the stocks of gold, no great harm can have been done by the tiny trickle which the appellants added to the ocean of paper in which we flounder. It is true that they have no authority to make notes at all, that they have used without permission the Crown's designs and forms of words. I imagine, therefore, that a civil action for damages might lie against them for breach of copyright, though the Crown will hardly be able to show that the circulation of their own commodity has suffered severely. But to the charge of felony we must oppose the doctrine of 'clean hands'. 'Who', as Sir Godfrey said in his eloquent address, 'can counterfeit a counterfeit?' The conviction is quashed, and the appellants must be discharged.

(28) REGINA *v.* HOCKEY

How Much can you Kill a Burglar?

(Before the Court of Criminal Appeal)

THE Lord Chief Justice, presiding said:

The appellant, Mr. Hockey, has the misfortune to be a good and courageous citizen who shot a burglar, so that the felon was wounded, arrested, convicted, and imprisoned. So impudent, expensive, and brutal have been the depredations of burglars and other robbers in recent times, so few of them have been apprehended and punished, that Mr. Hockey, it is said, expected to receive the applause of the State. In 1811 the courageous Mr. Purcell, of County Cork, resisted, single-handed, a band of nine night-robbers, armed with swords and fire-arms: he killed two of them, with a carving-knife, severely wounded three, and drove the rest away. For these brave deeds he was, very properly, knighted. But the times are different. Mr. Hockey has been found guilty of 'unlawful and malicious wounding'. It is true that he was not sent to prison, but the Court below ordered him to pay costs of £20. His solicitor's bill was already £30. The ordinary citizen, who does not read very carefully the sparse reports of these proceedings in the papers, cannot have been much encouraged to take robust and resolute action in a similar contingency. He will be doubtful of his duty, and anxious about the cost of doing it.

But it is not perhaps for Mr. Hockey, who has caused all the trouble, to come here and complain. What are the facts? Surprised in a bedroom at his quiet work, the redistribution of the national income, the burglar made off through a window. Mr. Hockey coolly went downstairs, loaded a shotgun, and took it to the front door. He saw the burglar moving across the lawn, and cried 'Stop!' The burglar stopped for a moment and then ran on. Mr.

Hockey fired and wounded the felon so that he could not get away. He was tried and sentenced to three years' imprisonment. For this admirable event Mr. Hockey, and no other, was responsible. But for him, the burglar would probably be preying on the sleeping citizens still. Yet he has been convicted of an offence, and his grateful country has made him pay the costs of the prosecution. He has appealed.

The law that governs this kind of affair was correctly stated by counsel for the Crown. If an able-bodied citizen sees a felony being done (and burglary is a violent felony) it is not merely his right but his duty to arrest the malefactor if he can. He must not, of course, allow himself to be influenced by personal pique or resentment, however little he may care to have burglars about his house. He must remember throughout that the felon has probably had an unhappy youth, was warped by a cruel charwoman, or fell from a tree in boyhood. He must not use more than 'reasonable force'; that is, if he is compelled to strike the burglar, the blow should be so regulated as to have a sufficiently discouraging effect without inflicting perhaps a lasting wound on a sensitive mind: while, of course, any physical lesion or trauma should be avoided. Lord Mildew said, in *Rex* v. *Batley* (1939): 'To be quite sure that any violence he may be obliged to exert will fall within the limits of "reasonable force", the householder, as a rule, should provide himself with boxing-gloves and be careful not to strike the felon in the face.' If he is compelled by circumstances to use a weapon, he must again make a careful choice of one that will not be unreasonably rough, selecting, for example, any blunt instrument to hand rather than one with a cutting edge or penetrating point. He may use a fire-arm only in the last resort, that is, when it is clear that by no other means can he secure his proper end, defeat the intruder and detain him till the police arrive.

Subject to the observance of these conditions and precautions, it is his duty, I repeat, to arrest the felon. But,

before he sets about this task, he must acquaint the burglar
with his intentions, and assure himself of the burglar's. The
usual formula (approved, I believe, by the Rules Committee) is: 'You should surrender. It is my duty to inform
you that I propose to arrest you for the felonious offence of
burglary. Kindly be seated while I telephone to the police.'
The counsel for the defence drew the Court's attention to
the celebrated case of *Rex* v. *Rungle*, affectionately known
to the legal profession as 'Codd's Last Case'. In that case
an outraged householder threw a garden-fork (which he
kept beside the bed) at a departing burglar who had dis-
obeyed the order to 'Stop!' The burglar died. Our late
lamented brother Codd carefully surveyed the authorities
and rightly complained of the incertitude he found. One
respected text-book says:

> 'The question whether and how far it is justifiable to
> kill a burglar is by no means clear. If violence on the part
> of the burglar be reasonably apprehended, it is not
> murder to shoot him dead with intent to kill him, but
> whether it is justifiable to kill *merely in defence of property*
> is doubtful.'

Mr. Kenny too, in his *Outline of Criminal Law*, says:

> 'When the wrongdoer is not going so far as to assault
> a human being, but is *only interfering unlawfully with
> property*, the possessor of that property (though he is per-
> mitted by the law to use a moderate degree of force in
> defence of his possessions) will *usually* not be justified in
> carrying this force to the point of killing the trespasser ...'

But he goes on:

> 'Such a justification will not arise unless the tres-
> passer's interference or resistance amounts to a felony,
> and moreover to a felony of some kind that is violent,
> such, for example, as robbery, arson or *burglary*.'

We can hear the sighs of earnest students as they pass to the next sentence:

'And even these extremely violent felonies should not be resisted by extreme violence unless it is actually necessary; thus fire-arms should not be used until there seems to be no other mode available for defeating the intruder and *securing his arrest*.'

Our brother Codd's response was characteristically robust: 'They're trying to whittle down our ancient rights. It's all part of this namby-pamby stuff about crime.' Finally, he said:

'I declare the law to be as follows:
It is the right and duty of any householder, or any other honest citizen, who finds an undoubted burglar in a dwelling-house, to arrest him. He may, and should, order the burglar to stay quietly on the premises till any necessary arrangements have been made. If the burglar disobeys this order and attempts to make off, the honest citizen may use any force that he considers necessary and any weapon that is at hand to stop him: and if the result is death it is justifiable homicide, not murder or even manslaughter.'

With some reluctance this Court must overrule and reject Codd J.'s pronouncement. It is not in accordance with the tender spirit or the enlightened thinking of the time. Property is not the sacred cause that it was: for many it is almost a crime. Burglary is technically a 'violent' felony: but in this case the only violence in fact was the manipulation of a latch, and at the moment of the shooting the malefactor was peacefully departing. Thus the use of fire-arms 'merely in defence of property' was quite unjustified. There remains the question, tiresomely pressed by counsel for defence, whether the shotgun was not, in the words of the admirable Kenny, the only 'mode available' for 'securing the intruder's arrest'. It is true that it did have that result, but, as we have seen, there were other 'modes available'. The prisoner could have given chase, uttering persuasive words. This he failed to do.

Such behaviour must not be encouraged or condoned. It must be recognized that every burglar has a mother and, through the ill-treatment of society, is likely to be a sufferer from psychological lesions. If it were once to get about that householders were able and willing to pursue the successful robber with fire-arms, the burglar, in self-defence, would be compelled to carry a pistol, a great inconvenience to his profession and a danger to others. In these hard times, when Full Employment and the Redistribution of the National Wealth are the principal hopes of the State, the Courts must be careful not to interfere with either.

The appeal is dismissed: the appellant will pay £100 by way of costs. That will teach him, perhaps, to do his duty.

(29) TROUT, M.P. *v.* CELESTIAL PUBLICITY LTD. *and* BROOT

END OF A NONSENSE

I

THE House of Lords today discussed a conundrum on the law of defamation which has long provoked and puzzled our leading jurists.

The Lord Chancellor said: This is an appeal by Sir Wesley Trout, M.P., from a decision by the Court of Appeal (Lord Justice Rutt dissenting) reversing a decision of Mr. Justice Plush in the Queen's Bench Division. The facts are simple. The appellant, a retired man of business, stood for Parliament at the recent by-election for Hammerton (West). He was 'adopted' not long before the election, was new to the neighbourhood, as well as to political life, and had little time to captivate the fifty thousand electors. The respondent company offered their aid. The ordinary methods, they said, of poster, canvassing, and public meeting, always expensive and exhausting, would in his case be quite ineffective as well: for if he travelled and talked all day and all night he would still be unable to make his presence, his personality, and opinions, sufficiently felt. They suggested, therefore, the use of the air. One plan was to fly a helicopter slowly over Hammerton, at the lawful height, and to lower the candidate, by a long rope, to roof-level, or near it, in a comfortable chair, from which he could address the unfortunate citizens without fear of interruption or correction, through the barbarous instrument known as a 'loud-hailer'. This, as your Lordships heard with horror, was successfully done more than once. Another plan, which is the cause of this litigation, was to advertise the candidate's name and nobility over the borough by a procedure known as 'sky-writing'. Here, it appears, an aircraft picks out some simple message in huge letters formed of smoke or vapour, high in the sky. Whatever the message, the spectacle of the soaring machine is sure to capture the attention of every street for many miles. The respondents first sent up a pilot, Mr. Broot, to 'write' upon the pale-blue dome of heaven the words ALL OUT FOR TROUT; and this was a big success, doing more to get the candidate's name into the people's heads than numerous posters and meetings. The next was TROUT IS ALWAYS RIGHT. Unhappily there was a calligraphic error, and the last word began with a T, making it TIGHT. It was a fine still day, the message hung in the sky for half an hour, and was read by vast hilarious crowds. The pilot apologized, no malice was suspected—after all, a man flying at a great height, vertically or upside down, may easily make literal mistakes— and the next day Mr. Broot was ordered aloft again. This time the message was SEND TROUT IN: but the appellant was horrified, and the crowds were delighted, when the last word was done, to read SEND TROUT GIN. 'What a bungler!' thought the innocent appellant: and that was all he thought. The machine passed on to another part of the sky where it was to write a second battle cry: VOTE FOR TROUT THE PUBLIC FRIEND. This, according to the respondent company, was designed as a pleasant parallel to 'the Public Trustee' and a sly reply to the tall talk of Sir Wesley's rival about the benefits of Public Ownership. But the respondent Broot wrote clearly on the sky VOTE FOR TROUT THE PUBLICANS FRIEND. (He even tried, according to the evidence, to depict an apostrophe after the 's' in PUBLICANS.) He then flew off to a distant airfield, landed, and left the country at once.

Later, it emerged that Broot was a supporter of a small but subversive political party, and had a personal spite against Sir Wesley, from one of whose factories he had been dismissed some years earlier. 'Celestial Publicity Limited' were innocent, in fact, but were technically responsible for Mr. Broot's behaviour: and Sir Wesley sued both for defamation. Sir Wesley is not, in fact, a teetotaller, and indeed is reasonably tolerant of the use of alcohol (as wine is now described), but no more. The seat is a 'safe' one, and the accusations in the sky were not enough to lose it: but he complains they have stuck. Small boys cry after him 'Boozer!' or 'Trout, the human fish!' On the other hand many electors, it seems, thought the better of him: and many who did not thought that he had been hardly used and voted accordingly.

The trouble is—not for his country, we may be sure, but for himself—that he was successful in the election. Nor, having 'retired', can he claim that he has been injured in any professional capacity. In other words, he could offer no evidence that he has suffered any actual damage from the celestial insults of which he complains. That would not matter if they were indubitably in the nature of libel, if Mr. Broot had written his foul words on a postcard or published them in a newspaper. For then, damage or no, he, and his employers, without any doubt, would be liable: and such was the finding of Mr. Justice Plush. But the respondents claim that the defamation, if any, was no more than a slander, so that some damage must be shown: and such was the finding of the majority of the Court of Appeal (Lord Justice Rutt dissenting).

Your Lordships, then, must wearily consider once more the question to which, for so many decades, so many judges, juries, and jurists have given so much time, thought and toil: have we here a libel or a slander? We shall, I fear, be discussing it for many decades more: for a Defamation Bill, now well on its way to the Statute Book, does little to modify, and nothing to remove, an old but accidental distinction which many good minds regard as vicious and valueless, which does not exist in Scotland, but is preserved like a sacred relic in this part of our island.

My Lords, I need not tell you, but I must—for the instruction of less learned men and the full employment of typists and printers—what that distinction is. Upon the

best authority, a text-book, in libel the defamatory statement is made in some permanent and visible form, such as
writing, printing, or effigies: in slander it is made in spoken
words or in some other transitory form, whether visible or
audible, such as gestures, hissing, or other inarticulate but
significant sounds.

In which category are we to place insults which are
conveyed by smoke or vapour high above the earth's surface? They are visible: they are in the form of legible letters:
they are described by the respondents themselves as 'writing' of a sort. But they are certainly not 'permanent': they
begin to dwindle as soon as they are made, and in ordinary
conditions of wind and weather are not decipherable, perhaps, for more than ten minutes. After that they are a
memory, no more. No man can say to his wife or child
'Come out and see what they have written about Trout';
for there is nothing to see. Vapour is not like a postcard, a
paper, a caricature, which can be passed from hand to
hand. It is much more like a rude word, or derogatory
speech, 'gone with the wind', or, in the words of the authorities, 'transitory in form'. On the other hand, these
particular insults were conveyed to the minds of millions
and will remain there longer, it may be, than anything that
they read on a postcard or even in a newspaper. My Lords,
I think it will be convenient if we now have lunch and
continue our discussion on another day.

The House adjourned.

II

The House of Lords considered again the appeal of Sir
Wesley Trout, M.P., in the Sky-writing Case. Sir Wesley
complained of defamatory messages 'written' in the sky, in
vapour, during a by-election.

The Lord Chancellor, continuing, said: It is not disputed
that the smoke-signals or characters were defamatory. The
only question is, are they libel, as was held by Mr. Justice

Plush, or slander, as the Court of Appeal (Lord Justice Rutt dissenting) decided? Should they be treated as 'permanent', like a letter or postcard, or 'transitory', like a hiss, hoot, or derogatory speech? In the first case the appellant will receive the damages awarded by the court of first instance: in the second his suit will be at last dismissed.

Learned counsel have referred us to some cases of which all that can be said is that they belong to the same department of doubt. There was the famous case of *Chicken* v. *Ham*, where a man deliberately caused opprobrious words to be recorded and published by means of a gramophone. There were two trials of the action and two appeals to the Court of Appeal, which held on the first occasion that the wrong was slander and on the second that it was libel. In your Lordships' House my illustrious predecessor and Lord Arrowroot were for slander, and the late Lords Lick and Sheep for libel: the late Lord Goat was about to give his opinion, which would, presumably, have been decisive, when, unhappily, he perished of heart failure. The second of two contradictory decisions of the Court of Appeal, therefore, was allowed to stand, precariously—a not entirely satisfactory climax to an enjoyable year or two of litigation.

Lord Lick in that appeal referred to the case of *Silvertop* v. *Stepney Guardians*, 'where a man trained a parrot to say three times after meals "Councillor Wart has not washed today". It was held that this was a libel.' A minor jurist has unworthily complained that no record is to be found of *Silvertop* v. *Stepney Guardians*. But the learning and character of the late Lord Lick are too well respected——

Lord Wool: It was one of Lick's own cases. I know what happened. There was a fire that night at the reporter's house. Old Lick could hardly remember his name: but he never forgot his own judgments. The parrot's all right.

The Lord Chancellor: Just so. The House is obliged to Lord Wool. But the repetitive parrot—like the repetitive gramophone—has an element of continuity which cannot be found in brief and fugitive vapour-writing. Then there was the more recent case of *Temper* v. *Hume and Haddock* (M.L.C., 1951). There the insults were conveyed by flag-signals in the International Code, the flags being displayed sometimes for a few minutes only, sometimes for a few hours at most. Here, you may think, we are nearer to temporary defamation by vapour. Unhappily, the jury disagreed about the facts, and Mr. Justice Codd (now defunct) was unable, or perhaps unwilling, to pronounce an opinion on the question of law. Your Lordships have never had a similar case before them, and so have no decision of their own to guide them. Parliament has declined to abolish the distinction between libel and slander: and your Lordships, I conceive, are bound to abide by it. I think that this was a slander, and the appeal should be dismissed.

Lord Wool: Stuff and nonsense! With great respect to my noble friend the Lord Chancellor, I disagree. Not only with what he said but the way he said it. Evidently he doesn't like the Common Law: but he's afraid to say so. I'm not. God bless me! Who made the Common Law? The judges. Who are we? The top judges. And who's put the Common Law right when it's old and silly? Why, we, of course. I thought it pitiful to see our good Lord Chancellor prowling about, like a dog at the dust-bins, in the Courts below, trying to find some mouldy old decision to comfort him. Then he bleated that Parliament had not abolished the crazy quibbles about libel and slander. Well, it has done a bit, just a nibble or two. But we invented them, and we should put an end to them. You're all afraid. I'm not. I'm 73. But I'll race any of you across Westminster Bridge. Where was I? Oh yes. You say, in this case, there was 'no actual damage'. Therefore the poor chap can't recover. God bless me, isn't it enough to have small boys calling 'Boozer!' after you? How would any of your Lordships like it? I don't care whether you call this libel or slander—it was defamation, the man has suffered, and the appeal should be allowed.

Lord Middle: I do not agree. It will be a sad day for British justice if ever we interrupt the orderly march of precedent and case-law. Nor can I dismiss so lightly as Lord Wool the ancient distinction between written and spoken abuse or vilification. It does not, I know, exist in Scottish law: but then, I understand, most of the Scots are more or less speechless. In England, everywhere, it would be disastrous if a writ could issue for every foolish or unfriendly word. Turning to the present appeal, I find, like the Lord Chancellor, that insults in smoke or vapour have not the solid and enduring character which is required in the case of libel. They are more like the signal-flags, and less like the trained parrot or the gramophone, both of which, I should say, were libellous. This was a slander and the appeal should be dismissed.

The House adjourned. The score is now 2–1. Lords Off and Laburnum have still to give their opinions. In legal circles the betting is heavy, and most of the money is on slander.

III

The House of Lords considered for the third day the Sky-writing Case, in which Sir Wesley Trout, M.P., claims damages for defamatory messages expressed in smoke. Lord Wool, at the last hearing, vigorously declared himself in Sir Wesley's favour: but the Lord Chancellor and Lord Middle came down on the side of slander—and the respondents. Score 2–1. Betting 6–4 on slander.

Lord Off: I do not agree. I have reached the same conclusion as Lord Wool, but by a different route. He is not, I think, quite just to the judges of the past. The distinction of which he complains is due to an historical accident. Slander, in ancient days, was dealt with by the feudal, and later by the ecclesiastical courts. Then printing came in, and the apprehensive Star Chamber made the new invention its particular care, so that an action for libel has retained some of the criminal character of that Court's proceedings, and no proof of damage is required. We should still, I think, make some distinction between garden-wall gossip and widespread defamation. The trouble is that our distinctions are now out of date. Other mechanical inventions have followed printing, and there may be more to come: but the Courts, having no guidance from your Lordships' House, are still applying the ancient rules of the Common Law which are evidently inappropriate to the age of the gramophone, the film, the talking-film, the radio, the loud-hailer, and now the sky-scribbler. The test should be not the method, or even the duration, but the area and the occasion of the defamatory act. The Bill now before Parliament goes a little way in this direction. 'The broadcasting of words by means of wireless telegraphy' is to be treated as 'publication in permanent form'.[1] But this will not assist the man who is vilified by loud-hailer, gramophone or sky-writer. In my judgment, wherever a mechanical instrument is employed, the area and the importance of the defamatory act is likely to be greater (about the trained parrot I express no opinion), and the wrong should therefore be considered more offensive in degree, and, for convenience, *prima facie*, be classed as libel. I find that there was here a libel, and the appeal should be allowed.

The score was now two Law-Lords all, with one to go. Excitement was intense as the aged Lord Laburnum began to speak. He said:

My Lords, I am only 87: but I am not going to race my brother Wool across Westminster Bridge. Still, my memory's pretty good. My mind goes back more than twenty years—I think it was 1928 or '9—to the case of *Sparrow* v. *Pipp*, where your Lordships' House (including myself) stood by a young puppy of a puisne judge who had cocked a snook at the Common Law of defamation. His

[1] Sections 1, 2, 3, of Defamation Act 1952.

name was Wool. The Lord Chancellor of those days—I forget his name—used language very different from that which has fallen from the noble occupant of the Woolsack today. He said: 'Your Lordships have the power to amend the Common Law provided that you are willing to abandon in some degree the mechanical adhesion to precedent which has been for centuries the foundation of our judicial practice. We may as well begin with the law of libel.' Very good. But here we are, twenty-four years later, still splitting the same old hairs. Of course—and here I agree with Wool —the simplest thing is to stop all this talk about 'special damage': then we could stop distinguishing between libel and slander. Why should a man have to prove that he has lost a job or been turned out of a club? Damage to reputation, to character, to pride, is not a material thing to be measured and calculated like damage to a motor-car, or the supply of gas to a house. If many people have been led to believe bad things about you which are not true that should be enough. My Lords, you are all afraid of letting loose a lot of flimsy and frivolous actions, I know: but judges and juries can be trusted to discourage those. Let's do a little deeming. My Lords, I declare the law to be as follows: In these times there is no libel, there is no slander; there is only defamation. In any clear case of defamation it shall be deemed that there is damage, whether spiritual or material, 'actual' or 'special', until the contrary is shown. After all, if a man hits you in the face you do not have to prove that you are dead or disabled. It is sufficient that there has been an unjust and unprovoked assault. Of course, if the defamatory defendant can show that the plaintiff has suffered little or nothing the plaintiff may be discouraged with costs: but the scurrilous defendant will be discouraged too. People will be more careful what they say, and litigation, in my opinion, will be less, not more. In this case I deem accordingly. The appeal should be allowed and Sir Wesley Trout should have his damages.

It was. He did.

NOTE—The hearing of this case began on 22 August 1952 and was concluded on 29 October. On 30 October the new Defamation Act (presented by Mr. N. H. Lever, M.P.) received the Royal Assent. Section 2 materially modified the distinction between libel and slander but not to the extent demanded by Lord Laburnum. The Section reads:

'In an action for slander in respect of words calculated to disparage the plaintiff in any office, profession, calling, trade or business held or carried on by him at the time of the publication it shall not be necessary to allege or prove special damage, whether or not the words are spoken of the plaintiff in his office, profession, calling, trade or business.'

This is a great improvement of the law, and shows that Parliament had taken note of the long series of cases mentioned by the Lord Chancellor in Trout's case. Whether the new Section would have saved the plaintiff Trout his protracted and expensive litigation, is not absolutely certain. He was not 'at the time of the publication' holding any 'office' for he had not yet been elected. Nor, having retired, had he any 'trade or business'. But is a politician, seeking election to Parliament, 'carrying on ... a profession or calling'? Presumably yes. But an unscrupulous defendant might well have argued that Trout, who had never sought election before, was not entitled to the benefit of the Section. More interesting litigation may be expected, and it would have been better, many feel, if Parliament had made a clean sweep of the distinction.

(30) REGINA *v.* HADDOCK

'Who Giveth This Woman?'

Mr. Albert Haddock gave evidence today in the appeal from his conviction by the justices of Rivertown, under the Act of 1860, for brawling in church.

Sir Anthony Slatt, Q.C. (cross-examining): Then, I believe, the Vicar said: 'Who giveth this Woman to be married to this Man?' What happened next?

Haddock: I said 'As a matter of fact, *I* do.'

Sir Anthony: Loudly?

Haddock: I believe in speaking up, sir.

Mr. Justice Plush: Quite right. What should he have said, Sir Anthony?

Sir Anthony: My lord, no words are prescribed. The question 'Who giveth ...?' is followed immediately by these directions: 'Then shall they give their troth to each other in this manner. The Minister, receiving the Woman *at her father's or friend's hands*, shall cause the Man with his right hand to take the Woman by her right hand,' and so on. My lord, in my submission, it is not intended that the 'father or friend' shall use any words: and, in fact, as a rule, he is content to make a formal gesture and quietly stand aside.

The Judge: But how, then, is anyone to know who he is?

Sir Anthony: My lord, it is assumed that the person making the gesture——

The Judge: 'Assumed'? But he may be an imposter—some violent bully who by duress or drugs is forcing an unwilling woman into a union which is repugnant. I think Mr. Haddock was quite right to make himself, and his consent, manifest. Did he 'announce his identity' as the telephone book says?

Sir Anthony: Yes, my lord. But that, my lord, was not all the accused said.

The Judge: Oh? What else did you say, Mr. Haddock?

The Witness: 'I am Albert Haddock,' I said, my lord, 'the father of this beautiful girl: and I am very glad of this opportunity to say a few words. I may say it's the first chance I've had to say a few words, without insult or interruption, for about six months. It is a singular fact, worthy of study by the anthropologists, that a month or two before his daughter's marriage, the father, the husband, the bread-winner, who has made the whole affair possible, is afflicted with imbecility—that is, in the estimation of the female members of the tribe. They fuss and buzz about like a swarm of bees, arranging, planning, arguing, advising, whispering in corners, yelling over the telephone, buying this and ordering that. The only person never consulted, never allowed to open his mouth, is Daddy, who "doesn't understand". Daddy is only fit for footing the bills. Yes, Vicar, I do give this Woman away, but I'm also giving the wedding-dress, and three, at least, of those horrible brides-maids' dresses. I can't stand yellow—they all know that. "Pale blue," I said, "anything but *yellow*," I said. But oh, no—"Daddy doesn't understand"—and there they are, poor girls, like a clutch of canaries. What's more, I'm giving the party afterwards. I'd like to discuss that. I never know why it's the *bride*'s father who has to cough up for the reception. I speak feelingly, Vicar, because, as you know, I've seven daughters. Doris is the fourth to get married, and there are still three to go. Next time—and I give you all fair notice—there'll have to be some other arrangement. Fair do's.'

The Judge: I have five daughters myself, Mr. Haddock. I know what you mean.

The Witness: Thank you, my lord. Well, 'Don't think I begrudge the money,' I said, 'it isn't that. But if I have to cough up every time, I might at least be allowed to have my way about the bridesmaids' dresses. *And* about the wine. I don't like champagne—hardly anybody does, if the truth were told. Horrible drink. "Let's be different," I said, "let's have a nice still Hock—or some of the Alsatian.

Much better for everybody—and nobody who matters will miss those ridiculous bubbles." But oh, no—it's "Daddy doesn't understand."'

The Judge: The Court is with you. But, Mr. Haddock, I am not quite clear. Did you actually say all this?

The Witness: Yes, my lord—or something like it.

The Judge: Excellent. Go on.

The Witness: 'And *then*,' I said, my lord, 'the extraordinary thing is this! On the day of the race—I mean the match—at the last minute, when the poor bride is hysterical and as likely as not to throw herself out of the window —*all* the women who have been bossing the show for six months go off to the church and leave her alone in the house. *And who with?* Why, with the incapable *man*—the half-witted Father! I can tell you, it was a job to get poor Doris to the starting-gate at all. I had to use the *sal volatile*, and that's a drill I'm not familiar with. How I suffered!'

The Judge: How it all comes back! Go on.

The Witness: It was about then, my lord, that I noticed the Vicar whispering to the verger, who made a stately exit. 'However,' I said, 'thanks to me, we made it.'

The Judge: You made what?

The Witness: The starting-gate, my lord. But just as we were coming round the turn into the nave—all in step with the music, and going well—we'd rehearsed it several times, my lord—some lunatic female dashes out of her pew and hisses 'You're on the wrong side—you're on the wrong side.' 'I'm not,' I said, 'Go away.' 'I ought to know,' she said, 'I've done this five times.' Then she disappeared. Well, she was wrong, of course, my lord, but it shook me—put us out of step. We get to the top, and I stand there looking like a riderless horse—that's all right—but when we get to my little bit, there's nothing for me to say. Suddenly I thought 'If I've got to go through all this three more times, there must be better arrangements.'

The Judge: You mentioned this in your address? It was in the nature of a dignified protest?

The Witness: Yes, my lord. 'I'm not being obstructive,' I said, 'I said I'd give Doris away, and so I will, though after all this many a man would change his mind, and where would you all be then?'

The Judge: Mr. Attorney, where would they all have been then?

Sir Anthony: Milord, without further instructions, I should not like to say.

The Judge: Very well. And that was all?

The Witness: Yes, my lord. No, my lord, there was one more thing. I'm glad you reminded me. I said a word about the *time* of these ghastly affairs. *Months* ago, my lord, I said '*Don't* have it at two o'clock!' But, of course, Daddy didn't understand, and two o'clock was precisely the time the frantic women chose.

The Judge: Why do you object to that?

The Witness: Well, my lord, just because two young folk want to get married, I don't see why all their friends should be expected to miss a whole day's work and put on tails and toppers at twelve noon. The last lawful hour for weddings used to be 3.0, but many years ago Parliament very wisely passed a new law permitting them up till 6.0. Well, 5.30 would do very well—that's what we did with June and Joyce. By the time the cake-cutting and all that is over it's a reasonable hour for a drink—even champagne. Three o'clock in the afternoon is a disgusting hour for drinking—especially champagne.

The Judge: I think you're so right.

The Witness: My lord, when the other two were done, we had a nice stand-up supper, with a band and dancing. The bridal pair took the first dance alone—a very pretty picture; and June, I remember, even danced with her contemptible Papa. About 9.30 or 10.0 they tootled off to the Savoy, or somewhere, leaving us all happy; and the next day they went abroad. That's the thing. Now, with a two o'clock affair the wretched guests are left high and dry in their ridiculous clothes at half-past four in the afternoon—

dressed up for a Midsummer Night's Dream with Titania and Oberon gone. There's nothing to do but have another drink, and after champagne any other drink is lethal. All because the couple insist on rushing off to some foreign country this afternoon. 'Heaven knows' I said, 'where these two are going—nobody tells Papa, of *course*—but if they're going to Sicily, why couldn't they go to Sicily tomorrow? After all, they've caused all this costly fuss—they're going to spend their whole lives together, and it wouldn't be a bad thing if they started it by showing some consideration for others. I call it rather selfish.' And about then, my lord, Constable Boot stole up the nave and took me away.

The Judge: In my opinion this prosecution should never have been brought. There is, as the Attorney-General has pointed out, this undoubted and surprising hiatus in the marriage service. Everywhere else all concerned are told precisely what to say and do—'The Man shall answer "I will"' and so on. Here a question is prescribed but no answer is provided. The question, presumably, has some importance, or it would not be put at all. Some answer therefore must be intended; Mr. Haddock was expected to say something: but what he should say was left to his discretion. It may well be, as he has suggested, that originally this moment was designed as an occasion for the bride's father to deliver a patriarchal address, giving to old and young the benefit of his experience and wisdom. One witness thought that the whole business of 'giving away' was a barbarous relic of the father's proprietary interest in his young—the head of the tribe 'giving' his daughter in exchange for twenty fat oxen, and so on. I prefer, myself, to think that it is a wholesome safeguard against the malefactor, strengthening the evidence of true consent. But there the question is, and I have only to decide whether what Mr. Haddock said in answer to it was 'riotous, violent, or indecent'. I think, on the contrary, that what he said, though perhaps insensitive and tactless here and there, was in substance sound and sensible. Certainly, I can find no evidence of anything that amounts to brawling. The Attorney-General, I know, is fussed about 'creating a precedent'. The Church, he says, is afraid that if Mr. Haddock is discharged all the fathers will do as he did. I have no fear of that: few fathers have the fortitude of Mr. Haddock. Besides, if necessary, the service can be amended. The prosecution is dismissed. All possible costs to be paid by the Crown.

(31) INLAND REVENUE v. HADDOCK

The 'Bottle' Case

MR. JUSTICE ROUGH to-day gave judgment in this fascinating case. He said:

This, I think, is one of the innumerable actions which the Inland Revenue should never have begun. One of the singular and baleful features of the recent industrial troubles was the unshaken pertinacity and punctuality of that Department. At a time when the main communications of the nation were dislocated or idle, parcels forbidden, and letters and telegrams discouraged, the terse red menaces of the tax-collector seemed to reach their targets as easily as ever. At a time when business and professional men were suffering loss and threatened with ruin by strikes with which they had nothing to do, the tax-collector still thought it fitting to demand from them large portions of any money they had left in the bank. In such a state was the defendant, Mr. Albert Haddock. First, he says, the newspaper strike diminished his opportunities to earn money by the pen. Then the dock strike held up several ships which were to carry in their holds large quantities of his many masterpieces to the United States and other foreign lands. Last came the railway strike which prevented the distribution of his books even in the United Kingdom, reduced the size of the newspapers, and prevented or discouraged the people from attending in their usual numbers his fine and numerous theatrical productions.

At the very peak of all this trouble, it appears, the Inland Revenue demanded of him the payment of a sum which must make his relations with his bank, already precarious, impossible. Moreover, they sternly named a date after which, failing payment, legal proceedings would be taken. At first, Mr. Haddock told us, he was tempted to ignore this impudent threat. He is not, he said, one of those unfeeling monsters who think only of themselves. Indeed, he assured the Court, every morning on rising he says three times, aloud: 'Thank God for the Welfare State!' But, he added, at the age of nearly sixty-five he does feel from time to time a momentary reluctance to hand over most of his earnings for the benefit of those who are so well off that they can stop work whenever the spirit moves them, and so lacking in the finer feelings that they do not care what injury they do to their country. They expect, he said, and are permitted, to enjoy, while they are idle, not only the ordinary public services but the so-called 'social' services to which the direct taxpayer is compelled so heavily to contribute.

'I asked myself,' the defendant said (Q. 2347), 'whether in the circumstances it was right to encourage such behaviour by making such a payment. Was it not perhaps the national duty of every taxpayer to fight the strike fever by withholding his taxes? For the logical end would be that the Revenue would be diminished and the social services reduced, so that the strikers would feel at last the impact of their folly'—in other words a strike against strikers. 'I confess,' said the defendant frankly, 'that beside this patriotic anxiety there may, for a moment only, have been in my mind the selfish thought that I might thus postpone for a month or two my inevitable end, bankruptcy through the taxes. But then,' he continued, in a moving passage (Q. 2489), 'I thought of the wan faces of the strikers' mothers and wives, unable to do their Pools, the wails of little children cruelly disappointed of the promised television set: and I put those other thoughts aside.'

The Court, on the whole, commends this decision, though it is not quite sure. But Mr. Haddock, having escaped from one dilemma, now found himself in another. The public had repeatedly been enjoined by the Government to send no parcels and no unnecessary or avoidable letters through the post during the railway strike. The sum demanded of the defendant, though in his eyes enormous, was without doubt less than a drop in that great ocean the national revenue. 'I asked myself,' Mr. Haddock said again (Q. 2534), 'whether it would be right to clog the channels with so trivial a communication.' This time the answer was No. But ingenious as he is patriotic, it appears, the defendant hit upon a device which would discharge with honour, he thought, both his obligations. He lives beside the tidal Thames, at Hammersmith. Somerset House, the plaintiffs' headquarters, stands upon the same historic stream about nine (statute) miles farther down. He therefore wrote a cheque for the required amount (crossed, I need hardly say, 'a/c payee'), placed it in a bottle, sealed and clearly labelled the bottle in indelible ink: *To* THE INLAND REVENUE—*Somerset House—please forward*. In the presence of witnesses he committed the bottle to the river at the top of the tide on Friday, 3 June, that is at about 2.12 p.m. by British Summer Time. He then telephoned to the plaintiffs and warned them to be on the look-out between 5.00 and 6.00 p.m., when, according to his calculations, the cheque should be passing the plaintiffs' premises.

But, in addition, he took the trouble to inform them that this would not be their only opportunity to collect the cheque. The ebb tide at this point runs out for about seven hours, and the flood runs in for about five. If they failed to gather the bottle on the first transit, it would, he calculated, pass Somerset House again on the flood at about 12.00 midnight, when the moon, nearly full, he said, would be high in the sky. It might that night go up as far as Chelsea, but about 04.40 (well after sunrise) it would, on the ebb, pass the plaintiffs' office again. Thereafter, by simple calculations, its gradual departure down the river could be followed for many days.

The cheque has not yet come to hand, and the Crown has rashly instituted these proceedings. The Attorney-General (not at his best, by the way) says that Mr. Haddock has not discharged his debt; that, if he had such worthy scruples about using Her Majesty's mails he should himself have delivered the cheque at Somerset House. But this discloses, it seems to me, a lamentable misconception of the plaintiffs' function. Their officers, for good reason, are called '*Collectors* of Taxes'. It is their business to go out into the highways and byways and gather in the revenue. No man would think himself worthy to be called a collector of butterflies if he sat in an office and waited till the butterflies came in. Recent practice, and some recent legislation, it is true, may seem to have condoned some slackness in this Department. Theatrical managers slavishly and at some expense collect the Entertainments Tax instead of compelling the Crown's officers to attend and do their dirty work themselves. The system known as Pay As You Earn exposes employers to labours even more costly and surprising. But these deplorable exceptions cannot be accepted as the rule. In this case the plaintiffs should have hired a boat and done their best to collect the cheque. One word to that fine force, the River Police, might have been even more effective. In fact the plaintiffs took no such precaution, and they ignored, it appears, the elaborate tidal information kindly provided by Mr. Haddock. The explanation given by the Crown is that they regarded the defendant's action as frivolous, and that in any event the River Thames is not a recognized or proper channel for the payment of taxes. This is astonishing. The Thames, that mighty highway, the first great stream of Western commerce, of London's greatness and England's wealth, deserves no insult from any quarter, least of all from the British Treasury. But there is more. Many an important message has been placed in a bottle and delivered safely by the tidal waters. If a shipwrecked mariner or castaway delivered to the same powerful but uncertain agency his last will and testament, duly framed and attested, who can doubt that the Courts would accept and enforce it? I can see no difference between a will and a cheque. If I found that the defendant was at fault in any way I should have to find as well that the plaintiffs were guilty of contributory negligence. But I do not. I find that the defendant has done all that, in the circumstances, he could. The cheque, through the sloth or carelessness of the Crown, may have escaped to sea; but it is likely still to come to rest upon some civilized shore and be delivered to the right address. If this does not occur within a reasonable time, say two or three years, the matter may legitimately be raised again and the cheque presumed to be destroyed or lost. But meanwhile, I find for the defendant. Costs of every kind will be paid by the Crown.

NOTE—Some years later, in 1961, there was a happier episode in the long struggle between Haddock and the Inland Revenue. After a lengthy exchange of views Mr. Haddock received from the Office of the Special Commissioners of Income Tax, Thames Ditton, Surrey, a letter concluding thus:

'... but I am to add that if it is not received within that period the papers will be referred to the Solicitors, Inland Revenue, without further warning.'

Mr. Haddock, within the period, despatched the following cheque, duly 'crossed' and stamped:

To NATIONAL AND GRINDLAY'S BANK LIMITED
    54 Parliament Street, S.W.1. February 9 1961.

Dear Bankers, PAY the under-mentioned hounds
The shameful sum of FIVE-AND-EIGHTY POUNDS.
By 'hound', of course, by custom, one refers
To SPECIAL (INCOME TAX) COMMISSIONERS;
And these progenitors of woe and worry
You'll find at LYNWOOD ROAD, THAMES DITTON, SURREY.
    This is the *second* lot of tax, you know,
On money that I earned two years ago
(The shark, they say, by no means Nature's knight,
Will rest contented with a single bite:
The barracuda, who's a fish more fell,
Comes back and takes the other leg as well).
    Two years ago. But things have changed since then.
I've reached the age of three-score years and ten.
My earnings dwindle: and the kindly State
Gives me a tiny pension—with my mate.
You'd think the State would generously roar
'At least, he shan't pay SURTAX any more.'
Instead, by this unChristian attack
They get two-thirds of my poor pension *back*.
    Oh, very well. No doubt, it's for the best.
At all events, pray do as I request:
And let the good old customs be enforced—
Don't cash this cheque unless it is endorsed.

                                        Albert P. Haddock

The cheque was passed through the Bankers' Clearing House and cashed. But Mr. Haddock was delighted by the arrival of the following receipt:

    Office of the Special Commissioners etc.

It is with pleasure that I thank
You for your letter, and the order to your Bank
To pay the sum of five and eighty pounds
To those here whom you designate as hounds.
Their appetite is satisfied. In fact,
You paid too much and I am forced to act.
Not to repay you, as perchance you dream,
Though such a course is easy, it would seem.
Your liability for later years
Is giving your accountants many tears.
And, till such time as they and we can come
To amicable settlement on the sum
That represents your tax-bill to the State,
I'll leave the overpayment to its fate.
I do not think this step will make you frown;
The sum involved is only half a crown.

                                                      A. R. Grove

Touched by this evidence of humanity in harsh places, Mr. Haddock replied:

I thank you, Sir, but am afraid
Of such a rival in my trade:
One never should encourage those—
In future I shall pay in prose.

(32) REGINA *v.* WILPOT
MEMBERS' PAY

(Before the Lord Chief Justice and the Judges of the High Court sitting in banc)

THE Lord Chief Justice to-day gave judgment in this important case concerning the recent increase in the remuneration of Members of Parliament. He said:

This is in the nature of a test case which the Court has considered at the request of the Speaker of the House of Commons. The defendant, Mr. Henry Wilpot, was elected to the House of Commons by the delighted citizens of Burbleton (West) in 1952. At that time the annual sum received by Members of Parliament—I use that cautious expression for reasons which will appear later—was £1,000 a year. In the present year there have been two or three debates concerning the inadequacy of this sum and the propriety of an increase. It was touching, one witness told the Court, to see what brotherly love and forbearance was shown in these discussions by Members of all parties, who in other subjects are accustomed to address each other as if they were snakes or tigers. It was in the end resolved by a large majority that an increase to £1,750 per annum was desirable and fitting. This decision was accepted and executed by Her Majesty's Government and is now in force. It was proved before us that the defendant has received, and accepted, the first instalment of what the common people would call his 'rise'.

With the ethics of these affairs this Court has nothing to do. Indeed, it would ill become Her Majesty's Judges, who have recently received a belated improvement in their own position, to criticize the Members of Parliament, who also find themselves hardly pressed by the heavy expenditure of the State and the cruel taxes for which they are responsible. Our task is only to interpret the law.

Now, in 1707, in the reign of Queen Anne, was passed
the Succession to the Crown Act. Section 25 provides that
if any Member of Parliament

> 'Shall accept of any office of profit from the Crown,
> during such time as he shall continue a member, his
> election shall be and is hereby declared to be void, and
> a new writ shall issue for a new election, as if such person,
> so accepting, was naturally dead; provided, nevertheless,
> that such person shall be capable of being again elected.'

The purpose of this arrangement, I think, is clear. For
one thing, there may be some suspicion of nepotism or
corruption, some question of unfitness in the appointment,
which the sovereign people at a popular election may
examine and condemn. For another—and this perhaps is
more important—there has been a drastic change in the
relations between the Member and his constituents. They
chose a man who would serve them faithfully—and in those
days serve for nothing—who would devote to their interests
all his time and talents. Now, they find, he has sold his
talents, and much of his time, to the Ministers. For all his
fine professions at the election, the hope of profit, the greed
for power, was hidden in his heart. He may, for all they
know, have sacrificed his principles to secure his post. He
may have put it out of his power to pursue with vigour the
policies, the promises, for which they gave him their votes.
Accordingly, they are given this opportunity to call him to
account, to elect him again, if they are satisfied, and reject
him if they are not.

In this case it is argued that these wholesome precautions
ought to apply, and legally do apply, to Mr. Wilpot. Again,
there has been a drastic change in his relations with the
people of Burbleton (West). They elected one man, and
now they have another. Any ordinary man whose annual
remuneration is suddenly advanced by a half—and there
are not many—at once moves into another world. The
defendant, in the box, admitted that at the election he said

nothing about the inadequacy of the Parliamentary 'pay', nothing of any intention to press for an increase. On the contrary, according to the evidence, he asked with passionate eagerness to be sent to Parliament, though well aware of the terms and conditions of that employment. He also promised in many ways to secure an improvement in the lot of the poor: but these undertakings, through no fault of his own, perhaps, have not all been fulfilled. Further, the electors are now entitled to suspect that the man they chose for selfless service and philanthropic purpose had all the time in his heart the desire for profit and the intention to pursue it. In these circumstances it is not at all surprising if the electors wish him to vacate his seat and offer himself for election again. The question is, is that the law?

The Attorney-General, who appeared for the defendant, developed some arguments which may appeal to his Parliamentary colleagues, but will not, I fear, enhance his reputation at the Bar.

Sir Anthony Slatt, Q.C.: Milord, with great respect——

The Lord Chief Justice: Quiet, Sir Anthony.

He contended that the £1,750 was not 'profits and gains' but an 'allowance' towards the expenses of a legislator. If that were so the whole sum would be free of income tax. But where a Member has other sources of income the Parliamentary 'pay' is lumped with them for purposes of income tax and surtax and, in fact, in many cases he enjoys the use of very little of it. The Court does not, as a rule, concern itself with the speeches of Members of Parliament: but here we take judicial notice of the fact that in a recent speech the Chancellor of the Exchequer referred more than once to the Member's 'salary'.

Then Sir Anthony said that membership of the House of Commons could not be described as an 'office'. In my opinion it can, for, according to the *Oxford English Dictionary*, an office means 'A position or place to which certain duties are attached, especially one of a more or less public character; a position of trust, authority, or service under constituted authority; a place in the administration of government, the public service, etc.'

The Attorney-General argued then that if the defendant held an 'office of profit' he could not be said to hold it from the Crown. He is not in the employ of Ministers; indeed he belongs to the Opposition: and the money was voted by the House of Commons, in the name of the people. Yes, but it was the Crown, that is, the Ministers, who made the proposal. The Members may carry resolutions till they are tired: but without the deliberate initiative of the Crown these payments could never have been authorized or made. Technically, therefore, there is an opening for some of the very suspicions which prompted Section 25 of the Act of Queen Anne. Mr. Wilpot and his friends may not be employed by the Crown, but they are beholden to the Crown. For all the elector knows there may have been some improper agreement or menace. The defendant and his friends may have undertaken not to oppose some Government measure if this increase of salary were moved by the Ministers—they may have threatened to obstruct the Government business if it were withheld.

There is no evidence of any such thing: but that matters not at all. In most cases, in this honourable land, it will be found upon examination that such precautions were unnecessary: but that is not to say that they ought not to be scrupulously observed. Whatever ingenious play may be made with words and precedents, Mr. Attorney, I find that in essence, in the conditions of the time, the facts are of the same character as our wise ancestors had in mind in 1707. The consequences must be the same. Mr. Wilpot, and any other Member who has accepted the increase of salary, whether he voted for it or not, have vacated their seats, and new writs must issue for new elections. We are told that this may cause something like a General Election: but that does not concern the Court. The Members should have thought of that before.

(*All the Judges concurred.*)

NOTE—In the Greyhound Gimcrack Speech of 1962 Mr. Albert Haddock (with what relevance is not clear) made the following remarks:

'Last Thursday the Prime Minister received a deputation of Members of the House of Commons to discuss a rise in their remuneration. Well, I spent nearly fifteen years "inside" myself—fourteen years hard—a long sentence for a literary man. When I went in—twenty-seven years ago—the prize money was £400: it is now £1,750 and they are asking for "added money" of something like £1,000. Knowing something of their lives and labours I think that they ought to have it.

'But I am extremely dubious about some of the devices and subterfuges that have been suggested. It is said that the poor Members feel shy about asking for a rise for themselves, and putting it through. But this is something that is done by the directors of every company and business in the land, without, so far as I know, any invincible embarrassment. They submit their modest demands to the shareholders, and surely, somehow, the Members could do the same.

'Nevertheless, this show of girlish reluctance does our Members credit. But what are the remedies proposed?

'One is that the Member of Parliament should count as a Civil Servant— rather a come-down, I should have thought—that he should creep, unnoticed, up the income-ladder as the higher Civil Servants do; and this is regarded by many as a reasonable comparison ...

'The second line of thought is even more surprising. It is that, in some way or other, the salaries of the Members should rise according to the cost of living. This is the most impudent proposition since the first Gold Brick. For who causes most of the cost of living? The Ministers and the Members. I propose an opposite principle—and if they are not careful I shall lead a deputation to the Prime Minister and lay it before him—I propose a real "sliding scale"—*that as the taxes rise the Members' salaries should go down.* That would get them out of the starting traps! ... If anyone here is drinking the people's beer let me tell him that he or his host is paying what amounts to a purchase tax of 130 per cent. Brandy is a mere 200 per cent: but if there is any gouty old gentleman here who can take nothing but whisky the tax on his medicine is something like 468 per cent. And at any moment, if some teetotaller in the Treasury thinks it good, all these taxes—the unfair Dog Tax too—can be increased by another 10 per cent. Who makes, or suffers with hardly a whimper, these barbarous arrangements? The Members of the House of Commons who are complaining of the cost of living.'

(33) REGINA v. FEATHERS, FURBLOW, AND PHILANTHROPIC POOLS LTD.

THE LAW OF THE PIN

MR. JUSTICE PHEASANT began his summing-up to the jury in this lengthy trial to-day as follows:

Members of the Jury—Now and then, from the waste of dreary disputes and offences which occupy Her Majesty's Assizes, there emerges a criminal cause of electric attraction and importance. Such is the case before us now, not only for the novel points of law which it uncovers but for its social background. Here for once, it appears, the greater part of the population are interested in the matter of the trial and will rejoice at, or resent, our decision.

On the material Monday, as you have heard, the accused man Feathers, a plumber, was informed by the accused company Philanthropic Pools that he, and he alone, had won, with 23 points, a 'first dividend' in the football results competition of the preceding Saturday—a sum of £261,214. The man Furblow, a newsvendor, was also told by a kindly emissary that he had won the second dividend, £101,403. These rewards, it appears, were exceptional: the drawn matches had been few and for the most part unexpected. A Mr. Albert Haddock, who had 22 points, was awarded, as a third dividend, the paltry prize of £863.

Before they received any money from the company the defendants Feathers and Furblow were interviewed by the newspapers. Both, as is customary, we understand, began by announcing that money meant nothing to them, that their winnings would make no difference to their simple way of life, that, after a brief visit to the metropolis with their wives, they would return to their usual employment. They then disclosed the secrets of their success. Mr. Feathers said that he had written on slips of paper the names of all teams beginning with A, B, C, and L, placed them in a lucky hat and desired his niece, aged 11, to extract ten of them. Mr. Furblow said that he had asked a stranger in a tavern to choose any twelve numbers between 1 and 54. He added proudly that he had been using this method for the last seven years. Before that his custom was to place the coupon upside-down before him, close his eyes, and make hopeful marks with a pencil.

One who read this information with especial interest was Mr. Haddock. This competitor, as he testified later, had attained his 22 points by a careful study of the 'form'. He had noted the relative positions of opposing teams in the League Tables, the results of their recent matches, and the corresponding matches in previous years: he had consulted the expert advisers of eight newspapers on the previous Sunday, three evening papers on Tuesday, and a sporting paper on Wednesday and Thursday. He now telegraphed to the Claims Department of Philanthropic Pools:

> UNDERSTOOD YOU WERE CONDUCTING COMPETITION IN FORECASTING REPEAT FORECASTING STOP PUBLISHED METHODS OF MESSRS FEATHERS AND FURBLOW CLEARLY SHOW THEY WERE EMPLOYING METHODS OF AN UNLAWFUL LOTTERY STOP CLAIM THEY SHOULD BE DISQUALIFIED AND FIRST DIVIDEND AWARDED TO ME WHO USED ONLY SKILL AND JUDGEMENT ACCORDING TO LAW ALBERT HADDOCK x3/13.

To the general astonishment, and the natural annoyance of Feathers and Furblow, the defendant company acceded to this request, and their cheque for £261,214 was duly presented to Mr. Haddock by Miss Angel August, an actress. The company, as they have explained to the Court, had long been worried by the number of winning entrants who had publicly attributed their success to practices similar to those of Feathers and Furblow. Some have employed a pin, some, less industrious, an old-fasioned toasting-fork. Some have scattered shot, or brown sugar, on their coupons, and used it as a guide. Others have used the

Letter System. These take some message such as God Save The Queen Long May She Reign, and select eight matches in which the first letters of the Home teams spell out that message. One of the numerous Royal Commissions on Betting and Gaming referred to two winners of very large prizes whose 'method of selecting the matches to be included in their forecast was to choose those matches which corresponded with the dates of the birthdays of members of the family'. None of these methods, said the company, even when they took the form of a loyal greeting to the Throne, could be dignified with the name of 'forecast', a word which is frequent in their Rules. No competitor before Mr. Haddock had objected.

Feathers and Furblow were unable to sue the company, because of a passage in the Rules providing that nothing in any pool transaction shall be 'legally enforceable or the subject of litigation'. They then, in an understandable fit of pique, laid an information against the company for conducting an unlawful lottery. The police took over the prosecution and put them in the dock as well for 'playing, throwing or drawing' at a lottery.

I must not attempt to influence you in any way: but I have no doubt myself that you will find them guilty. A 'forecast' is a mental process. It is described in the *Oxford English Dictionary* thus: 'To estimate, conjecture or imagine beforehand the course of events or future condition of things.' Mr. Feathers neither estimated, conjectured nor imagined: he used no skill or judgement. He simply drew, with the assistance of his niece, some scraps of paper from a hat. Mr. Furblow drew his numbers similarly from a stranger. Now, as one of the Royal Commissions remarked, 'The characteristic feature of a lottery is that it is a distribution of prizes by lot or chance.' Who can doubt that as far as these two men were concerned that was the character of this transaction, that but for the intervention of Mr. Haddock they would have been large winners in a lottery?

But in your lively minds, members of the jury, I see this

question stirring: Does it follow, if these two men are convicted, that you must find the defendant company guilty?
I must instruct you to the contrary. The company, you may
well conclude, are conducting a *bona fide* competition for
persons interested in forecasting the results of football
matches. It was, and is, their intention and desire that the
prizes shall be won by serious-minded competitors using
such skill, judgement and technical information as they
may possess or can acquire. This they have sufficiently
shown, you may think, by their disqualification of Feathers
and Furblow, which was a highly unpopular act. But then,
you may inquire, if they are not conducting an unlawful
lottery, how can Feathers and Furblow be condemned for
taking part in one? That is the kind of question over which
the law of our land rides easily and proudly. There are
many cases where a guilty act or element can be imported
into an innocent enterprise without involving the enterprise
itself. A man may write obscene answers to a cross-word
puzzle or draw lewd pictures in the margin, so as to expose
himself to a prosecution; but the newspaper will not be
blamed. A man by some trick might continue to consume
intoxicating liquor on licensed premises after permitted
hours: but the publican, if he had done his best, would not
be held responsible. In certain matrimonial causes it has
been established that A committed adultery with B, but not
B with A, though that, I fear, is not so close a parallel. Here
again these men have imported evil into an innocent
activity. They, and it is feared a good many others, have
done their best to convert a respectable competition into a
criminal gamble. If they have to pay any penalty it need
not obviously be applied to their victims too.

'The part' said Lord Mildew 'does not necessarily infect
the whole.'

Do not, by the way, pay much attention to the ingenious
argument advanced for the defence by Sir Adrian Floss. Sir
Adrian observed that in the Treble Chance Pool, for reasons hidden from the Court, the task is to forecast Eight

Draws in a single line; that as a rule there are 54 matches in the list; that there are no fewer than 1,040,465,790 ways in which 8 matches can be selected from 54. Therefore, he said, the use of skill and judgment cannot, in fact, greatly affect the result. Indeed, they may be a positive disadvantage: for he who follows 'form' will miss the unforeseeable, exceptional results, the 'outsiders', as it were, which produce the highest 'dividends'. These, he said, can only be caught by a happy chance: so that Feathers and Furblow, though they used no skill, at least showed some judgment. Mr. Haddock, on the other hand, said that he always did better when he studied 'form' and so on than on the rare occasions when, by way of experiment, he 'used a pin'. Mr. Haddock, I thought, gave his evidence with singular clarity, credibility and charm. All must now be as clear to you as the many miles of mud that lie under the Thames between Westminster and the Nore. Pray retire.

The jury retired.

Feathers and Furblow were found Guilty. Philanthropic Pools were acquitted.

NOTE—See too the strange prosecution of *Philanthropic Pools Promoters Association Ltd.*, initiated by a Member of Parliament of intrusive mind and inadequate knowledge in 1963. The harsh winter of 1962–3 gravely interfered with professional football for eight weeks or more. On several Saturdays more than thirty matches (out of say fifty to sixty) were postponed, all bets were declared void, and the stakes credited. In order to maintain the interest of their clients, the employment of their staff, and their contribution to the revenue (a tax of 33 per cent. on all stake-money) the pools promoters devised an ingenious arrangement which became known as the 'Phantom Pools'. They announced in the Press that:

'In the event of more than thirty matches being postponed the pool will not be void but will operate in the case of those matches which are played on the basis of the actual results: and in the case of those matches which are postponed on what a *panel of experts* decide would have been the results had the matches been played, using their own skill and basing their decisions on such considerations as current form, past performances and other relevant matters: and their decision will be final and binding.'

The five 'experts' were all famous retired footballers except one, a well-known referee—Messrs. Ted Drake, Tom Finney, Tom Lawton, Arthur Young (of Scotland) and Arthur Ellis. They went into action in four consecutive weeks under four different 'non-participating' Chairmen.

The prosecution said that this was a mere illegal lottery. Every entry on a football coupon is a bet, or a series of bets. 'A bet is a promise to give money or money's worth upon the determination of an uncertain or unascertained event in a particular way, and (unlike a lottery) may involve skill or judgement.' (Royal Commission on Lotteries and Betting 1932-3 paragraph 11.)

Here, the prosecution said, when there was no football match there was no 'event', and accordingly no 'bet'.

The Court (Ermine J.) dismissed this reasoning as faulty. 'The "event" on which the bets were made and the prizes were distributed was the determination of the five experts. That, it is quite clear, was by no means a matter of "lot or chance".'

Mr. Albert Haddock, who on one occasion acted as 'Chairman', confirmed that the practice of the 'Panel' accorded with the promise. (Q. 2456) 'They were provided with all possible statistics—tables showing the relative position of Team A and Team B in their "division" of the league, and whether "the trend" was up or down—records going back over ten years of former conflicts between the same teams—other tables showing the results of recent matches, "Home" and "Away", number of goals scored "For" and "Against" and so on. All these were faithfully considered, with other special particulars, the size and slope of grounds for example, which might be inimical or uncongenial to a visiting team. To some extent, too, the matter of "sequences" was discussed—the number of times that this or that team had lost "at home" or won "away". After weighing all the evidence they pronounced a careful verdict on every match.' The witness added: 'They did not give the slightest attention to the views of any newspaper "prophet", but trusted entirely to their own knowledge and judgment. This may explain some of the criticisms in the Press.'

Now, the ordinary citizen can obtain, I understand, if he is diligent enough, exactly the same facts and figures as were available to the five experts: and by using the same 'skill and judgment' (if he has them) may well arrive at the same results. Moreover, after a week or two of the proceedings he will be studying not only the 'form' of the football teams but the 'form', so to speak, of the experts. He will know, or think he knows, the workings of the 'Panel's' minds (whether, for example, they give more weight to 'current form' or 'past performance'), and another element of 'skill and judgment' comes in. Thirdly, if he is a thorough man, he will, before he marks and posts his coupon make a careful study of the weather reports in every part of the country and try to determine which of the matches, if any, are likely to be played, for this, in some cases, may modify his forecasts. 'No "chance or lot" in all this,' said Mr. Haddock. 'The pin, for once, is useless.' In many ways, he thought, as a regular practitioner, the 'phantom' pools were much less like a lottery than the 'real' ones. This was confirmed by the fact that in none of the four 'phantom' weeks were there the large dividends—sometimes amounting to £100,000 and more—which are frequently yielded by the 'real' matches, when a number of surprise results make 'the form' look foolish. The prosecution then contended that in spite of the exercise of 'skill and judgment', both by the experts and the forecasters, the dominant element in this affair was chance. In the first week the top 'dividend' (for an investment of 2d.) was £22,000, in the second week it was £190—in the third £3,875, and in the fourth £1,023. Yet the same five experts were in action on each occasion. This showed that their judgment, however conscientious, was in effect capricious and could not in fact be predicted by the most informed and careful wagerer. In the case of the ordinary wager, on an 'event', a horse-race, for example, which actually takes place, the whims of chance can defeat the best of skill and care, but the wager will remain a good one. But where the 'event' is the judgment of five mortal men on thirty or forty imaginary football matches, so strong an element of chance reduces the transaction to a lottery, for which the elaborate business of 'experts' was merely an ingenious and insufficient cloak.

Alternatively, said the prosecution, all these wagering contracts should be declared void as being contrary to public policy, for the reason that, if the protective frills are cut away, the foundation of them all is not a determinable fact but a speculative fancy. Such a wager deliberately made and signed by informed individuals might bear examination. But here there was only a general notice of the conditions, the amended Rules and so on, published in the Press, which might well have been missed or misunderstood by thousands of those who filled their coupons and contributed their money. It must be against public policy, said prosecuting counsel, that large sums of money should be distributed by way of alleged wagers so ill-defined in form, so unsubstantial in subject-matter and so tainted by chance.

'This reasoning,' said Ermine J. 'did not impress the Court. Pretence and fancy are by no means alien to the British way of life, or indeed to public law and custom. The Statute Book, even the Common Law, is full of "deeming". Babies which are in fact illegitimate are deemed to be legitimate. Every citizen is deemed to know the law. Every Briton is deemed to have been born at midnight, though in fact he may not have come into existence till 4.30 the following afternoon. For many months every year the whole nation pretends or deems that the sun has crossed the meridian of Greenwich one hour earlier than it does in fact. There is here too the same duality of fact and fiction as is seen in the football affair: for the aeroplanes over London are using Greenwich Time, a factual time, but the railway-clocks below them are set to a fancy time. As for "the distribution of money", see what fanciful things are done by way of Death Duties to an extinct author's copyrights. They said to the son of one: "This book of your father's was made into a film, and that did well. This other book is rather like it and is sure to be filmed—you must pay Estate Duty on that assumption." Fortunately, the son was able to produce a letter from the film censor saying that the book could not possibly be filmed. Otherwise he would have had to pay. There's deeming for you! The Phantom Pools in my view are merely one more legitimate form of deeming. For the rest, I hold that there is a sufficient element of skill and judgment in these arrangements to make the wagers lawful. The difference in the dividends in the various "phantom" weeks is easily explained: the forecasters must have varied in the degree of skill and judgment that they used. The prosecution is dismissed.'

(34) BOARD OF INLAND REVENUE *v.* HOE

Born to be Taxed

(Before Mr. Justice Puce)

This is a test case of high importance. The Solicitor-General, Sir Roger Wheedle, for the Crown, said:

My lord, the defendant, Sir Rigly Hoe, has to answer two of the gravest accusations in the British catalogue of wrong-doing: first, that he deliberately avoided the payment of certain taxes, and second, that he refused to pay certain sums lawfully demanded by the Inland Revenue.

Until this unhappy affair, my lord, the defendant was a man of blameless and indeed distinguished reputation. At his university he secured first-class honours in Science, Political Economy, History and Philosophy. He has been a director of many well known industrial firms and one or two banks, and, until recently, was Chairman of British Concentrated Chemicals and Engineering. He speaks five foreign languages. He has written several successful books, history, biography, scientific speculation. He has acquired much money and paid large sums into the Exchequer. The residue was invested in well-chosen stocks and securities. He enjoys good health. The Board of Inland Revenue had a right to expect that a citizen so able and experienced would be a fruitful target for taxation for another ten, or perhaps fifteen, years.

But, my lord, at the age of 60 Sir Rigly suddenly, and arbitrarily, retired from all gainful occupations. He sold, at good prices, every one of his stocks and shares, and, as he shamelessly admits, proposes to live upon the proceeds till the day of his death.

The Court: Is this man now living in idleness and vice?

Sir Roger: No, my lord. By his own account, he has never been busier. For he has chosen—wantonly chosen, if I may say so—to devote himself to charitable and unpaid public service, so many forms of which exist in this country. He is chairman of the local bench of magistrates, unpaid, a Borough Councillor, unpaid, one of the Board of the Thames Conservancy, unpaid, a Trustee of the National Maritime Museum, unpaid, and the Tate Gallery, unpaid, a member of the Royal Commission on New Planets, unpaid, of agricultural and other committees, all unpaid. In short, my lord, he might be said, in the Biblical phrase, to have 'bestowed all his goods to give to the poor'.

The Court: He sounds rather a busybody. But what's wrong?

Sir Roger: A great deal, my lord. A man of his powers ought to continue in gainful employment, to the enrichment of the revenue, as long as his physical and mental condition permits.

The Court: Oh? I see.

Sir Roger: The Inland Revenue, my lord, has been defrauded in two ways. First, they have lost the revenue from the dividends yielded by the securities he held.

The Court: But somebody bought them. He's paying now.

Sir Roger: Yes, my lord, but the defendant's capital is on current account, and, not being invested, is yielding nothing. Secondly, they have lost the tax upon the high earnings which he would have received if he had remained in gainful employment. He does not even write any books.

The Court: But, look here, the fellow can't be made to work.

Sir Roger: No, my lord, but he can be deemed to work.

The Court: I never like deeming.

Sir Roger: My lord, by the Finance Act 1960 new powers were given to the long-suffering Board of Inland Revenue. They can now question any manipulation of stocks and shares the purpose of which appears to be the avoidance of tax, or the gaining of 'tax advantage'. The defendant, we submit, in deliberately divesting himself of taxable securities, had no other purpose.

The Court: Yes, I see that. But what's to be done?

Sir Roger: My lord, the Board has assessed the defendant to income and surtax, first, on the income that he would have enjoyed if he had retained his securities, and second, on the sums that he would have earned if he had remained in gainful employment

The Court: Imaginary sums? That's a bit harsh, isn't it?

Sir Roger: My lord, the doctrine of Notional or Hypothetical Gains is now well-established. My lord, to take one example, if an author dies penniless his widow is nevertheless required to pay Estate or Death Duties on the estimated values of the dead man's copyright works: and that estimate is based on the royalties considered likely to accrue after his death, though none may in fact accrue, and there is nothing in the bank wherewith to pay the duty.

The Court: Oh, well, an author? That's fair enough.

Sir Roger: My lord, the defendant has refused to pay: and that is the case for the Crown.

Sir Rigly (in the witness-box): It's a free country. My time and my money are much better spent than they were before. And saving is anti-social.

The Court: I say, you mustn't say things like that! Stand down.

After further argument on the Doctrine of Notional Income his lordship said:

It is a long time since I took a Revenue case, and I am greatly indebted to the Solicitor-General for his excellent exposition of modern thought and practice. Without it I might well have fallen into the same old-fashioned errors which have evidently bedevilled the defendant.

From time to time, as civilization advances, there is formed a new conception of the individual citizen and his place in the general pattern. Convenient labels mark the change. There was the Economic Man, who was moved only by considerations of personal gain. There was the Reasonable Man, beloved by the law, who cautiously avoided trouble, to himself or others. Each of these Men retained a vestige of personal freedom and decision. But now we have the Tax Magnet or Revenue Man, who is important only as an instrument of taxation. In ancient days the tax, or tribute, was the mark of a slave or subject race. As freedom grew and spread, the tax was resented and resisted. Then came a phase in which the tax was granted by the free citizen to the Crown as a kind of favour, for the prosecution of unavoidable wars.

Some traces of this notion rather laughably remain. The Queen, when she gives the Royal Assent to a Money Bill, 'remercie ses bons sujets, *accepte leur benevolence*, et ainsi le veult'. There is sometimes heard, among the ignorant, the historic cry of 'No taxation without representation', and in theory still the faithful Commons decide, in special Committees, how much money shall be granted to the Crown, and how it shall be collected. The informed know that none of this has the slightest relation to reality.

If every subject elected ten Members of Parliament instead of one his *benevolence*, his taxes, would remain the same. But still, till recently, the illusion of individual freedom remained. More than one of my learned brethren on the Bench have declared that the subject is entitled so to arrange his affairs that they do not 'attract taxation'—a charming choice of words—and is not to be blamed if he does. All that is past. We are back in the age of the subject race.

The Treasury, that subtle body of men, have succeeded in shifting the moral values, in adding insult to injury. No Village Hampden would win applause today—he would be told that he was merely increasing the burdens of his fellows. When the Chancellor of the Exchequer reduces by a fraction a savage tax he does not apologize but speaks of 'giving money away'.

Finally, by the Finance Act of 1960 it was established that the subject may *not*, in certain areas of activity, arrange his affairs so that he does not attract taxation; from this it follows, the Solicitor-General says, that he has a duty to arrange them so that he does. I think Sir Roger is right; and the defendant, like any other Tax Unit, must pay the sums demanded, or go to prison. I dismiss the plea of unpaid public service. This is often a form of self-indulgence or personal vanity, and in any case should be confined to those who are unable to earn large taxable incomes.

The governing Section in the Act of 1960 applies only to transactions concerning stocks and shares. But, no doubt, in later enactments the principle will be extended. Twenty-five years ago, I remember, the entire 'Budget' amounted to about £800,000,000. To-day, I am told, more revenue than that is raised by the taxes on tobacco alone, enough to defray the whole expenses of the National Health Service. Evidently those who do not smoke or drink are shamefully avoiding taxation, and failing in the citizen's first duty. There is now no reason, it seems to me, why they should not be 'deemed' to smoke and drink, and pay accordingly. By their behaviour they are seeking 'tax advantage'.

The simplest thing would be to do away with all the tiresome details and distinctions, one tax on this, no tax on that. The State should say 'Every citizen shall pay £X a year, whether he drinks, smokes, bicycles or motors, plus £Y, a proportion of his income' and leave the Treasury to fill in X and Y. May I add that no citizen over 70 should pay anything at all.

NOTE—Asked what he meant by his extraordinary remark: 'Saving is anti-social' Sir Rigly Hoe recited some lines by the poet Haddock:

'Save, save, they say, and put away
What you would like to spend today!
Don't drink—or smoke—or go abroad,
And all the parties will applaud.
But when the money's in your banks
Expect no more the nation's thanks.
Your earnings now have changed their name:
They're CAPITAL—a cause for shame,
While any yield that they may bring
Is DIVIDEND—a filthy thing:
And, what is really quite a bore,

It's UNEARNED INCOME—which pays more.
Give some away to poorer men?
Oh, no—you're DODGING TAXES then.
In short, the patriots who save
Remain in error till the grave:
So die as quickly as you can
And pay DEATH DUTIES like a man.'

(35) REGINA *v.* DARK *and* HADDOCK

'CHEAP LITERATURE'

AT Bow Street to-day the Chief Magistrate, Sir Raven Wren, gave a vigorous decision in the Privileged Libraries case. He said:

This was an information laid by the British Museum, the Bodleian Library, the University Library, Cambridge, the National Library of Scotland, the National Library of Wales, and the Library of Trinity College, Dublin, against Mr. Alan Dark, a publisher, for an offence under Section 15 of the Copyright Act, 1911. One Haddock, an author, is charged with conspiracy, incitement, aiding and abetting, and all that kind of thing.

This, I suppose, is the most impudent prosecution that ever came before this Court. It is a shameless attempt to enforce through the criminal law what can only be described as a piece of statutory robbery against some of the best and poorest citizens, the authors and publishers of our land.

Section 15 of the Copyright Act, 1911, provided, astonishingly, as follows:

'(1) The publisher of every book published in the United Kingdom shall within one month of the publication deliver, *at his own expense*, a copy of the book to the trustees of the British Museum, who shall give a written receipt for it.

(2) He shall also, if written demand is made within twelve months ... deliver a copy of the book (to each of the five other prosecutors).'

Subsection (6) provided penalties:

'If a publisher fails to comply with this section he shall be liable on summary conviction to a fine not exceeding

five pounds and the value of the book, and the fine shall
be paid to the trustee or authority to whom the book
ought to have been delivered.'

Observe that it is a criminal offence for a publisher to fail
to give his goods away for nothing; and for that offence the
honest Mr. Dark now stands in the dock.

All this is not, unfortunately, new: it goes back to an Act
of 1775, and even farther. Sir Thomas Bodley, it seems,
obtained a grant from the Stationers' Company of every
work printed in the country in 1610. According to a Royal
Commission of 1878 the other obligations dated from the
time of Charles II and an Act of 1662. The publishers
affirmed, in 1911, that 'the exaction is the remnant of an
enactment connected with the literary censorship established after the Reformation and intended to prevent the
publication of heretical, blasphemous, immoral or seditious
books.' The Royal Commission of 1878, by the way, recommended that the provisions should be repealed except
so far as they related to the British Museum. The 1911
Section did not become law without protest from authors
and publishers, and there were long and strong debates in
the House of Lords,[1] led by the great Lord Gorell.

The Copyright Act, 1956, repealed nearly all of the Act
of 1911, but carefully preserved this Section, with one other.
It seems to me that here is a shocking tale of gracious
gestures abused and exploited. It was one thing, two or
three centuries ago, when the libraries were young and
struggling, for the Monarch or the Stationers' Hall to give
them special privileges. It is quite another thing to-day,
when these great libraries have the force and sometimes the
funds of the State behind them, to impose by Act of Parliament compulsory charity on authors and publishers who
stand alone, without subsidy or assistance from any quarter.

Nor is this, as we had thought, a small affair. More than
23,000 books were published last year in the United King-

[1] Hansard (Lords), Vol. X, Cols. 173 and 468.

dom; and most of these are in fact demanded and delivered. It may be right, the defendant Dark conceded, that the British Museum should have every book that appears, and he delivers all his own books to the Museum himself. But he made much the same complaint that was made by Lord Gorell, who said that 'in course of time it has become the practice of the other libraries to apply for a copy of every book published, including a vast mass of printed matter which cannot possibly be of any use to them'. A single agent, it appears, serves the five libraries and with some exceptions demands everything—'to be on the safe side'. Thus, taking 23s. as the average price of a modern book, we conclude that the six prosecutors are receiving free about 140,000 volumes, or £160,000 worth of books, for which the publisher receives no profit and the author no royalty. Dark gave the Court some special examples of hardship. Suppose, he said, that out of the goodness of his heart he prints an expensive and almost certainly unprofitable volume of the folios of Shakespeare—fifty copies at fifteen guineas—it is no trifling injury to be required to give away six of those precious copies: and there are publications even more expensive than that. In no other country are so many free copies exacted.

Another publisher, with evident reluctance, told us about one of the prosecutors, Trinity College, Dublin. When Eire left the Commonwealth the publishers naturally inquired whether they were still bound to supply this alien college with their authors' books for nothing. Our Minister of Education, it seems, desired them to 'make no fuss', and to continue to bestow their books as a 'cultural gesture'. The publishers generously agreed: for Trinity College has strong links with England. By the Act of 1956, Parliament, in its wisdom, continued, at the publishers' expense, the benefaction to Trinity College, Dublin.

Goaded, he admits, by one of his authors, the defendant Haddock, Dark has declined to deliver to the six prosecutors copies of one of Haddock's fascinating works, *Re-name The*

Stars. Haddock, in evidence, said that as a patriot he was proud of the British Museum; that as an Oxford man he was devoted to the great Bodleian; that his father was a student at Trinity College, Dublin, that his middle name was Patrick, that he felt a firm affection for the Irish. He would be delighted, as an act of grace, to present his books, if they are needed, to these three libraries himself, as he does in fact to the House of Commons. But, he added, 'There comes a time when sentiment must stand aside for justice. This law is an important example of the attitude of the State and Parliament to the literary craft and trade. Everything is rightly done for those who need books; but there is not sufficient thought for those who produce them. We have become a nation of book-borrowers, with a vast and splendid library system; but authors and publishers can only live by the sale of books. The "free" Public Libraries issue on loan, for nothing, 460,000,000 books a year—this enormous figure has grown from a mere 76 million in 1924. Parliament, in 1892, forbade the Public Libraries to make any charge to the borrower: and that is still the law. A single book (with one re-binding) may be issued to 200 citizens: but for this one volume the author will receive a single royalty of 1s. 6d. to 2s. 6d., and the publisher a similar sum; while the people have enjoyed £200 worth of reading without payment, except through the rates. When the Copyright Act of 1911 was before the House of Commons, one Member, Mr. Booth, said that "he had had communications from all over the country, from working men, who properly consider it an attack on their right and privilege to *cheap literature*."[1] That is very fine: but authors and publishers conceive that they have a right and privilege to earn their living and pay their bills. In small but civilized Denmark the harsh lot of the authors has been recognized and relieved through a Government grant by way of "Library Royalties". Here ...'

At this point I had to check the witness for irrelevance.

[1] Hansard, Vol. XXVIII, Col. 1903.

But his roving testimony satisfied me at least that the action of the two defendants was more in the nature of a political demonstration or protest than an assault upon the ancient prosecuting libraries; and this has assisted me. I am bound, formally, to find both men guilty. Dark, accordingly, will pay a fine of 1s. plus 15s. the value of the book, to each of the first five prosecutors. (I except Trinity College, Dublin, on the grounds of public policy, which must forbid the payment of a fine to a foreign institution no longer in the Commonwealth.) But there will be a stay of execution for ten years, which should give Parliament time to alter the law. I hope there will be no long delay; for if every publisher takes it into his head to do as Mr. Dark has done we shall have 23,000 prosecutions on our hands, and the law may begin to look pretty silly.

The man Haddock is bound over to be of good behaviour, but not for very long. The entire costs of the prosecution will be paid by the prosecutors.

NOTE—Mr. Haddock, in a statement after the case, said:
This has been described as one of the oldest living controversies. The student will enjoy the three eloquent and informative debates in the House of Lords, 1911, notably a passage in Column 196, Volume X:

'THE LORD ARCHBISHOP OF CANTERBURY: My Lords, I stand before your Lordships in an unwonted capacity—as a member of the Board of Trade. I do not know who the other members are, or whether they ever meet.'

All the great names appeared. 'In 1836' Lord Curzon, Chancellor of Oxford University, revealed, 'the curators of the Bodleian Library were offered five hundred pounds by the Government to surrender their privilege, but so much value did they attach to it that they declined the offer....' The Scots, strangely enough, were not so shrewd. Under a Statute of Queen Anne (1709) Scotland had five libraries on the free list, but they agreed to be bought out.
No noble Lord paid the slightest attention to the Royal Commission of 1878, though it was mentioned. Lord Gorell, champion of the book-producers, merely, and mildly, asked that (except for the British Museum) there should be 'some control or some check upon the right to demand *every* book that is published'—as there was to be, and is, in the case of Wales.
Lord Cromer quoted an article written by the poet Southey in 1819:

'The publishers were told that the public bodies would exercise their claims mildly and liberally, that they would take lists and only call for such books as they absolutely wanted, that their main object was to *establish* their right, but trust them, and it should be seen how they use the power. See, indeed, how they use it!'

'In the course of time,' said Lord Cromer, ninety-two years later, 'it has become the practice ... to apply for a copy of every book published, including a vast mass of printed matter which cannot possibly of any use to them' and much that is not 'really necessary or desirable for the libraries.' (Col. 178.)

He mentioned the expensive and limited editions; for example:

'the *Bridgewater Gallery* ... the cost price of which was fifty guineas ... The publishers are making a present of goods which they value at two hundred and fifty guineas, and I think it is asking a good deal of them.'

He was very severe about:

'*The Story of Emma, Lady Hamilton*, published at thirty guineas ... This work consists of a story of Lady Hamilton's youth and contains reproductions in photogravure of a number of those celebrated pictures of Romney representing this remarkable lady as Circe, Euphrosyne, the Nun, St. Cecilia, the Spinster, and several times as a Bacchante. I can hardly conceive a work of a less academic character or one less necessary for the tuition, instruction, and edification either of the authorities at the Universities or of those students who flock for instruction and study to the Bodleian Library.' (Col. 181.)

But Lord Curzon vigorously replied:

'The noble Earl ... spoke of the Bodleian Library as if it were purely an academic institution existing solely for the instruction of Dons and under-graduates. He even put the case of the history of Lady Hamilton and asked what was the good of giving a book of that sort to the Bodleian Library. It would, he said, hardly appeal to the Dons—about which I am not at all certäin—and it ought not to appeal to the undergraduates, about which I am even less sure. But ... the Bodleian is more than an academic institution. It is ... a great national institution, one of the principal repositories of literature in this country.' (Col. 184.)

He continued:

'Is it wise, even admitting the special character of the British Museum, that you should treat that as the only great national repository of published books in this country? Supposing some great conflagration were to occur and the British Museum were to be wrecked and its contents destroyed, what a lament-able thing it would be if there were no other institution to which to turn than that which you had unfortunately lost!'

No one will quarrel with that. We simply ask why such 'national institutions' should be kept alive by the publishers, and to a lesser degree the authors. Sir Henry Craik, a University Member, said in the House of Commons, in 1911, on the proposal to add Wales to the free list: 'My objection is not to the grant of books, but to the grant being made in the form of a tribute from a particular trade.'

Lord Curzon said: 'I do not think it is anything more than a slight burden.' But in 1911 perhaps 7,000 books were published. In 1962 the figure was 23,200 and the average price about 23s. As production and prices continue to increase so will the burden on the book-producers.

Lord Curzon said:

'The question is whether it is a burden that they can legitimately be ordered to bear. I think it is for these reasons. In the first place, publishers as a body gain enormously by the privileges (?) conceded to them in the Copyright Act ... and those privileges are really enhanced under this Bill. Publishers, on the whole, and authors with them, are placed in a better position. It is, therefore, not unreasonable to ask that they should make some return to the public for the privileges that they enjoy.' (Col. 185.)

Lord Haldane too had said, moving the second reading:

'It is complained that it is a burden on publishers to supply these books. So it is. But it must be remembered that publishers are getting protection under this Bill of a new kind.' (Col. 46.)

Some of us remember the same reply being given in Whitehall during the passing of the Copyright Act of 1956. 'We are giving you something in this Bill. Why make a fuss about the free books?'

The publishers gave way, meekly muttering the last lines of Hymn A & M 224:

> 'O happy band of publishers,
> Look upward to the skies,
> Where such a light affliction
> Shall win so great a prize.'

The argument is impudent, and does not impress. We are duly grateful to Parliament for the laws of copyright; but what we enjoy through them is not properly described as 'privileges'. They are protection against cheating and stealing such as the law provides for other forms of property. No such tribute, we believe, is demanded of scientific inventors who 'enjoy the privileges' of patent law. There have been special statutes concerned with 'poaching': but the grateful landlords were not, and are not, required to send thank-offerings of game, in perpetuity, to the Exchequer.

Lord Curzon, leaping like some nimble chamois from one effrontery to another, said:

'If I were a publisher I would rather be disposed to welcome the *gratuitous form of advertisement* for important books which I thus obtained.' (Col. 185.)

This was the cry of the infant B.B.C., and is now the cry of the Public Libraries. 'Not much cash, old boy. But look at the publicity!' We wonder what the motor manufacturers would say if they were told: 'You will all be compelled by law to give six of your new models to the State. But cheer up! Just think of the advertisement.'

In 1961 Mr. Nigel Fisher, M.P. took the matter up, in vain. One junior Minister made the surprising assertion that 'We have not so far received any complaint from the publishers.'

On 11 July, in reply to a supplementary question in which Mr. Fisher asked whether 'the cost to the authors and publishers is about £100,000 per annum,' Mr. Maudling, for the Board of Trade, said:

'I think that my hon. Friend is possibly over-estimating the burden on the publishers.' (Not in the least.) 'In 1952 the Copyright Committee said:

' "In view of the long-standing nature of the privilege and obligation and what we feel to be the comparatively slight burden it creates for the publishing trade as a whole in relation to their turnover it did not recommend the discontinuance of the custom." I think that on the whole, I would agree with that.'

We may observe that if the burden on the publishing trade is comparatively slight it would be unnoticeably infinitesimal as an item in the expenditure of the State. Whatever may be thought of the dimensions of the burden we are shocked by the fact that since the Royal Commission of 1878 no official body has admitted the iniquity of the principle. But if the principle is admitted where are these exactions to stop? We foresee a day when the 'red-brick' Universities (there are twenty of them already, and more imagined) will say, with some force: 'Why should the ancient places alone have these privileges? We babies need them even more. Why should we not get our books for nothing from the publishers? Are we not as deserving as Trinity College, Dublin?'

Would free books for twenty-six libraries (a mere £700,000) still be regarded as a 'comparatively slight burden'?

Authors are less affected directly, but everything that touches the publisher touches them; and they should, perhaps, protest more than they do. No individual author loses more than six royalties for each new book (or new edition): but the total loss of royalties must be between £15,000 and £16,000 a year, and, failing all else, it would be a pleasing gesture if the State made over such a sum to the Society of Authors.

(One Minister in 1961 made the astonishing statement that the present arrangements 'need not penalize authors at all', meaning that the publishers should add the cost of royalties to the cost of providing, packing and despatching 140,000 free books. It has always been the custom to exclude from royalty payments books given away, whether compulsorily to the privileged libraries, or voluntarily to newspapers for review and public purposes. No author expects, or would think of asking for a royalty upon them.)

Authors use the libraries themselves, and are grateful. They have too, like the publishers, a strong sense of service to the public. They think themselves fortunate that the purpose of their work and calling is to instruct or entertain, or please in other ways, their fellow-men. But, also, we favour fair-play and decent dealing. Too often, it seems to us, our gentle feelings are abused by the rulers, or taken too much for granted. This ancient business of the free books is a gross example. We should all support the publishers in resisting statutory robbery, and never let the grievance die.

The expression 'Copyright' Libraries, by the way, is a meaningless misnomer: the privileged libraries acquire nothing in the nature of copyright.

(36) HADDOCK v. THE ARTS COUNCIL OF GREAT BRITAIN

WHAT IS THE ARTS COUNCIL UP TO?

(*Before a Divisional Court*)

MR. JUSTICE LARK, giving judgment to-day, said:

This captivating bicker began with a polite writ of *Quaere transgressit* requiring the Arts Council of Great Britain to show cause why it has exceeded the instructions and conditions which govern its existence.

The Council was incorporated by Royal Charter on 9 August 1946:

'for the purpose of developing greater knowledge, understanding and practice of *the fine arts exclusively*, and in particular to increase the accessibility of the fine arts to the public ... to improve the standard of execution of the fine arts and to advise and co-operate with ... Government Departments, Local Authorities and other bodies on any matters directly or indirectly concerned with those objects ...'

The sixteen Members of the Council are appointed by the Treasury, from which it receives an annual grant. Among other laudable activities it finances the performance of Grand Opera and Ballet at Covent Garden and Sadler's Wells; it supports the London Philharmonic, the Hallé and other symphony orchestras; the Old Vic and Nottingham Theatre Trusts, the English Stage Company, the Birmingham Repertory, and other repertory theatres all over the country. The public funds, we were told, between 1945 and 1956 contributed £1,778,000 towards the losses sustained by the Covent Garden Opera House, so that the questions raised in the case are of more than academic interest.

A notable omission from the objects of the Council's aid is 'literature'—and this is one of the plaintiff's grievances. But in recent years a slightly helping hand has been held out to Poetry. In 1961–2 the total expenditure was £1,598,201. Of this sum £1,216,937, or 76 per cent., went to Music: £256,007 (or 16 per cent.) to Drama, and only £79,000, (or 4·9 per cent.) to Art. Poetry got £4,581 (or 0·3 per cent.): the small remainder went to Festivals and Art Clubs.[1]

Thus 92 per cent. of the money went to Music and Drama, and less than 5 per cent to Art. The State patronage of Music, by the way, was not quite so generous as it sounds: for what it bestowed with one hand it took away with the other by an uncivilized tax on musical instruments. As Sir Malcolm Sargent stands with baton poised at the opening of the Pathetic Symphony he may well feel grateful to the Treasury which is helping to keep his mighty orchestra in being: but he will reflect with melancholy that every instrument about him (except the piano) has paid a purchase tax, and sometimes a Customs duty as well. In 1961–2 £830,000 went to Covent Garden, but about £900,000 was raised by the tax. In addition about £7½m was yielded by the tax on records.

One day, like a little April breeze, there appeared before us the patriotic and familiar figure of Mr. Albert Haddock. He contended, very plausibly, that the activities I have mentioned could not properly be described as developing 'the fine arts exclusively', were therefore *ultra vires*, and indeed unlawful. To one question that he put to the Court there seems to be no answer: 'If "Literature" is excluded from the benefactions of the State, by what right is Poetry admitted?' Poetry is, after all, only a special section of Literature. A simple dictionary definition describes Literature as: '*Books of artistic merit written in memorable prose or verse.*' 'Prose', we observe, comes first: and the best prose,

[1] See *Government and the Arts*, a pamphlet issued by the Conservative Political Centre.

we take it, has as much 'artistic merit' as the best verse. Mr. Haddock assured the Court that he was not opposed to Poetry (except modern poetry), still less to Opera and Ballet. Challenged then to justify his application for a writ, he said that he had been the author, or part author, of numerous musical plays, which, though not continuously dismal, had as sound a claim to rank as 'Fine Art' as many of the musical plays performed at Covent Garden and Sadler's Wells. In none of his own plays, he admitted, does the heroine perish through tuberculosis or self-inflicted wounds in the last act; and this failing may well have raised a prejudice against him. But, in fact, not one of his works had obtained the favour of the Arts Council, or been performed with the aid of public money: and this he resented. We think too well of Mr. Haddock to receive this complaint very seriously, but at least it gives him a place in court.

The question, then, that we have to answer is: 'What is meant by "the fine arts exclusively"?' The surprising thing is that it has not been positively answered before. Many years ago the project of a Ministry of the Fine Arts was discussed: but I cannot recall that anyone told us which the Fine Arts were. There is today a Royal Fine Arts Commission—and another, by the way, in Scotland. But their terms of reference direct them, rather vaguely, to 'questions of public amenity or of artistic importance', which might mean no more than the design of postage stamps, lamp standards, or public conveniences. In 1862 was passed the Fine Arts Copyright Act: but this was concerned with the copyright in original drawings, paintings, and photographs, and does not help us much. (Does photography, by the way, claim to be a fine art?) But in the Scientific Societies Act 1843 we find the very phrase which is troubling us to-day. A society may claim exemption from the rates if (among other conditions) it was instituted for the purpose of literature, science, or *the fine arts exclusively*: and here perhaps we may stumble on a clue.

At the present time, if Parliament had occasion to pass

an Act concerning the Fine Arts, we may be sure that our meticulous legislators would insert an interpretation clause, identifying the arts affected. The Parliament of 1843 did no such thing. It seems to have assumed that everybody knew what the fine arts were: and the explanation may be that at that date everybody did. This, like many of my observations, is not so crazy as it sounds. The expression 'fine arts', according to the evidence, was a translation, apt or not, of the French '*beaux arts*': and the *beaux arts* were the three 'arts of design'—painting, sculpture, and architecture. These, I believe, are still the only arts taught and practised at the famous *École des Beaux Arts* established in Paris in 1816. (What a lot I know!) In a recent case the Master of the Rolls, a charming fellow, read a passage from the seventh edition of the *Encyclopaedia Britannica*, published, he said, in the years 1830 to 1842—mark the date:

'The term Fine Arts may be viewed as embracing all those arts in which the power of imitation or intention are exerted, chiefly with a view to the production of pleasure by the immediate impression which they make upon the mind. But the phrase has of late, we think, been restricted to a narrower and more technical signification; namely, to painting, sculpture, engraving and architecture, which appeal to the eye as the medium of pleasure; and, by way of eminence, to the two first of those arts.' 'It appears,' added Sir Raymond Evershed, 'that the entry which I have just quoted was contributed by no less a master of our tongue than Mr. William Hazlitt.' I could have done as well myself, I think: but here is our clue. This, I am satisfied, was the meaning of 'the fine arts' when the Act of 1843 was passed: and the question is whether the Courts, without further instruction from Parliament, are entitled to give it a new interpretation to-day. There are judges, it is clear, including the Master of the Rolls, who would like to do so if they had a chance. Many fiddling little societies have sought exemption from the rates under the Act, and have been resisted with characteristic tenacity and craft by the

Inland Revenue. Most of the cases have been decided on other points, so that none of them has yielded a confident answer to the main conundrum. In a case of 1897 it was *assumed* that music was a fine art: but the point was not argued, and the authority, though accepted, is unconvincing. In the Court of Appeal there have been some liberal speculations. 'I am prepared,' said Lord Justice Jenkins, 'to treat the fine arts as including, e.g. poetry, eloquence and music, as well as such arts of design as painting, sculpture and architecture ... It is possible that dramatic art should be included ... I see no justification for holding that dancing can never rank as a fine art.' Lord Justice Birkett has said, 'I am not ready to accept the contention that dramatic art cannot be included in the fine arts ... If for example a theatre produced plays like *Twelfth Night* I think there might be a considerable argument on the matter.'

I am tempted to follow these generous gropings. But, after all, they are no more than the *obiter dicta* of much more eminent men: and I do not feel qualified in this case to translate them into firm decisions. If I did I see that I should soon be in trouble. Suppose that I pursued the line of thought suggested by Lord Justice Birkett, I might be driven to find that *Tosca* at Covent Garden qualified as an example of fine art, but that some rancid play without music presented under the same auspices at the Arts Theatre, Burbleton, did not. But then I should be descending from the functions of a judge to those of a dramatic critic. Surely it is for the Court to say whether, in general, this or that art deserves the name of fine, not whether this work or that is a worthy child of the art.

In that conviction I find that in law the words 'the fine arts exclusively' have the same meaning as they had, I *think*, in 1843, that is, painting, sculpture, engraving and architecture. It may well be that by an accident of litigation music must now be admitted as well: but that decision concerned pure music, and need not necessarily be extended to music adulterated by Italian tenors or the fleshly allurements of the ballet. Accordingly, all the activities of the Arts Council other than those I have named are *ultra vires* and must be abandoned. If I am wrong it is for Parliament to make the matter clear. If I am right the figures quoted earlier reveal a shocking state of affairs—only 5 per cent. of the funds available are devoted to the purposes intended.

Mr. Justice Swallow: With some reluctance, for I like *La Bohème* and Margot Fonteyn, I concur.

Mr. Haddock: May it please your lordships, I assume that there will be an order that all the public money disbursed on this unauthorized business be refunded by the Council?

The Court: Oh, Mr. Haddock, do you think so?

Mr. Haddock: Yes, my lord, formally, at least. But, upon certain terms, I should readily agree to a stay of execution or even to an order to the contrary effect.

The Court: Oh, would you? Upon what terms?

Mr. Haddock: My lord, you have correctly assessed my prime purpose in this well-meant litigation. The Charter of the Arts Council must be revised. Either this tosh about 'the fine arts exclusively' should go out, or else 'the fine arts' be officially defined. One way or another, if it be the purpose of the State to support Music, Opera, Ballet, 'legitimate' Drama, and Poetry, let this purpose be clearly asserted. Most important, my lord, 'Literature' should be added to the list of beneficiaries, Literature, perhaps the most enjoyed and, by the State, the most ill-used of all the arts. Here, I submit, there should be some special arrangement between the Treasury and the Arts Council, such as exists for Covent Garden Opera House. An annual payment representing one penny for every book issued by the Public Libraries (460,000,000 in 1961–62) would be a good beginning, and would be administratively the simplest solution of a complex problem. Other sums would be added by way of compensation to the author for the vast and State encouraged increase in the borrowing of books—something too for the statutory robbery of book-producers under

Section 15 of the Copyright Act 1911 (the miscalled 'Copyright' Libraries). Something too——

The Court: Yes, yes, but, Mr. Haddock, the Court has no power to impose any such conditions.

Mr. Haddock: No, my lord, but if you made the order requested, but granted a stay of execution for, shall we say, six months, Her Majesty's Ministers might in that time be able to make the necessary arrangements. You might then be disposed to amend or withdraw your order about returning the mis-spent money—and all would be well.

The Court: Very well, Mr. Haddock. You are generally right. It shall be as you say.

(37) (*Ex parte* HADDOCK)

Stamp out 'Stampery'

Her Britannic Majesty Queen Elizabeth II and Her Majesty's Principal Secretary of State for Foreign Affairs v. the Republic of Lebanon, the Hashemite Kingdom of the Jordan, the United Arab Republic, the Island of Cyprus, and the rulers of Holland, Italy, France, Denmark, Switzerland, Germany, Ceylon, Spain, Greece, Yugoslavia, the Commonwealth of Australia and Canada and the United States of America.

At the International Court to-day the President delivered the unanimous judgment of the Court in the Haddock passport case. He said:

In this dispute the original complainant is a British citizen, one Albert Haddock, who asked for a declaration that his passport has been injuriously and wrongfully used by the officials of foreign countries. We were unable to hear him in person, however, for this reason: on the last page of the document it is stated that '*this passport remains the property of Her Majesty's Government in the United Kingdom*'. This was warmly denied by the man Haddock on the very reasonable ground that he had paid one pound for the original passport and another ten shillings to have it renewed. If it was not 'his' passport in the fullest sense, he contended, why was he required to pay for it? If, on the other hand, it was Government property, it was the British Government's duty—and interest—to protect it. This view eventually prevailed, and the dispute now lies between one sovereign State and many others.

The passport in question consists of two passports, not one. They are sealed together by the British Foreign Office in a bulky blue container which is almost impossibly large, says Mr. Haddock, for any pocket present in normal male attire. Further, this two-volume affair, though it may impress the more simple-minded officials, confuses them as well. 'Why,' they say, 'has this traveller *two* passports, and *two* photographs, strikingly dissimilar?' 'Should he' they wonder 'be treated with exceptional respect, or with some suspicion?'

The explanation goes to the root of the case. Each of these passports has 32 pages—another example, by the way, of the magic of the number 32 (there are 32 pieces on a chessboard, 32 points of the compass, and 32 teeth in the mouth of a grown man). Four of these pages are devoted to official information and 'observations', including a description and a photograph of the *'titulaire'* or 'bearer'. Two are reserved for 'renewals'—which are necessary in the United Kingdom after five years: and two at the end are headed 'Foreign Exchange for Travelling Expenses'. The remaining 24 pages are headed 'Visas', and that, says the complainant, is the only purpose of them. No page, he pointed out, is reserved for 'stamps'. Yet, in the first of these two passports only 8 pages are occupied by visas, and 16 pages by the 'stamps' of petty officials at the many places visited by the *'titulaire'*.

In 1958 Mr. Haddock applied for a visa for the Republic of Yugoslavia. The Yugoslavian Embassy in London replied that this could easily be arranged, but unfortunately there was no space left available for a visa in the passport. Accordingly, though the document was still valid for a year or two more, Mr. Haddock was compelled to apply, prematurely, for a new passport, at a cost of 20s.[1] Further, since the first passport contained a still valid visa for the United States, the two documents had to be united in the vexatious manner already described.

All this costly inconvenience is directly, and, we think, correctly attributed to the sixteen pages of 'stamps'. Now this is not merely the complaint of a single State or a single individual. In recent years 'the stamping pestilence', as it has been vividly described, has spread throughout the

[1] The charge is now 30s.

world. Every minor official or policeman who lays his hand upon a passport conceives that he has a right to violate a virgin page of it with a 'stamp', sometimes illegible, sometimes meaningless, and often upside down. Each, it seems, is determined to make his mark, as vulgar travellers like to scribble their names on the walls of historical monuments. In Mr. Haddock's new passport, we observe, only four of the pages marked VISAS are in fact occupied by visas, but eight are disfigured and rendered useless by 'stamps'. In a fortnight's visit to the Middle East, we see, he suffered no fewer than ten stamps—four from Lebanon, two from Jordan, two from Cyprus, and two from Syria: the last-named country affixed to his passport as well a coloured stamp which advertised a forthcoming International Fair at Damascus. This, the plaintiffs truly say, might well form a dangerous precedent. The next thing may be the stamping of visitors' passports with religious texts or political propaganda. But every 'stamp' they say, unless requested by the *titulaire*, is an unauthorized invasion and mutilation of property.

The defendant States reply that the practice is convenient to them. Its precise purpose was not made clear, and, clear or not, is irrelevant: for trespass to property can never be justified by convenience. It may be well at this point to recall the basic conception of the passport. The issuing State examines the 'bearer' and decides whether he is worthy to travel abroad with the State's particular commendation. It gives, upon the passport, such facts as are necessary to identify 'the bearer'—his photograph, his occupation, the date and place of his birth, his height, the colour of his eyes and hair. Nor is this all. Where a *visa* is required, the country to be visited, through its Embassy in the country of the traveller, takes the greatest pains to assure itself that he is not a felon, a spy, or an otherwise undesirable person. To secure visas for the Lebanon, for Jordan, and Syria Mr. Haddock had to expose his ancestry and past life on several forms, to supply more photographs, a vaccination certificate and, in one case, a declaration of his religious faith. Accordingly, when he arrives, the local authorities have a right to assure themselves that he is the rightful holder of the passport, and the visa, so meticulously issued: but that is all.

On the first page of the document before me, in archaic type, appear some stately words—words which with slight variations, we were told, have appeared in every British passport issued in the past 150 years:

> *Her Britannic Majesty's*
> *Principal Secretary of State*
> *for Foreign Affairs*
> *Requests and requires*
> *In the name of Her Majesty*
> *All those whom it may concern*
> *to allow the bearer to pass freely*
> *without let or hindrance*
> *and to afford the bearer*
> *such assistance and protection*
> *as may be necessary.*

The man Haddock, in his evidence, reminded us of the words of the Lord Chancellor in a famous British case of 1929:

'*The passport is in fact productive of more "lets and hindrances" than any other circumstance of a journey abroad ... What was a privilege has become a duty; what was a talisman has become an instrument of torture; what was intended to facilitate free movement has become an engine of obstruction.*'

In recent years, according to many witnesses, a new routine or ritual of tyranny has been built about it. At every turn the traveller is compelled to copy out on forms and cards the particulars of his life already recorded on his passport. The purpose of this is never explained. Perhaps it is designed to catch the dishonest in a lie. But a rogue who has obtained a passport—and a visa—by giving a false date and place of birth is likely to stick to the same tale throughout. In fact, as the man Haddock testified, the invading spy, the absconding scientists, the criminal, the crook, the Communist, pass through the frontiers and defences as easily as beer through the body.

Worse, we are informed, there is a growing practice by which the visitor's passport is taken away from him and delivered to the local police for stamping, for copying, and suspicious examination. In some countries, a witness said, it can only be recovered on payment of a fee or bribe: it is firmly stated in Mr. Haddock's passport that '*this is a valuable document and should not be allowed to pass into the hands of any unauthorised person*'. But how is the traveller to tell whether a sweating stranger in an open shirt, often without any semblance of uniform, is 'authorised' or not? The only safe course is to declare, as the Court does now, that except in case of a criminal offence, no foreigner should take a traveller's passport out of his possession. We further declare that all this stamping of passports is contrary to international unity and law and should be discontinued. We trust that the body called UNESCO will take such steps as are necessary to make this declaration effective. We are aware that many thousands of persons find gainful employment in the idiotic and offensive practices which have been disclosed. But the travellers are still more numerous.

NOTE—Mr. Haddock, in a statement after the case, said:

It is hoped that the Governments concerned will take steps to carry the principles of this judgment into effect. The British Government could set a good example by abandoning its claims to 'property' in the passport. This impudence is comparatively new. I have here an expired passport issued in 1945. At the end I read:

'This passport is a valuable document ... It should not be altered in any way or allowed to pass into the possession of any unauthorised person.'

Nothing about 'property': the document, evidently, belongs to the holder. This, then, was considered good enough in 1945, at the end of a World War.

My double passport, though, which was exhibited to the International Court, and is an important historical curiosity, tells a different tale.

On the first half, dated 1949, there are these new words as well:

'This passport *remains the property of His Majesty's Government* in the United Kingdom, and may be withdrawn if the holder ceases to be entitled to the protection of His Majesty's Government.'

Thus, without notice, and, so far as I know, without explanation, the property in the passport suddenly passed from the citizen to the Crown. But the citizen was still compelled to pay for a document which had ceased to belong to him, and, if I remember rightly, had to pay more.

In the second half of my double passport, dated 1958, we take one more step to tyranny: The words now are:

> 'This passport remains the property of Her Majesty's Government, and may be withdrawn *at any time*.'

'Thus Freedom narrows slowly down——' It is not often, though, that the process is so clearly seen in a single official document. The new formula must mean that a policeman can come to my door and say: 'I want your passport, please' without giving any particular reason—and without returning my money. I must warn H.M.G. that on that day the officer will be sent away with strong and scornful words. The power to grant passports is without doubt an attribute of sovereignty; but so is the power to grant knighthoods. Once granted they cannot be taken away. No Government Department would dream of sending a policeman to 'withdraw', 'at any time', my Birth or Marriage Certificate, my Dog or Radio Licence. A motor Driving Licence can be suspended or cancelled by order of a court where offences have been committed, for a motor vehicle is a danger: but even this is not described as 'the property' of the Crown. The passport is a very different affair. It is not 'a licence to travel'; for in time of peace no such licence is necessary. There is still no law, no regulation, which compels the traveller to carry a passport, or forbids him to leave the country without one. Nor is it a permission to do some dangerous thing like firing guns or riding motor-bicycles. It is more like the birth or marriage certificate, evidence of identity and respectability. This at least was recognized by formula 1949 'may be withdrawn if the holder ceases to be entitled to the protection of His Majesty's Government.' But formula 1958 '*may be withdrawn at any time*'—abandons the last elements of that gracious favour which was the origin of the passport. It reduces the citizen to the status of a ticket-of-leave man.

This arrogant assertion, then, must go, and the passport become again, *prima facie*, the property of the holder, as it used to be. The travelling Briton will then be in a stronger position to resist the petty official abroad. He can say: 'This is *my* passport, and I will not permit it to leave my possession. It is not to go to the police, it is not to go ashore: if anyone wishes to see it he can come aboard. No British policeman can take my passport away—why should you? *And will you stop stamping it?*'

An enterprising newspaper could render a great public service by sending some man of spirit on a leisurely voyage round the world, with orders to record, inspect and question all orders received anywhere, and to make a moderate nuisance of himself. The ordinary traveller, however sure of his rights or angry about his wrongs, is often reluctant to make a fuss. He may miss his connexion, lose the rooms he has booked, keep fellow passengers waiting in the queue, embarrass his wife and family. Our newspaper-man would care for none of this. He would never be in a hurry, and could miss his connexions with calm. He would refuse to let the Spanish hotel send his passport to the police—and see what happened. He would refuse to fill up endless forms with unimportant particulars, or fill them falsely or facetiously—and see what happened. In most cases nothing would happen, for the practices have no point or purpose, the officials are well aware of this, and if the bluff was resolutely called would have to confess it. Now and then the travelling nuisance might be arrested but he would be ready for that. And what a travel-book he could write when he got home!

(38) THE QUEEN *v.* MORTIMER

The Laws of Sunday

THERE was a startling turn to the Sunday Entertainment case at Bow Street this morning. In the dock was Mr. R. Mortimer, charged with an offence against the Sunday Observance Act, 1781, which forbids the opening of any house, room, or place for any public entertainment 'to which persons are admitted by payment'. According to an information laid by the Sunday Society, Mr. Mortimer was the promoter of a charity football match in aid of the Lawyers' Widows and Orphans Fund, in which twenty-two leading figures from stage and screen took part.

Mr. Luke Goody, Secretary of the Sunday Society, gave evidence for the prosecution. The Chief Metropolitan Magistrate, Sir Richard Strong, said: You, or your Society, originated this prosecution. But how do you know that the offence took place? Were you there?

Mr. Goody: No, sir. On the Lord's Day I never leave my home. I read no newspapers. I allow the eating of no cooked food. I do not even answer the telephone, for this means labour on the Lord's Day.

Sir Richard: But if the unfortunate operator has to ring you three or four times, in vain, you have caused a lot more labour on the Lord's Day. (The witness did not reply.) Very well. At first-hand you can tell me nothing about the offence. Is there anyone here who can tell us more?

Witness: Yes, sir, several of my workers were present.

Sir Richard: Let them be called.

Mr. Wagwash, of the Sunday Society, testified that the match took place as alleged.

Sir Humphrey Baise (for the defence, in cross-examination): Can you swear that any payment was made by the spectators?

Witness: Yes.

Sir Humphrey: How do you know?

Witness: I entered through a turnstile and paid five shillings for admission.

Sir Humphrey: When was the entertainment concluded?

Witness: At four o'clock.

Sir Humphrey: How do you know?

Witness: I was there.

Sir Humphrey: So you were present from first to last? Watching a football match? Do you think that is a proper way to spend the afternoon on the Lord's Day?

Witness: I was doing the Lord's work.

Sir Humphrey: The Court may have other opinions. This prosecution has been lodged by your Society under the Sunday Observance Act, 1781?

Witness: Yes, sir.

Sir Humphrey: Are you familiar with the Act of 1677?

Witness: I have read it. It is rarely used. You have to get the consent in writing of the chief of police, two justices of the peace, or a stipendiary.

Sir Humphrey: A pity. Let me read what it says: 'No tradesmen, artificers, workmen, labourers, or other persons whatsoever'—*or other persons whatsoever*, Mr. Wagwash— 'shall do or exercise any worldly labour, business, or work of their ordinary callings upon the Lord's Day, or any part thereof (works of necessity or charity only excepted).' You are aware, Mr. Wagwash, that the defendant, and those who assisted him, were engaged in an act of charity?

Witness: So they say. But the stars don't give these exhibitions for charity. They do it to get themselves publicity, and in that way they are really working.

Sir Humphrey: So your Secretary said in one of the newspapers. Not a very charitable judgment: but I am glad to have had it repeated in open court. Now, Mr. Wagwash, you have been described by your Secretary as a 'worker' for the Society. Is that correct?

Witness: Yes sir.

Sir Humphrey: Are you a paid worker?

Witness: Yes.

Sir Humphrey: You get an annual salary?

Witness: Yes.

Sir Humphrey: How much?

Witness: That's my business.

Sir Humphrey: Very well. Have you any other business?

Witness: Sir?

Sir Humphrey: Any other regular employment?

Witness: No.

Sir Humphrey: Now, Mr. Wagwash, how would you describe your work?

Witness: Well, sir, we are always on the watch——

Sir Humphrey: For forthcoming breaches of the law?

Witness: Yes, sir. We study the newspapers. We follow up reports from local sympathizers. We write warning letters to the promoters, and so on.

Sir Humphrey: I see. And if these are not successful you attend the scene of the offence on Sunday, make notes, collect evidence, and so on?

Witness: Yes, sir.

Sir Humphrey: What made you act as you did last Sunday?

Witness: Instructions from Mr. Goody, sir.

Sir Humphrey: Just so. Now Mr. Wagwash, would it be fair to say that on the Sunday in question you were 'doing or exercising worldly labour?'

Witness: No, sir, it was labour for the Lord.

Sir Humphrey: But you were paid for it?

Witness: Clergymen are paid.

Sir Humphrey: But you are not a clergyman. I do not doubt your sincerity, Mr. Wagwash. But you have chosen to earn money by this business of watching, protesting and, on the Lord's Day, spying.

Witness (hotly): It's *not* spying.

Sir Humphrey: Very well—collecting evidence. Would you agree that the earning of money—except perhaps by clergymen—was a 'worldly' occupation?

Witness: Not in this case. It depends on the motive.

Sir Humphrey: Oh, does it? Then why are you so hot against the defendant, whose motive was charity?

Witness: That's different.

Sir Humphrey: Very well. You still don't agree that you were 'doing worldly labour' on Sunday last?

Witness: No.

Sir Humphrey: But at least you will agree that, in the words of the Act of 1677, you were doing 'work of your ordinary calling' on the Lord's Day?

Witness: No.

Sir Humphrey: Perhaps you don't understand the word 'calling'. In the dictionary I have here it is described as 'trade, profession or vocation'. Did you not tell the Court just now that you have no other 'trade, profession, or vocation'?

Witness: That is so.

Sir Humphrey: Very well. Then this must be your 'ordinary calling'. But perhaps you rely on one of the exceptions. You would not suggest, I think, that your Sunday spying was a work of charity. Would you say that it was 'a work of necessity'?

Witness: Yes, sir. The law must be enforced.

The Chief Magistrate: At last I agree. Sir Humphrey, we need not trouble you more. Your able questioning has made it clear to my mind that the evidence supporting the prosecution was obtained by unlawful means, and it is to that extent severely tainted. The late and celebrated Lord Darling said once that the right way to be rid of a bad law was not to ignore but to enforce it. As a salaried magistrate I am qualified to authorize a prosecution under the Act of 1677, and I shall do so now. Not the unfortunate Mr. Wagwash only. I find repelling the picture of the first witness, Mr. Goody, sitting piously in his home on the Lord's Day, doing nothing, but sending his minions forth, to risk their souls, if no more, by this unpleasant, and, I believe, illegal espionage. He is at least an accessory before the act, and should appear with Wagwash and the other 'workers' before this Court this afternoon. As for the defendant Mortimer, I am bound to find him technically guilty, but he is unconditionally discharged.

Later today Goody, Wagwash and three others were found guilty of offences under the Act of 1677 and were fined 5s. each. The Society was ordered to pay the costs in all the prosecutions.

Interviewed, Mr. Goody said 'It is a cruel dilemma. We must produce evidence. But if it is illegal to collect it, what are we do to?' 'Don't pay them,' a reporter suggested. But it is not certain that this precaution would be enough.

(39) REGINA *v.* CLATTER

THE QUEEN IN THE CITY

In the Court of Criminal Appeal to-day the Lord Chief Justice said:

This is an appeal of a novel character. Though at first sight it appears impudent, it springs from the sound roots of our legal history and must be seriously considered.

On May 26 at the Old Bailey the appellant Clatter was found guilty of capital murder and was duly sentenced to death by Mr. Justice Thrush——

Sir Humphrey Baise, Q.C.: My lord, with great respect, the word 'duly'——

The Lord Chief Justice: I am grateful to Sir Humphrey. 'Duly' was a slip. Indeed, here is the nub of the appeal. We are not asked to consider the facts or the general conduct of the case: no complaint is made of the summing-up, or the evidence admitted. The simple ground of the appeal is that Mr. Justice Thrush, though I myself directed him to preside as a Judge of Assize over this and other criminal causes, had no jurisdiction to pass sentence of death on the appellant.

The strange facts are as follows. The jury returned to deliver their verdict. The Clerk of the Court put the usual question: 'Have you considered your verdict?' But as the foreman of the jury opened his mouth to reply, a message was laid before the Clerk, bearing, in block capitals, the words:

THE QUEEN IS COMING TO THE CITY

Such a communication, to any ordinary citizen in that neighbourhood, could bring no sensation but loyal delight. But to the Clerk of the Court, as he explained in evidence, it was the cause, at that moment, of alarm and dismay. It is well understood, at least among the legal profession, that Her Majesty is the prime fountain of Justice, the head of the judiciary, as she is of the Church of England. It is at her command, and as her deputies, that we do what we can to administer justice. Accordingly, when she herself is present in the immediate neighbourhood it would be presumptuous for any of us to continue our humble search for justice and right. As Her Majesty approaches Temple Bar, the word, as a rule, is passed in good time to all the judges of the Central Criminal Court, and every judge, with loyal alacrity, steps down from his Bench, at whatever stage the case before him may have arrived. Indeed, in olden times, many a judge was seen scampering out in wig and robes to see the Queen go by.

These thoughts raced through the mind of the unfortunate Clerk of the Court. 'My first instinct,' he told us, 'was to get the proceedings stopped at once. But since I had put the solemn question "Have you considered your verdict?" to follow it at once with the command "Don't answer" would, I felt, make for confusion, and might be the cause of unfitting mockery. Moreover, the message did not say that Her Majesty was in fact within the boundaries of the City, and it was my hope that the case would end before her arrival.'

The shorthand note of the evidence given by the Clerk of the Court then continues (Q. 443): 'The foreman of the jury said: "We find the prisoner guilty." At that moment another message was thrust before me:

THE QUEEN HAS PASSED TEMPLE BAR

'I now felt it my duty to act at once. But Mr. Justice Thrush was already preparing to deliver sentence. My Lord, I stood and whispered to the judge "*The Queen! the Queen! passed Temple Bar!*" But, my lord, this is rather difficult—my lord, his lordship did not hear.'

The Court: We fully appreciate your delicacy, and your dilemma. Our brother Thrush, though his intellectual powers are still unrivalled, has not, naturally, the hearing of a very young man. And at that moment, no doubt, he was intent upon his distressing duty. Yes?

The Clerk: His lordship began 'Prisoner at the bar——', I thought it my duty to try again and I said, more loudly, 'The Queen! Passed Temple Bar'.

'That is what I said,' said his lordship, with a glance of some severity. I then desisted. His lordship completed the sentence, and ordered the officers to take the prisoner below. He then administered a strong but not unexpected rebuke to me for interrupting him at so solemn and distasteful a moment. When I had explained the circumstances he made a most gracious apology, adding, my lord: 'God bless me! Where are we now?'

My lord, a further message had now arrived with the information that Her Majesty was making only a brief visit to the City, in order to take luncheon at the Inner Temple, of which she is a Bencher. I therefore suggested that when she departed his lordship should pronounce sentence a second time, when he would have full jurisdiction again and all would be in order.

The Court: What did he say to that?

The Clerk: My lord, he said: 'I'm damned if I do all that again.'

The Lord Chief Justice continued: This Court feels considerable sympathy for our brother Thrush. In an ordinary case of this kind, where a judge has admitted evidence, not knowing that through the adjacence of Her Majesty he has no jurisdiction, it is easy to hear the evidence again. (See *The Queen against Stubbs*—1909 2 A.C. at pages 401–10.) But here is a very different affair. One sentence of death in a single day—or week—is as much as most of us can stomach: but to deliver two, one before the midday adjournment and one thereafter, would be repugnant to all of us. Moreover, the learned, but very human, judge may well have put himself in the mind of the prisoner. A criminal brute he evidently is, and he well deserved to hear those terrible words of condemnation; but what opinion would he, or anyone, hold of the ways of British justice if he had been required to hear them again, after the midday meal, on the technical ground that the judge had no right to say them the first time? I might, of course, instruct Mr. Justice Thrush, after a reasonable interval for recovery, to return to the Old Bailey, send for the appellant, and condemn him to death once more. But, apart from my regard for the learned judge, this might expose the appellant to a period of jeopardy and doubt which would cause comparisons with the worst excesses of American dilatory procedure. This I decline to do.

What, then, is our proper course? This Court, strangely and sadly, has no power to order a new trial: but in this case there would not be the slightest virtue in it, if we had. The Solicitor-General, Sir Roger Wheedle, suggested that we should avail ourselves of the *proviso* in the Act of 1907 which created the Court. That Act said that though we may find a trial faulty we may allow the result to stand, provided that there has been 'no substantial miscarriage of justice'; and a sentence we have power to amend. But, Sir Roger, it is common ground in this case that the trial had no fault; so that question does not arise. We can neither confirm nor amend the sentence here, for there was no sentence at all. By ancient tradition and sound doctrine, everything that was said or done by the learned judge after Her Majesty entered the City was null and void. We are confronted, as it were, with a dog without a tail, and are invited to correct that state of affairs, though we have no power to manufacture tails.

It seems to me that we must respectfully have regard to the central fact on which our difficulty is founded. That fact is the temporary propinquity of the Monarch to the Central Criminal Court, which made it not merely unseemly but impossible for the learned judge to do what he did, or purported to do. It would be insufferably presumptuous for this Court even to guess what the Monarch would have said and decided, if she had in fact sat upon the Bench that day, as long ago some of her predecessors did. But suppose that during the midday adjournment our learned brother Thrush had obtained access to Her Majesty, confessed his fault, and humbly besought her guidance. Can we doubt that the royal instinct would at once have inclined to mercy, that the royal mind would have at once recalled the ancient maxim *In errore semper clementia*? We therefore think that this appeal should be allowed and Mr. Clatter should be freed. If he commits another murder he must not expect to be so fortunate again. But I have a feeling that he won't.

Pheasant, J., and Table, J. concurred.

(40) REGINA *v.* STROOL

THE SPLIT SENTENCE

AT the Old Bailey to-day, before Mr. Justice Grail, Sir Luke Lintel, Q.C., opened the case for the defence in the sensational trial for bigamy of Reginald Strool, 43, commercial traveller. There were many dramatic exchanges between Court and counsel.

Sir Luke: My lord, the fact is, my unfortunate client has a schizoid condition.

The Court: A what, Sir Luke?

Sir Luke: Schizophrenia, my lord.

The Court: You don't have to shout, Sir Luke. I can hear you clearly—when you use clear language. You mean a split mind?

Sir Luke: Yes, my lord.

The Court: But don't we all?

Sir Luke: My lord?

The Court: One morning I travel to court with the keenest interest and zest. The next I detest the thought of administering justice, and would much prefer to stay at home.

Sir Luke: Yes, my lord, but on the second day you do in fact attend the Court and discharge your duties. Your responsibility is unimpaired. The prisoner's sense of duty, as will be shown in evidence, has dwindled to the verge of disappearance; and therefore he is not accountable for his actions.

The Court: I could easily allow my sense of duty to dwindle.

Sir Luke: With great respect, my lord, I doubt it. Your lordship's case-history, I dare to hope, is very different. When the prisoner was nine, my lord, his father locked him in a dark cupboard for three-quarters of an hour.

The Court: Good gracious! What was the offence?

Sir Luke: Putting the cat in the coal-box.

The Court: Ha! 'The punishment fits the crime.'

Sir Luke: Maybe, my lord, but it was a traumatic experience which, as you will hear from the medical evidence, was of lasting effect. My lord, the prisoner's ambivalent relations with his father led to a fixation on the mother, who took his part.

The Court: You mean he was fond of Mum? Very proper. So am I.

Sir Luke: It is not quite so simple as that. My lord, you may have heard of the Oedipus complex?

The Court: I have. I seem to remember that Oedipus, when he heard the bad news, put out his own eyes. Does your client ever feel impelled to do that?

Sir Luke: Not so far as is known, my lord.

The Court: Very well. But in 1956 this man married Lily Somebody and in 1958 he married Henrietta Somebody Else. What has Oedipus to do with that?

Sir Luke: My lord, there was a psychosomatic lesion——

The Court: Caused by the cupboard?

Sir Luke: Yes, my lord—and other episodes—deep-seated lesion. And the result, in a sense, I am instructed, is that every woman stands in place of the mother. He feels the need for comfort and protection. All women are mother-surrogates.

The Court: Yes, yes, but he can't marry them all. Doesn't he know that it's wrong to marry two women?

Sir Luke: Yes, and no, my lord. Psychodynamically, no. My lord, as the evidence will show, before he married Henrietta something told him that it was wrong. But forces that he was quite unable to resist impelled, indeed, compelled him to go through with it.

The Court: What forces?

Sir Luke: First, there was the transferred son-to-mother urge which I mentioned before—a trend to the female, *gynaecophilia*, my lord.

The Court: Oh, yes, I remember that.

Sir Luke: Secondly, my lord, when at school, the prisoner

was regarded as effeminate by his companions, a 'sissy', my lord, in schoolboy language. His first marriage was, no doubt, a psychical response to the challenge, a subconscious expression of the schoolboy's retort of triumph, my lord, 'Sucks to you.' But it was insufficient: remnants of the old guilt-anxiety and inferiority-feeling subsisted, and these reinforced the urge to marry again.

The Court: My sacred aunt!

Sir Luke: I beg your pardon, my lord?

The Court: Nothing. Proceed.

Sir Luke: If your lordship pleases. Thirdly, my lord, my client suffers from indelible delusions. He believes that he has lived before—a very common form of mental maladjustment.

The Court: Oh, yes, I knew a charming old gentleman who was convinced that he had been Lord Nelson.

Sir Luke: Very apt, my lord. But in this case there is a novel feature. The prisoner has been not one but many persons; and these persons belong to two distinct homogeneous categories, which are diametrically opposed in character. Sometimes, my lord, he is Lord Byron or Casanova. At others he is Mr. Gladstone——

The Court: Poor chap.

Sir Luke: ——George Washington, St. Francis of Assisi, and others. On every important occasion, he says, he can hear the two sides debating in his brain what his conduct ought to be: and if, for example, Lord Byron triumphs in a dispute with Mr. Gladstone it is physically impossible for him to resist Lord Byron's advice.

The Court: You are doing very well, Sir Luke. But would not all this come better from the prisoner?

Sir Luke: My lord, the medical evidence will fully support what I have said. But I do not propose to put my client in the box.

The Court: Oh? Well, no doubt you know best.

Sir Luke: My lord, the reason is very simple. My client, it is clear, is possessed of two distinct personalities. One of these, in common parlance, has a better 'character' than the other. One, that is, is more likely to adhere strictly to the truth than the other. But, my lord, no one can tell—certainly not my client—which of those two, at any given moment, is likely to be dominant. Indeed, the evidence suggests that at times they change places on the stage, at very short intervals. I should not therefore care to take the risk of putting in the box a witness who might well be capable, though without wrongful intent, of erroneous testimony.

The Court: Very well. What are your client's relations with his wives?

Sir Luke: Significantly ambivalent, my lord.

The Court: What is the meaning of that pestilent word?

Sir Luke: 'Having two values', my lord, like a pink gin at the 'Crown and Anchor' and a pink gin at the Savoy Hotel. In the field of mental therapy it was used by the famous Swiss psychiatrist Bleuler to designate alternate feelings of love and hate for the same person. Stekel preferred the term 'bipolarity'. My lord, one day the prisoner is buying flowers for Lily's birthday, the next he may be bitterly abusing her: one day, with Henrietta, he is dutifully washing-up, the next he smashes the crockery. Fortunately, because of his occupation, he is seldom in the same house for many days. Lily is established in the South of England, Henrietta in the North. It often happens, my lord, that a period of hate for Henrietta coincides with one of love for Lily, and vice versa. So, in practice, at least, the happiness of the two wives is well served by the present arrangements. But here again the bilateral pattern of the personality is exhibited. Call Dr. Frogg.

Dr. Silas Frogg said: I have examined the prisoner in his cell on sixteen occasions. It is a classic case of phrenetic fission. There is a multiple psychosis, my lord, precipitated by cumulative traumata—father-repugnance—mother-imago transferred—derision reaction—and bifocal hallucination. My lord, under the Word Association Test——

The Court: What is that?

Dr. Frogg: The patient is asked to give the first spontaneous thought associated with a particular stimulus-word. The answers are often revealing to the trained inquirer. But this man invariably gave *two* answers instead of one, a symptom-expression of a cleavage even at the subconscious level. To the word 'mother', for example, he replied 'love' and 'cow', to the word 'wife' 'one' and 'two'——

The Court: You say, doctor, that the prisoner has two personalities?

Dr. Frogg: Yes, my lord. There is a psychocerebral caesura, a bisection of the ego, a——

The Court: And therefore he is entitled to have two wives?

Dr. Frogg: I do not say that, my lord. But he has, I am sure, a dominating delusion fantasy that he is.

The Court: Not always, surely? Thank you. Sir Luke, your argument, the evidence has greatly impressed me. But I should like to be clear about the dual personality. In these interior conflicts which you have so vividly described—Casanova against Mr. Gladstone and so on—one side or the other, I take it, definitely prevails?

Sir Luke: Yes, my lord.

The Court: And if, and for so long as, Mr. Gladstone is the conqueror, your client is a decent, conscientious, even a congenial person—'buying flowers', you said, 'dutifully washing up'?

Sir Luke: Yes, my lord. But, of course at any moment Lord Byron may take charge——

The Court: Yes, yes, but *until then*—he has the feelings of a normal person, including regret, perhaps remorse, for the behaviour of his other half?

Sir Luke: That is very likely.

The Court: Now, Sir Luke, how did the facts of this case come to the notice of the authorities?

Sir Luke: My lord, the first wife, Lily, stumbled on the truth and informed the police.

The Court: And this, of course, was many years after the

crime? I am wondering, you see, Sir Luke, why in one of his lucid, Gladstonian interludes your client did not himself inform the police?

Sir Luke: My lord, no man is required to incriminate himself.

The Court: 'Himself'? No, Sir Luke. But that, surely, would not have been the position? This would have been Mr. Gladstone informing dutifully on Casanova—a different personality, as you have explained so well?

Sir Luke: My lord!

The Court: You see, perhaps, I think, the way in which my mind is moving. You may be able to persuade the jury that the wilder section of your client, the section which bigamously married Henrietta, cannot at law be held responsible for its actions. But the other section, as you have shown so clearly, is rather different. I tell you what, Sir Luke, I am going to direct that the indictment be amended by the addition of another count—'misprision (or concealment) of felony'.

Sir Luke: If your lordship pleases.

The Court: I do. I please very much.

His lordship then addressed the jury. The jury found both the prisoners guilty.

The Court: The sentence for each offence will be three years' imprisonment: and since we are concerned here with 'two distinct personalities' the sentences will run consecutively.

Sir Luke (fainting)*:* My *lord!*

(41) REGINA v. HADDOCK

The Law of Sitting

Mr. Albert Haddock to-day appeared at Bow Street on a summons for assault and battery by Rowena Stuke, 20, of Chelsea, who was dressed in black silk trousers, sacking and sandals.

Haddock, giving evidence, said: 'I am the President of the *Friends of the Police*.'

Sir Adrian Floss (defending): What are the rules of this Society?

Haddock: There is only one rule—to give aid and comfort to the police whenever that is clearly the duty of a decent citizen.

Sir Adrian: You are also, I believe, the President of the *Friends of Women*? What is the purpose of that body?

Haddock: To give aid and comfort to females in distress or danger—females bewildered by railway termini or underground labyrinths or Button B, females who lose their tickets or drop their parcels, females in doubt at pedestrian crossings or in one-way streets. And so on.

Sir Adrian: Very well. Will you tell the Court, in your own words, what happened on the date in question?

Haddock: Apprehending from the newspapers that our services might be required, I directed the members of both my Societies to attend at Piccadilly Circus.

Sir Adrian: Was anyone else present?

Haddock: Yes, sir, a multitude, some of them, as I feared, females in evident distress—and about 2,000 police officers.

Sir Adrian: What did you do?

Haddock: Near to me, with her back to me, I saw a fallen woman——

Sir Adrian: Fallen?

Haddock: I presumed that she had fallen, sir, for she was

seated in the middle of the highway. I judged that she stood, or rather sat, in danger from any vehicles that might approach, and also from the feet of the crowd.

Sir Adrian: Did you then take any particular action?

Haddock: Yes, sir. Placing my two hands under the prosecutor's arms, I gently raised her to a standing position. She turned her face to me with a charming smile, but on seeing me she scowled instead, and said: 'You ——, will you ——well leave me alone?' She then subsided to the ground. I again did what I conceived to be my duty. She repeated some of the expressions to which I have referred and said: 'I want to be arrested.' I said: 'That, madam, is nothing to do with me. But it is my duty as a citizen to assist the police in clearing the highway. Also I am President of the *Friends of Women.*' She then broke away, ran to another part of the road, and sat down. I followed and respectfully raised her again: I cannot describe to the Court the fury of her countenance, nor should I care to repeat some of the observations which fell from her lips.

The Court: Better not.

Haddock: When she was half-way to the standing position she called to a passing policeman: 'Officer, arrest me!' The constable replied: 'No, lady, I can see you're in good hands. You take her home, sir.' The prosecutor then appeared to become discouraged and allowed me to escort her to the Underground station. But she took my name and address—and here we are.

The Stipendiary Magistrate: I am happy to say at once that the Court applauds the motives of Mr. Haddock in this strange affair: and we are tempted at once to advise all good citizens to do likewise. But his behaviour did not appear in the same favourable light to the prosecutor, and we have to consider whether what he did amounted technically to an assault. An assault has been defined as 'an unlawful attempt, or offer, with violence to do a corporal hurt to another. A "battery" is an injury done to the person of a man in an angry, revengeful, rude or insolent manner. In other words,' says the same authority,[1] 'an assault is a movement which attempts, or threatens, the unlawful application of force to another person; while such an application itself, when actually effected, constitutes a battery.' But there are degrees of force. A mere push or tap on the shoulder may amount to a battery, though a friendly tap, to attract attention, will not. On the other hand a friendly touch in the nature of a caress, may be an assault, if it be not welcome. The circumstances of every case must be the guide. There is no suggestion here that the defendant's handling of the prosecutor was prompted by any improper amorous feelings. On the contrary, the prosecutor's attorney maintains that it was done in 'an angry, rude and insolent manner'. Mr. Haddock replies, and we believe him, that he acted throughout with gentleness and courtesy, using no force more than was necessary to raise a fallen woman from the Queen's highway. The prosecutor says that all this politeness—'these smooth and smiling attentions', as her counsel put it—was but a mask for insolence and rudeness. She, it appears, is against being destroyed by a nuclear bomb, and Mr. Haddock is in favour of it. Thus, while pretending to assist, he was in fact deriding and thwarting her, and so his apparently courteous approaches were battery in law and fact.

Now this is taking us rather far. It is true that an action apparently innocent and good may be made mischievous and wrong by the revelations of a malign or improper motive: a seeming compliment may be sarcastic or bitter, and the highest salute we know, the kiss, can be wicked and even criminal. But there is no evidence whatever that Mr. Haddock was moved by any secret cunning or ill-will. Throughout his evidence he made no reference to nuclear warfare; when challenged on the subject by prosecuting counsel he answered that he was opposed to every kind of warfare; and since the whole is greater than the part he

[1] Kenny on Criminal Law.

must be supposed to be an even more fervent advocate of
'peace in our time' than the prosecutor.

Malice, then, being set aside, the question remains: Was
he entitled to use such force as he did? I have no doubt that
he was. The exercise of force against the body of another
man is by no means always unlawful. One of the
occasions—indeed it is first in the list—when reasonable
force is legally justified is in the furtherance of public authority. Another is in the saving of human life. In this case
public authority desired the clearing of the Queen's highway, and Mr. Haddock, in his humble way, was right to
assist. The second case is even stronger. If a fireman called
to a burning house drops a sack over a ratepayer's head and
carries him, upside-down, out of his home, no summons for
assault and battery is likely to succeed. If Miss Stuke had
stepped off the pavement, looking the wrong way, in front
of a speeding motor-car and Mr. Haddock, with the utmost
violence, had snatched her back, nothing but applause and
gratitude would have come his way. The present case, it
seems to me, is different only in degree. Mr. Haddock, as
often before, was absolutely right, and I hope that other
men of public spirit will follow his example. Thus may these
sedentary exhibitions be reduced to reasonable proportions,
and the police allowed to enjoy their well-earned leave. The
summons is dismissed; and the prosecutor, not for her
opinions but for her foul ingratitude, will pay all the costs
of everyone.

NOTE—See also the *Queen* v. *the Society for Nuclear Extinction* (1962). This was
a prosecution initiated by the Committee for Nuclear Disarmament. The defendant body (S.N.E.) takes the view that the human race is evil, foolish and incor-
rigible; that it is breeding excessively and without the slightest care; that it is
covering the planet with redundant babies, hideous buildings, and continual
noise; that the one hope for Earth is the extinction or near-extinction of the human
race, after which a new start might be made; and that a short sharp nuclear
conflict would be welcome. The C.N.D. had organized a Pentecostal Procession
from the British Deterrent Base to Whitehall. But soon after it moved off, 20,000
strong, it was brought to a halt by 10,000 supporters of the S.N.E. who were sitting
or lying in the highway and the adjacent fields. The marchers, bound by their
pacific principles, were unable to force a passage, and the procession was abandoned. The organizers admitted in court that the purpose and intention had been

for the marchers to sit down *en masse* in Parliament Square. The Judge reminded them of the old maxim that a complaint must come into Court 'with clean hands—or, in this case, may I say, clean seats'. They were the last persons who could be heard to complain of obstruction by sitting or reclining.

(42) REGINA *v.* WALTON: *ex parte* RUSK

A Tent in the Road

(Before a Divisional Court:
Amble, J., Plush, J. and Slattery, J.)

Mr. Justice Amble said: This strange appeal comes before us from the Court of the Chief Metropolitan Magistrate, where Mr. Ambrose Rusk was convicted of an offence against the Highways Act. Mr. Rusk, it appears, resides at Number 12 Green Gardens, a modest by-street in that large area of the Metropolis called Kensington. On a night in Spring a Constable Boot, making one of the rare patrols which our dwindling police are now able to provide in residential areas, was surprised to see a small tent erected near the pavement, but in the road, outside Number 12. Upon investigation, the officer found a young female person, aged 17, asleep in the tent upon a light 'camp' bed. The young person turned out to be the fourth daughter of Mr. Rusk who accepted full responsibility for the erection of the tent in that place. 'My daughter Crocus,' he said. 'She's been sleeping there for weeks. Didn't you know? She's keen on camping and it keeps the cars away.' 'But the tent is an obstruction,' said the officer. 'What is it obstructing?' Mr. Rusk replied.

Later, Mr. Rusk, who conducted his own case, developed the point in his cross-examination of the chief witness for the Crown:

Q. 346. *The Defendant:* Constable Boot, at the relevant time, was there an unattended motor-car parked on either side of the tent?

Boot: Yes, sir.

Defendant: Was the street lined, on both sides, with unattended parked cars, mostly showing no lights?

Boot: That is so.

Defendant: Did you proceed against the owner of any of these cars for obstruction?

Boot: No, sir. There's no order against parking in that street.

Defendant: Was one of the parked vehicles what is called a caravan?

Boot: Yes, sir, to the best of my knowledge, it was.

Defendant: Was anyone sleeping in the caravan?

Boot: I did not inquire.

The trend of the appellant's argument, which was richly developed before us by his counsel, Sir Mowbray Spoon, is clear. Green Gardens, which was, till recently, a quiet street, empty at night but for a motor-car or two belonging to residents, is now a recognized and, it seems, authorized depository, an open-air garage, as it were, for motor-cars, very few of which are the property of the residents. They belong to citizens who are attending an adjacent cinema, who have come from the country to stay with relatives, to go to the theatre, or a banquet, or who live in the next street, perhaps, but because of the invasion of strangers can find no place for their own motor-cars there. Mr. Rusk has a small car himself, but, he said, can so seldom stable it at his own front door that, reluctant to trespass on the frontage of a neighbour, he now puts it in the nearest garage, a quarter of a mile away.

Few of the invaders, it seems, are so scrupulous. Some reply to any protest that, for once, they have the law and the police on their side. Others indignantly and even arrogantly proclaim that by reason of the high charges laid by the State upon road licences and motor-fuel they have some sort of notional right or interest in the public highways to whose maintenance they have contributed so much. This, I confess, is new doctrine to the Court. It seems rather like saying that the payment of entertainment duty entitled a man to spend the night at the theatre. But we need not argue about that: for however flimsy the claim in law, in fact, with police approval, every owner of such a vehicle is occupying and enjoying, by a kind of 'squatter's right', at his own pleasure, an area of land which is part of the public highway. Mr. Rusk says simply that he has an equal right to do the same, so long as he does not obstruct the traffic. Indeed, he says, he has a better right, for not only does he pay the motoring taxes too, but he is a local ratepayer and contributes at the rate of 4s. in the pound each year to 'Highways, Bridges, Street Improvements', etc.

This argument, at first sight attractive, will not, I think, bear close examination. There are many evident differences between Mr. Smith's motor-car and Mr. Rusk's daughter's tent. One is that Mr. Smith holds a licence to bring his vehicle on to the road, and Mr. Rusk has no licence to erect a tent there. The presence in the tent of an unprotected young woman in sleeping attire suggests to the Court only one of the many reasons why such a licence is not likely to be granted. The contention that there was no obstruction in fact can not prevail. We recognize constructive desertion in marriage, when the person charged has not in fact deserted: and so there can be constructive obstruction on the roads. The appeal should be dismissed.

Mr. Justice Plush said: I disagree, with delight. If one man may annex and occupy a portion of the public highway so may another: and it makes no difference if he employs a motor-car, a tent, a barrow, a perambulator, or a table on wheels. The presence of the young woman, whether asleep or awake, is irrelevant, an element of unworthy prejudice. If Mr. Rusk allowed a male guest to sleep in his car the police would have nothing to say, provided he were not intoxicated or meditating a felony. Many lorry-drivers, it is well known, snatch their rare moments of repose in their vehicles. Many a passenger snores in the motor-coach. There may have been someone sleeping in the caravan. If this sort of thing gives rise to any mischief there are laws 'in that case made and provided'. We are concerned with a charge of obstruction. I am aware that in the case of a motor-car there may be a conviction without evidence of actual obstruction. But there has been no such decision in the case of a tent: and accordingly, I hold, the appeal should be allowed.

Mr. Justice Slattery said: There is, on certain inland waterways, a civilized and charming custom by which the owner of riparian property is deemed to have a right to moor his own boat or vessel at the end of his own garden or estate; and will not there be charged the usual mooring fees. A similar understanding should prevail, and by custom has prevailed in the past, concerning the road-space immediately adjacent to every citizen's home. Mr. Rusk, it seems to me, has done no more than to make a formal assertion of a customary right, for which a parallel may be found in many actions concerning rights of way. The appeal should be allowed.

It was.

(43) THE QUEEN *v.* THE S.S. *EMPEROR DULLES*

MONEY IN THE CHANNEL

(In the Admiralty Court)

LORD MERRYMIND, the President of the Probate, Divorce, and Admiralty Division of the High Court, to-day delivered judgment in the Dover Strait case. He said:

In this case the steamship *Emperor Dulles*, on passage from the Persian Gulf to Hamburg and flying the flag of Panama, was closed and stopped by H.M.S. *Vole* about two miles East of the Dover Strait, and after some discussion was escorted into Dover Harbour, where she now lies under arrest. The *Vole* was engaged in her normal duties with the international patrol for the due enforcement of the English (and French) Channel Act, 1957. By that Act, and by the French *Loi Extraordinaire* 769 of the same date, Britain and France provided and proclaimed that the territorial waters of both countries would extend henceforth ten nautical (or $11\frac{1}{2}$ statute) miles from the shore. This means that Britain and France, between them, control the whole of the narrow strait between Dover and Calais; and by the Treaty of Boulogne they made some economical and enlightened arrangements for the joint defence and management of the Strait, including, of course, the collection of the appropriate dues from all vessels using the Channel.

The purpose and justification of those enactments, as explained in their preambles, were simple enough. The waters in question, with their strong and shifty tidal currents, are dangerous. They are bounded on two sides by high and inhospitable cliffs; they are flanked on one side by notorious quicksands; perilous shoals of sand and shingle, notably the Varne, $5\frac{1}{2}$ by $1\frac{1}{4}$ miles, lie in the fairway on the other; often the whole area is enveloped in fog. To secure a safe passage for the ships of the world both Britain and

France have provided, and still maintain, an elaborate system of lighthouses, lightships, and illuminated buoys. When the lights can no more be seen electrical stations give the ships their positions or bearings, and the diaphone, the siren, the reed-horn, the nautophone, the submarine oscillator, guns and explosives, bells, whistles and gongs, a noble orchestra, are ready to warn the mariner of danger. The Fleets of both countries, as well, still sweep the Strait for unexploded mines that may have survived from the last Great War. Special aircraft and naval vessels are always standing by for the assistance of shipping in distress.

But unless the ships of the world enter the ports of Britain or France, where they are liable to harbour dues, they contribute nothing to these costly precautions. The spectacle of enormous tankers in the Strait, carrying their profitable cargoes to other lands, and paying nothing for the services that make them safe, has long been irksome or worse to the people of Britain and France. That injustice is now corrected. The Strait is still open, without request or permission, to all vessels, except ships of war, provided that they give aid to those who aid them. The whirling beams of the South Foreland and Cap Gris Nez have long spoken to each other across the narrow waters; but now they flash, with the same authority, the same signal: *Il faut payer*.

All this is well known to everyone, except, it seems, the master of the *Emperor Dulles*, who, as an American citizen in a ship from Panama, might have been expected to find such arrangements familiar and acceptable. In the ordinary course, for the general convenience, the dues are paid through the banks when the notice of passage is given. But in case of default or evasion the Strait patrol-vessels are authorized to demand payment from the master. Captain Bubble, rather truculently, declined. The Commander of the *Vole* reminded him that the seas were free, and it was open to him to turn and proceed by way of the north of Scotland, where he would incur no charge. The master again refused; and here he is.

The question before the court is simple, and for this country, at least, admits only one answer. But Sir Robin Whangle, for the defendant vessel, hinted that the affair might be taken to some international tribunal; and in the hope that I may be able to avert so extravagant and futile a proceeding I had better indicate some of the many errors in Sir Robin's laborious and, if he will forgive me, rather laughable argument.

Sir Robin contended that the Dover Strait is open sea; that it is contrary to natural justice and the use and custom of the nations for France and Britain to claim rights of property and control therein; and that our treatment of the *Emperor Dulles* was tantamount to piracy. The description I have already given of the Strait is enough to show how little it deserves the title of 'open'; and the claim to which he objects would be by no means novel, if it were made. In the seventeenth century England asserted dominion over the whole of the Channel, Venice over the Adriatic, and Denmark over the whole space between Iceland and Norway. In the eighteenth century Denmark was still attempting to forbid fishery within sixty-nine miles of Greenland and Iceland. Such pretensions diminished, but they did not disappear. There is no doubt that marginal waters can in law be owned and occupied, provided always that the occupation is effective. For example, a State has undeniably an exclusive right to the fisheries in its own waters, and foreign fishermen are not surprised if they are chivvied away. The only question is: What is the extent of marginal waters? Some of the ancient jurists said 'a space bounded by the horizon'—which to a man on the beach may mean three miles, to a man on the cliff, thirteen. The measure most generally accepted was a marine league, three miles again; but this was founded on the supposed range of a gun of position, and can hardly be considered sacrosanct to-day. 'Perhaps', writes Hall in his *International Law*, 'it may be said without impropriety that a State has theoretically the right to extend its territorial waters from

time to time at its will with the increased range of guns.'
Britain has already been bombarded by a gun in France,
more than twenty miles away; and on the 'gun-shot' theory
might, without reasonable complaint, have extended her
limit to twenty miles. After all, the great light at the South
Foreland, for which she pays, may aid the mariner more
than twenty miles away. But with characteristic restraint
she has stopped at ten. Observe that now she lays claim to
half the Channel only: in the other half, so far as she is
concerned, navigation is free for all. The fact that France
is able to appropriate that other half merely illustrates the
narrowness of the passage and its fitness for international
control.

The flag of Panama, I understand, is seen so often on the
high seas because it assists the traders of other countries in
the avoidance of taxes: but it will not avail to rob this
country of her modest dues. Accordingly, in default of
payment within seven days, the *Emperor Dulles* will be confiscated. The usual writs will be nailed to the mast, and to
the master as well if he gives more trouble. As for you, Sir
Robin, go to the Hague, by all means—and I wish you joy.

44

COMMON TIME

THIS was the first appearance of Common Market problems in the British Courts. Five judges, Lord Plush presiding, sat on the Judicial Committee of the Privy Council to consider a matter specially referred to them by Her Majesty under Section 4 of the Act of 1833. Much interest was caused by the return to duty of Lord Wool, now aged 79.

Lord Plush said: In the month of April 1965 the United Kingdom, incautiously, as many thought, but with her habitual nobility, as all agreed, became a member of the European Economic Community. One of the purposes of the Community, as declared in Article 3 of the Treaty of Rome is '*the inauguration of a common transport policy*'. In July the European Commission, which manages the affairs of the Community from day to day, issued a '*Regulation*' that every transport system in the Community must use the same time and the same notation of time—20 hours, for example, instead of 8.0 p.m. This was merely an assertion of the obvious to the six original members, Germany, Italy, France, Belgium, Holland and Luxembourg, who use the same Standard Time, and the same convenient notation.

But British Time is one hour behind the common time of the European Community. This is no insular whim of ours. It is founded on the movements of the sun, which no manipulation of clocks, no bureaucratic itch for tidiness, can alter. Berlin, the most easterly capital in the Community, is in longitude 13° 25′ East: we are, very proudly, in longitude 0°. That is, the sun passes over Berlin nearly an hour—fifty-four minutes, to be exact—before it passes over London: and Man has always governed his rising, his sleeping, and the time of his midday meal, by the movements of the sun.

Unhappily, our fathers departed from these high truths

in the Summer Time Act which began the shameful tampering with clocks—shameful especially to Britain, whose local time, Greenwich time, is also a world time, the time in use among astronomers and navigators everywhere. As usual, early in 1965, Her Majesty's Government, by Order in Council, decreed that 'Summer Time' should endure from March 28 to October 24: and, Parliament acquiescing, it was so. During those months, therefore, the British railway time-tables tallied with the Continental tables. But the Regulation of the European Commission raised the question. What was to happen after October 24? The Regulation, for Britain, meant, clearly enough, not merely Summer Time that winter, but Summer Time, all the year round, for ever. Her Majesty's Government, as eager as a débutante to make a good impression, at once obeyed orders and presented to Parliament a Common Time Bill, which repealed the Summer Time Acts. Section One said:

(1) The time for general purposes in Great Britain shall throughout the year be one hour in advance of Greenwich Mean Time.[1]

They were compelled, however, for many good reasons, to enact again Section 3 of the Act of 1925:

(3) Nothing in this Act shall affect the use of Greenwich Mean Time for purposes of astronomy, meteorology, or navigation, or affect the construction of any document mentioning or referring to a point in time in connexion with any of those purposes.

The intention is queer but clear. The navigators of the world, including our own, will continue to calculate their positions by reference to Greenwich Time and the meridian of Greenwich: but the engine-drivers of Scotland and Northern Ireland will be governed by the clocks of Luxembourg and Prussia.

It is not the custom of our Courts to take notice of what

[1] See *Note*.

is said in Parliamentary debates, though I gather that in the interpretation of the decrees of Europe we may soon be expected to. But for our purposes it is necessary to record that the Government Time Bill was so hotly opposed in the House of Commons that it was withdrawn. On October 24, therefore, the British clocks will go back to Greenwich Time; the sovereign Parliament of the United Kingdom is, for the moment, in conflict with the European Commission—and we are asked by the Crown to advise upon the juridical position.

The intention of a Regulation is, without doubt, compulsory.

They shall, says Article 189 of the Treaty,

'*be binding in every respect and directly applicable in each Member State.*'

'Applicable.' The Attorney-General, to my intense dismay, suggested that this means that the Regulation already has the force of law in our land, whatever Parliament may say. Accordingly, Ministers propose to direct the British Railways, and all forms of public transport under their control, to conform with the Regulation: and they hope, it seems, that everyone else will voluntarily fall into line. (What will happen if they do not need not now be considered.) My Lords, I heard the Attorney-General's argument with almost invincible reluctance, and I now indubitably dismiss it. The sovereign authority in our land is Parliament still; and the Ministers' proposed action would be unconstitutional and wrong.

The word 'applicable' I take to mean 'should or must be applied', a kind of gerundive. If it is *not* applied a remedy is provided by Article 169. Where the Commission 'consider that a Member State has failed to fulfil any of its obligations under this Treaty' it shall first

'*require such State to submit its comments*'

and then

'*give a reasoned opinion on the matter*'

'*If such State does not comply with the terms of such opinion
... the Commission may refer the matter to the Court of Justice.*'

My lords, I find as a fact that we have failed to fulfil an
'obligation', and in law that we must submit ourselves to the
procedure of Article 169. Since I am not a Minister but a
judge I conceive myself debarred from offering advice upon
the nature of the 'comments' we should make to the Commission.

Lord Wool said: Well done, Brother Plush, but you've put
a foot wrong here and there. First, about the debate. It was
a splendid effort. Sometimes the House of Commons seems
to go mad and do something sensible *as one man*. Up they
rose, bless 'em, and said: 'Common Market be blowed!
We're not going to have a lot of land-lubberly continentals
mucking Greenwich Time about. Certainly we're not going
to abolish Greenwich Time in one clause and keep it going
in the next.' Gosh! as they say, what wallop! When this
Common Basket was going through some of us piped up
about our sovereignty, but they told us we were talking
through our coronets. No more loss of sovereignty, they said,
than in any other treaty. Lies, I said. In the common or
garden treaty you know what you've agreed to swallow, and
you don't swallow no more. In this lot we've got to swallow
anything they like to stick down our gullets. The Lord
Chancellor, I remember, in this House, said that the
ordinary British bloke would never be affected, wouldn't
know the Common Basket was on. Look at this, then—
Summer Time all the year round! Ain't that going to affect
the common Britons? The next thing, we'll have a 'Directive'
about driving on the right side of the road. That'll affect just
a few of us too. Might be a good thing. But we don't want
to be bull-dozed into it by a few bald busies in Brussels.

As for the comments, I'll tell you what. If they must
have a common time, let the Six Foreign Fellows come over
to *our* time. Then they'll all be in on Greenwich, and that's

a time worth keeping. Easy! It sticks out a nautical mile!

Lord Shackle said: I concur with Lord Wool: and, as a former President of the Admiralty Court, I feel free to suggest the kind of 'comments' that should be made to the European Commission. In 1884 the nations, assembled at Washington, agreed that the line of longitude 0° should pass through Greenwich, the finest compliment our country ever had. We may well share Greenwich Time with our continental partners, but to let it go would be the final folly.

The contention, my lords, is not merely patriotic but practical. By international agreement the earth's surface is divided into 24 'Zones' each 15 degrees of longitude in width: and each Zone uses Standard Time differing from Greenwich Time by an integral number of hours, *minus* or *plus*, fast or slow. Zone 0 lies between longitude $7\frac{1}{2}°$ East and longitude $7\frac{1}{2}°$ West. In this Zone, of which the centre is the meridian of Greenwich, all ships keep their clocks set to Greenwich Mean Time. Zone Minus 1 is between $7\frac{1}{2}$ and $22\frac{1}{2}$ degrees East longitude: ships in this Zone keep time which is 1 hour *fast* of Greenwich Time.

Now, my lords, five of the seven Common Market capitals are in Zone 0

	Longitude
London	0° 0′
Paris	2° 20′ E
The Hague	4° 18′ E
Brussels	4° 20′ E
Luxembourg	6° 7′ E

So are two of the E.F.T.A. capitals:

Oslo	7° 0′ E
Geneva	6° 10′ E

But all these (except London) employ on land, erroneously, I think, the time appropriate to Zone Minus 1—that is, one hour ahead of Greenwich. Thus a ship approaching the coasts of France, Holland or Belgium at 12.0 noon will find that the dock-side clocks say 11.0 a.m. This is unnatural and wrong.

Only two of the Common Market capitals are not in Zone 0—Rome 12° 28′ E and Berlin 13° 25′ E. Of the E.F.T.A. capitals Lisbon is 9° 7′ W but uses Greenwich Time—Copenhagen, 12° 35′ E, Vienna 16° 22′ E, and Stockholm, 18° 5′ E, are all in the neighbouring Zone − 1. Thus of the 13 Common Market and E.F.T.A. countries, 8, including Portugal, are naturally Greenwich Timers, and only 5 are naturally 1 hour ahead.

The 'common transport' provisions of the Treaty of Rome are to apply at first 'to transport by rail, road and inland waterway' (see Article 84). But paragraph 2, rather cautiously, says that 'The Council ... *may* decide whether, to what extent, and by what procedure, appropriate provisions might be adopted for sea and air transport.' No new provisions for sea and air transport will be appropriate or possible: for these are governed by world arrangements. Whatever is done on land in Western Europe the navigators by sea and air will continue to use Greenwich Time. It would evidently be sensible and practically useful if all Common Market and E.F.T.A. transport, land, sea, or air, used the same time; and that time, for the reasons given, can only be Greenwich Time, which is already, geographically, the natural time of the majority. The trains in the Channel tunnel, the ships and aeroplanes above it, the Golden Arrow, the *Queen Elizabeth*, the Boeing from New York, the Brussels train, the Riviera express, would use a common time. What could be better?

It will be said: 'But the European countries will have to put their clocks back one hour.' Why not? This is no worse a burden than Britain putting her clocks *ahead*: and since the Prime Meridian does not pass through these countries the change would not conflict with the cosmic scheme. In the Common Market Germany and Italy would be a minority of two. If necessary, they could remain in Zone − 1, and Austria and Sweden too—though it would spoil the symmetry of the thing.

It will be said then: 'What about Daylight Saving?' Many serious men regard the national tampering with clocks as a degrading confession of weakness. If the citizen desires to 'save daylight' he can easily achieve it, by rising earlier. It is not necessary to alter the clocks and cause Big Ben, a scientific instrument, to utter lies for many months. The Government have only to say: 'From March 29 all Government institutions will start work an hour earlier, and all private enterprises are expected to follow suit.' At present the traveller in the comparatively small space of Europe has to study a nautical almanac in order to discover (a) what is the Standard Time of this country or that and (b) whether it has an asterisk indicating that Standard Time has given way to Summer Time. All this confusion would go, in the confines of the European Community, at least— the clocks would tell the same tale all the year, in every aeroplane, at every air-port, in every ship and harbour. So great would be the general benefit that I should hope the Community would set an example to the world by formally prohibiting the trick called 'Summer Time'.

Greenwich Mean Time would thus recover its original and proper prestige and importance: and, apart from questions of practical convenience, our companions in Zone o might be as proud as we are, or should be, to think that their local time, on sea or land, was a world-time too. If the name of Greenwich stuck in any European throats it could be called Universal Time, as some have already proposed.

Lord Rutt said: I concur with Lord Shackle. All this may not appeal to land-borne Europeans. But what, I wonder, were our own representatives on the Commission doing?

Lord Wood: Treasury men, you bet! They agreed.

Lord Banner: I concur with Lord Shackle. When I was in the House of Commons a fine speech was made on the subject of perpetual Summer Time by a Member called Haddock. Hitler, he said, if he had won, would have had the line of longitude o° transferred to Berlin. And he concluded, I recall: 'Let us remember how much is meant by

Greenwich Mean Time. Let the Empire go if you must, but hold fast to the Prime Meridian.'

NOTE—In *Rex* v. *Slout* (1948) the defendant Slout, a publican, refused to obey the Double Summer Time Act and continued to open and close his premises according to Greenwich Mean Time. 'God's Time' he said 'is good enough for me.' He was convicted of selling 'intoxicating liquor' outside 'permitted hours', but appealed.

The Court of Criminal Appeal allowed the appeal. The Lord Chief Justice said:

'In the year 1880 it was enacted by statute that the word "time" in any legal document relating to Great Britain was to be interpreted, unless otherwise specifically stated, as the Mean Time of the Greenwich meridian. The Summer Time Act at present in force decrees that "the time *for general purposes* in Great Britain shall be two hours in advance of Greenwich Mean Time". The appellant, whose motives are of the highest, has contended plausibly that "general purposes" does not include the public sale and consumption of intoxicating liquor. This, he says, is a notably particular purpose, as is shown by the care which Parliament has taken to confine the pursuit of it to fixed and stated periods of time. No other activity of the citizen is so precisely limited to certain "permitted hours" every day of the year. In determining those hours Parliament, no doubt, had regard to the facts of Nature, and especially the movements of the sun. For example, on Sundays Mr. Slout was not permitted to open the *Blue Lion* till 12.0 noon, when the sun is, as the sailors say, "over the yard-arm". That, said Parliament, eight hours after sunrise in early July, was soon enough for public drinking on the Lord's Day. But now, says Mr. Slout, under the evil régime of Double Summer Time, he is expected to serve "intoxicating drink" on Sundays to all and sundry "at ten o'clock in the morning, God's Time"—only six hours after sunrise. On week-days the situation is worse, for his opening hour is 11.0, which means 9.0 a.m. by the sun—five hours after sunrise. Neither God nor Parliament, he says, can have intended or desired such an affront to temperance and decent behaviour.

'I must correct Mr. Slout on a technical detail. "God's Time" is not synonymous with Greenwich Mean Time, an expression which is clearly understood, I fear, by not more than 1 in 1,000,000 Britons. God's Time is Sun Time, or Apparent Time, the time shown by a sun-dial. But this, because of the varying velocity of the Earth in its passage round the Sun, is not a uniform time. It is subject to variations which may amount to sixteen minutes—earlier or later. This was not acceptable to tidy-minded Man, who required his hours and days to be of the same length always. He therefore invented "Mean" or Average Time. The Mean Time Day is equal to the average length of the Apparent Solar Day. The sun-dial agrees exactly with the clock for a second or two on only four days in the year. In November the sun is sixteen minutes ahead of the clock; at the end of July it is six minutes behind. As the late Mr. Hilaire Belloc wrote:

> "I am a sundial, and I make a botch
> Of what is done much better by a watch."

'Greenwich Mean Time, then, is a man-made institution: but it is founded (as "Summer Time" is not) on the true movements of the Sun. Mean Time reverently accepts and amends God's Time. Summer Time, single or double, impudently ignores it.

"Subject to that, I think the appellant has made a good case. In the Night Poaching Act 1828 there is a definition of "night"—it begins one hour after sunset and ends one hour before sunrise. This sensible arrangement is unaffected by such follies as Double Summer Time. Night-poaching is governed still by the wise definitions of Nature. In the Larceny Acts 1861 and 1916, on the other hand, "night", for the purposes of burglary, is "the interval between nine o'clock in the evening and six o'clock in the morning of the succeeding day". Double Summer Time makes nonsense of this, for 9.0 p.m. B.S.T. means 7.0 p.m. by Greenwich Mean Time, and this in high summer may be two hours before twilight. Evidently then, burglary should be excluded from "general purposes", for the essence of the offence is house-breaking in the hours of darkness. I hold, and so do my learned brethren, that the Licensing Laws concerning "permitted hours" should be an exception too. The appeal should succeed.'

Unfortunately, this decision was reversed by the House of Lords.

45

Brigitte Bardot M.P.?

Judgment was given in the Foreign Members' case to-day. Difficult questions of interpretation, in Common Market law, were involved.

Mr. Justice Owle said: The legal profession, or those at least who practise at the Bar, will ever give thanks for the entry of the United Kingdom into the European Economic Community. But those of us who sit up here may well be driven from the Bench untimely, so alien, odious, and unanswerable are some of the problems that the winds of Europe have blown upon our peaceful British shores.

By the Parliamentary Elections Act 1868 and later statutes the trial of controverted elections is confided to two judges of the Queen's Bench Division of the High Court, whose decision is final. My learned brother Fish and I are now required to judge and determine two odd petitions which followed the many by-elections of November 1965.

The Act of Settlement declared that no person born out of the kingdom could be a Member of Parliament: and though he may now be a naturalized Briton a Member, by our old-fashioned law, must still be a British subject.

But in 1965, upon our entry into the European Community, the Treaty of Rome was ratified by Parliament and thereupon acquired the force of, indeed it became, a British statute. One of the first of the 'purposes' declared in Article 3 is 'the abolition as between Member States of the obstacles to the free movement of persons, services, and capital'.

'Services', says Article 60, 'shall be deemed to be services normally supplied for remuneration,' and 'shall include in particular : (a) activities of an industrial character; (b) activities of a commercial character; (c) artisan activities, and (d) *activities of the liberal professions*.' Article 48 ensures 'the free movement of workers'.

2. This shall involve *the abolition of any discrimination based on nationality* between workers of the Member States as regards employment, remuneration, and other working conditions.

The general intention is clear. All callings, all occupations, are to be open, in any Member State, to the nationals of every other Member State provided they observe the rules. I myself this morning visited a Belgian osteopath, recently arrived. Many Italian doctors are already practising in Britain, though they may not, my own doctor tells me, be so well qualified as ours. Equity, the actors' union, has had to abandon its suspicious watch on performers imported from the Continent, for attractive young Frenchmen are now as free to take the stage as Britons. The prostitute from Paris has the same rights, if any, as her London sister. The legal profession, I believe, has not yet opened wide the doors, but, upon my word, I do not see how that can be avoided.

Following suit, as it were, five persons of foreign birth offered their services to the State at the recent 'Little' Election. Two were elected. Signor Garibaldi, the gentleman from Italy, is a well-known journalist and student of affairs. He also has a tenor voice and sang delightfully at his election meetings. Mademoiselle Bardot, the Court was told, is a public entertainer, but, like so many others of her profession, has shown a serious interest in political questions, and is opposed to bombs of a certain size and power. At all events, she secured more votes than any of the others. All those against her forfeited their deposits, including even a debonair young Liberal. It may not be relevant to the business of the Court, but both, it seems, have something to contribute, and Parliament should surely benefit from their knowledge of the Continent.

I find it hard to understand why the Attorney-General should appear in support of the adverse petitions, and urge us so eagerly to find that these two persons are disqualified.

For it was his own Government which planted this Treaty in our midst, and wished us to be one with Europe in everything. Sir Anthony first took the point that to be a Member of the House of Commons cannot be included among 'activities of the liberal professions'. But one of the definitions of 'politician' in the great *Oxford English Dictionary* is 'one who makes politics his *profession* or business'. Sir Anthony then made a stand on 'liberal'. But 'liberal' in this connexion originally meant no more than an activity that was 'worthy of a free man', as opposed to one that was *servile* or *mechanical*: and who will say that to be a freely elected member of a free Parliament should not be so described?

Sir Anthony then offered to call evidence from Brussels which would show that in the minds of the Treaty-makers the 'liberal professions' meant 'the arts and sciences, teaching, law, medicine', and so on. But as I had to remind him, and now remind the world, though this was once a foreign Treaty, *it is now a British statute*: and I conceive it my duty to interpret it as we interpret every Act of Parliament, by the plain contemporary meaning of the words. It is not our custom to peep round corners, to poke our noses into Parliamentary debates or the proceedings of committees, in order to discover what the lawmaker meant: and it will be an ill day when we do. 'No English judge,' Lord Mildew said in *Scott* v. *the Thames Conservancy* (1937), 'looks under the bed.'

The same argument arose when we considered Article 48, which covers the free movement and employment of foreign 'workers'. Sir Anthony grudgingly conceded that since the word is 'workers', not 'artisans', it may well include a Member of Parliament. But he drew the Court's attention to paragraph 4:

'The provisions of this Article shall not apply to employment in the public administration.'

and therefore, he contended, Mademoiselle Bardot, though possibly a 'worker', could not be a Member of the House of Commons.

A British Member of Parliament was called. I asked him if he thought that he was '*employed in the public administration*'. His hair stood on end. 'No,' he answered, curtly but correctly, 'I belong to the Legislature. The "public administrators" are the Civil Service, the judges, and so on, quite different—so different that they are not eligible for election to Parliament.' Again the Attorney-General asked leave to call evidence from abroad, about possible European constructions of the words: and again the Court refused. If I may quote Lord Mildew again: 'If Parliament does not mean what it says it must say so.' (*Bluff* v. *Father Gray*.)

We are now therefore confronted with two British statutes, one of which says that only British subjects shall be elected to Parliament, and the other says (in Article 7) that:

> '*any discrimination on the grounds of nationality shall hereby be prohibited*.'

I take it that the latter, being the later, must override the former. I therefore hold that Bardot and Garibaldi were duly elected.

Mr. Justice Fish: I concur. The case is plain.

Mr. Justice Owle: We shall certify accordingly to Mr. Speaker: and that, as they say, is that.

The Attorney-General: I am very sorry, my lord—but, my lord, my attention has just been drawn to Article 177 of the Treaty, the final paragraph:

> 'Where any such question'——

and this includes a question on 'the interpretation of the Treaty'——

> 'is raised in a case *pending* before a domestic court or tribunal from whose decisions no appeal lies under municipal law, such court shall refer the matter to the European Court of Justice.'

Mr. Justice Owle: '*Shall?*' 'Shall' indeed? No appeal here—that's right. But suppose it was the House of Lords?

And 'pending', you say. You mean that the Court has been wasting its time?

The Attorney-General: No, my lord. The European Court, I am sure, will read your judgment with interest and advantage.

Mr. Justice Owle: Don't over-excite me, Sir Anthony— Very well, Mr. Attorney. We shall certify to Mr. Speaker that for the present these persons are duly elected to the British House of Commons, but that at some future date somebody in Brussels may decide that they are not. And how, I wonder, will Parliament like *that*?

(46) HADDOCK v. THE CHANCELLOR OF THE EXCHEQUER

COMMON TEA

(Before the House of Lords)

THIS was an appeal to the House of Lords against a decision of the Court of Appeal reversing a decision of the High Court that a writ of *mandamus* should issue to the Chancellor of the Exchequer.

The Lord Chancellor said: I was a member of the Government which led this country into the European Economic Community: but though I studied the Treaty of Rome with care I confess that I did not foresee that it would give us quite so much enjoyable litigation. This case must have been a sorry shock to Her Majesty's Treasury which was perhaps of all the Departments the most eager to enter Europe. Yet let me say at once that these proceedings are a natural consequence of the Treaty of Rome which Ministers have signed and Parliament, by statute, has adopted. Since I am still one of those Ministers I propose to say no more.

Lord Gay said: One of the great purposes of the Common Market is 'fair competition'. The 'restriction or distortion of competition' is an evil frequently mentioned and met in the Treaty. Article 95, for example ('Fiscal Provisions') says:

> A Member State shall not impose, directly or indirectly, any internal charges of any kind in excess of those applied directly or indirectly to like domestic products.

Many reluctant Britons were reconciled to the Common Market by the prospect of enjoying Continental wines more cheaply after the removal of the customs wall between Britain and the Continent. Others glumly predicted that the British Treasury, ever itching to punish the people's pleasures, would find some way out of that. They were right. By the Finance Act of 1965 the excise duty on the liquids known as 'British Wines' was raised from 10s. 6d. per gallon to 26s. 0d. per gallon—which was the level of the Customs duty on Continental wine: and a new internal charge, described as a Public Health and Order Tax, was levied not on the importers but on the purveyors of wine, wholesale and retail. Since this applies to Commonwealth wine as well, the gifted gentlemen at the Treasury are now collecting more money from wines of all sorts than they were before, though they protest that it is not intended, and is not to be thought of, as 'revenue': and since the internal tax on all wines is exactly the same they have scrupulously complied with the terms of Article 95. They also, by the way, gave the new name of Public Health and Order Tax to the very heavy excise duties on home-grown beer, gin and whisky.

By the long-suffering British subject these manœuvres were sadly accepted as normal Treasury behaviour: but in the high institutions of the European Community they caused unfavourable comment. The wine-growers especially resented the suggestion that 'British Wines' could be described as 'like' products to Château Yquem, Château Lafite, Traminer, Liebfraumilch, or Lacrima Christi; and they complained that, whatever the name of the new tax, it would unfairly 'distort competition' between their own Community products and 'soft' drinks imported from America or tea imported from India and Ceylon. Some retaliatory, or, shall I say, corrective action was to be expected.

Article 99 says:

> The Commission shall consider in what way the law of the various Member States concerning *turnover taxes, excise duties, and other forms of indirect taxation*, including compensatory measures applying to exchanges between

Member States, can be harmonized in the interest of the Common Market.

And Article 100 says:

The Council, acting by means of a unanimous vote on a proposal of the Commission, shall issue directives for the approximation of such legislative and administrative provisions of the Member States as have a direct inci- dence on the establishment or functioning of the Common Market.

Accordingly the Treasury were required by the gentle- men in Brussels to give an account of the vast structure of indirect taxation on which the Revenue relies so much. But apart from wine the main attention of the Commission was given to tea. This is not, on the Continent, a name of such magic and power as it is in Britain: and the Preamble to the Council's interim 'directive' contained some caustic remarks:

'We observe that in the year 1960–1 the United Kingdom imported 535,457,409 pounds of tea: and 95 per cent. of them paid no tax at all. The total net revenue from tea was £469,648. The yield of the indirect taxes on other personal indulgences was rather different:

	Customs £	Excise £	Total £
Spirits	29,736,899	115,747,227	145,484,126
Beer	12,648,278	206,221,271	218,869,549
Wine	20,307,351	3,772,445	24,079,796
Cocoa, Coffee, Chicory	1,315,350		1,315,350
Tea	469,648		469,648

'The tax on brandy, we were informed, represents a purchase tax of 200 per cent.: on whisky, home-grown, it is 468 per cent., on gin, mainly home-grown, 400 per cent., on beer, mainly home-grown, 130 per cent., on a bottle of sherry, 80 per cent., on a bottle of Burgundy 53 per cent. or more: on "soft" drinks 15 per cent.: on tea (except for 5 per cent. of the imports) Nil.

'In 1960 the United Kingdom spent £176,087,576 on the importation of coffee, tea, and cocoa: on the purchase of foreign "Beverages" (including wines) only £42,031,207. But the revenue from wines alone was ten times the tax on coffee, tea, and cocoa.

'The Commission, and the Council, are unable to understand the British Exchequer's tenderness for tea. For it has been reported by the Community's Economic and Social Committee that:

> '*Tea in every industry and occupation is a prime hindrance to production and a major cause of industrial disputes*—the number, timing, and duration of the "tea-breaks", as they are called, the wages and welfare of those who serve the tea, etc. There are no "wine-breaks", it is fitting to remember, in French or German factories.'

(Lord Mildew said in *Haig* v. *the Inland Revenue*: 'Few men abandon their duties at eleven o'clock in the morning in order to drink whisky.')

'Accordingly, for the purposes of efficiency and financial stability as well as fair competition, acting unanimously on a proposal of the Commission, the Council issue to the United Kingdom the following *Directive*:

> 'All internal charges on Community wine are to be abolished and a customs duty on tea imported from outside the Community is to be imposed at the rate of 15 per cent., or such other rate as may yield the revenue of £20,000,000 a year.'

Now, my Lords, we have representatives both on the European Commission and the European Council: and since the 'Directive' was unanimous it follows that they must have supported it; but they are not bound, and may be forbidden, to disclose their reasons. Article 189 lays down that:

Directives shall bind any Member State to whom they are addressed, as to the result to be achieved, while leaving to domestic agencies a competence as to form and means.

In a statement to Parliament, the Chancellor said that he was considering the 'form and means', and it may be that he proposes to obey the 'Directive' in his forthcoming Budget. But some by-elections are expected to follow that and he may be tempted to prolong his consideration. The Friends of Tea are without doubt more numerous than the Friends of Wine. Ministers may explain that in the matter of the tea-tax they are acting under orders and against their will, but electoral reasoning is not invariably equitable.

In these circumstances a public-minded citizen, Mr. Albert Haddock, thought it right to act. He regards the Directive as just and desirable, having long resented the excessive and barbarous taxes not only on imported wines but on home-grown beer, gin and whisky: and he applied for a Rule *nisi* of *mandamus* calling upon the Chancellor of the Exchequer to show cause why he should not obey the 'Directive' in the next Finance Bill. Whatever the Court of Appeal may think, this is perfectly right and proper. Whenever a public authority is failing to discharge a public duty this admirable writ will lie: and under the conditions of the Common Market it can as well be addressed to a Government Department as to the London County Council. For all Government Departments have lost their former, superior status. The Chancellor is no longer 'a Minister of the Crown', responsible to Parliament. He is, in any matter governed by the Treaty, responsible to the European Economic Community, and, if the terms of the Treaty are duly observed, must do what he, or his 'Member State', is told. If he does not, if, through his act or neglect, he causes this country to 'fail to fulfil an obligation under the Treaty' this country may be hauled before the Court of Justice, and suffer both discredit and expense (see Article

169). If the Court of Justice finds that we have failed we shall be required (under Article 171) 'to implement the judgment of the Court'. If this 'Member State' still fails it is hard to say what follows: but under Article 172 the Council 'may confer on the Court of Justice full jurisdiction in respect of penalties'. In order to avert such international humiliations it is evidently open to any patriotic Briton to employ any legal remedy that exists, and none could be more suitable than the wholesome writ of *mandamus*. The appeal should be allowed.

Lord Luck said: I concur. This should be a lesson for the Treasury.

Lord Wool said: What a hope! I concur.

Lords Rutt and *Amble* concurred.

Bardot Regained

Before the House of Lords to-day another stage was reached in the Foreign Members' case. Signor Garibaldi and Mademoiselle Bardot have been active Members of the House of Commons for six months. Both have won high praise and popularity. Mademoiselle Bardot's maiden speech (on the Matrimonial Causes (Common Market) Bill) is still discussed with wonder at Westminster. She is one of the few women Members who venture boldly into that citadel of Man, the Members' Smoking Room, and are always welcome. Lord Rusk said to-day, in the course of his judgment: I have observed that many of your Lordships' House who, having once been Members of the House of Commons, are privileged by custom to use the Commons' Smoking Room, are exercising their rights with charming regularity.

Signor Garibaldi's speech on the Public Health (Common Market) Bill was an electrical success. The handsome Member from Milan sketched briefly the stories of the many grand operas in which he has appeared (in the tenor part): 'In every one, Signor Speaker,' he said, 'the heroine perishes at the end, of tuberculosis, of a bad cough, of malnutrition, exposure, injustice or neglect. Signor Speaker, I attend these operas, I sing the great arias, no more. All is now unreal. For I know that, under the social services of the English, in every story the heroine would be alive and well to-day. Signor Speaker, we must spread such services about Europe, about the world.' The Serjeant at Arms, Members observed, was in tears.

But outside, the best lawyers of Europe and Britain still debate the question: Were these two Members 'duly elected'?

Lord Bangle, presiding, said to-day:

We owe these odd proceedings to the vigilance and sagacity of two judges of the Queen's Bench Division, Mr. Justice Owle and Mr. Justice Fish, sitting as a special Court under the Parliamentary Elections Act 1868. Some months ago, they decided that under those articles of the Treaty of Rome which provide for 'the free movement of labour and services' and prohibit 'any discrimination on the grounds of nationality', two citizens of France and Italy had been properly elected to the House of Commons.

But at this point, a little late in the day, the Attorney-General drew the Court's attention to Article 177 of the Treaty of Rome. This gives the European Court of Justice power to make 'a *preliminary* decision concerning (*a*) the interpretation of the Treaty' and other matters.

> 'Where any such question is raised before a court or tribunal of one of the Member States, such court or tribunal *may*, if it considers that its judgment depends on a *preliminary* decision on this question, request the Court of Justice to give a ruling thereon.'

This, no doubt, may be a useful provision in commercial cases where consistency is desirable in the courts of the various Member States. But the final paragraph does not explain itself so easily:

> 'Where any such question is raised in a case *pending* before a domestic court or tribunal from whose decision no appeal lies under municipal law, such court or tribunal *shall* refer the matter to the Court of Justice.'

Mr. Justice Owle explained his difficulty thus:

'Our decision on these election petitions is final under the Act of 1868. At first, therefore, we were inclined to comply with the Article, and, having expressed our own opinion, to refer the matter to the European Court of Justice. But, I asked myself—and so did my brother Fish—to what purpose? It is not clear from the final paragraph what will follow the reference of this matter to the European Court: but I judge from the general sense of the Article that their decision will be "preliminary", at least in form. In other words the learned gentlemen in Brussels will make up their own minds, one way or another, but send the case back to this Court. But shall we then be expected to accept their decision? If we are, this means that a foreign Court, including one Briton only, will in effect have the final say on a question touching the composition of the British House of Commons. I find this possibility inexpressibly repugnant: for this is the jealously guarded privilege of Parliament itself. In 1868, to avoid the intrusion of partisan unpleasantness into such disputes, Parliament desired the High Court to settle them: but our powers are delegated powers only, and I do not feel that we have authority to delegate them again to any Court outside the kingdom. We therefore hold that Bardot and Garibaldi were duly elected, and that is final. Further we decline to refer this matter to the European Court, and against that decision you may appeal, Mr. Attorney-General, if you will. If a formal reason be required we simply say: This is not a case "pending"—for we have decided it.'

Accordingly, the two foreign Members presented themselves at the Bar of the House of Commons. There had been a question whether they could, or should, take the Oath of Allegiance. Mr. Speaker ruled that this was a matter for them: but since everyone in the European Community had now the same rights they had, presumably, the same obligations, including fidelity to the Heads of States. The two duly took the Oath and have been sitting and voting ever since.

But the Attorney-General appealed against the decision of Owle, J. and Fish, J. that they were not bound to refer the matter to the European Court. The Court of Appeal, by a majority, three judges to two, held that the two judges had decided wrongly. The Friends of Garibaldi and Bardot appealed.

My Lords, some of you, from the great Blitz of 1940 and

1941, and from many a maddening English spring or summer, can remember saying to yourselves: 'There seems to
be no real reason why this should ever come to an end.' I
confess that I have the same sensations when I regard the
impact of Article 177 upon the matter of Garibaldi and
Bardot. Your Lordships' House is the highest tribunal in the
land. To us, as a rule, in every dispute, men look for the last
and wisest word. But here, since 'no appeal lies from our
decisions' we were required by Article 177 to refer the
matter to Brussels, without ourselves saying a word. This
was a new and startling experience. But, my Lords, as you
recall, we set a good example and, with a good grace,
complied.

Three months later the European Court of Justice reported its 'preliminary decision', but without disclosing its
reasons. By five votes to four, I understand, they decided
that the provisions in the Treaty of Rome for 'free movement of labour and services' were not intended to cover
service in any Parliament, and therefore the persons Bardot
and Garibaldi should not have been elected and should now
be removed from Parliament.

My Lords, it is now, I suppose, our duty to report this
decision to Owle, J. and Fish, J. and direct them to try the
petitions again. But, do you know, that is not the course that
I propose to recommend to you. I think that Owle, J. and
Fish, J. were right. This is a matter for the sovereign British
Parliament and for nobody else: and long may Signor
Garibaldi, M.P., and Mademoiselle Bardot, M.P., remain
in our midst! My conclusion, I am aware, if you support it,
will put this 'Member State' in open conflict with the
European Community: and the consequences may well be
serious. But, do you know, my Lords, I do not care a button.
The fair exchange of goods is a splendid thing: on the
exchange of laws we stand to lose.

Lords Luck, Rusk, Banner and Rutt concurred.

(48) HADDOCK *v.* THE GENEROUS BANK LTD., COMPUTER 1578/32/W1, THE MAGICAL ELECTRONIC CONTRIVANCES LTD., AND THE CENTRAL ELECTRICITY BOARD

REIGN OF ERROR?

BEFORE Mr. Justice Squirrel in the High Court to-day Sir Cyril Tart, Q.C., opened for the plaintiff in this disturbing action, which is regarded as a test case on some novel points of law.

Sir Cyril said: My lord, this is an action for defamation, and the principal defendant is, perhaps, a computer——

The Court: Perhaps, Sir Cyril? But haven't you made up your mind?

Sir Cyril: No, my lord. With great respect, we hope that the Court will do that: for here is a new field of life and litigation, and I am unable to find any precedents with which to assist the Court, as I generally do.

The Court: You are always very helpful, Sir Cyril. Could we now have some approximate outline of the facts?

Sir Cyril: If your lordship pleases—as, may I add, your lordship habitually does. My lord, for many years my client, the plaintiff, has been a client of Generous Bank Ltd. In recent years the Bank has been employing a computer——

The Court: I never quite understand what they do.

Sir Cyril: My lord, I am instructed, if they are accurately fed with the requisite information they will answer almost any question that is put to them. Moreover, they will answer instantly a question which might occupy twenty expert men for many days. The defendant Computer is also capable of certain mechanical actions, the addressing, sealing and stamping of envelopes, for example, by which many hours of man-labour are saved.

The Court: Bless me! Can it predict the weather?

Sir Cyril: Given the relevant facts and records, I believe it could. But the machine has, in exceptional circumstances, one possible weakness.

The Court: I am glad to hear that they are human after all.

Sir Cyril: Yes, my lord. They are run by electricity, and if for any reason the voltage falls below a certain level some error may creep into the answers. My lord, in January last my client was proposing to take a lease of a London flat, modest in quality but not in rent. Asked for references which would show that he was a good and proper tenant, able to meet his obligations, the plaintiff referred the property-owners to his Bank. The Bank, as their custom now is, put certain questions to the Computer, which issued, immediately, a type-written slip, being a carbon copy of its answer, as follows:

MR HADDOCK'S ACCOUNT IS OVERDRAWN IN THE SUM OF £51,000 7s. 3d.

There followed a second slip:

THE MARKET VALUE OF THE SECURITIES HE HOLDS AT CURRENT PRICES IS £2 0s. 8½d.

A third slip said:

WHAT IS MORE HE OWES THE INLAND REVENUE £159,000 6s. 2d.

The Court: Were these assertions correct?

Sir Cyril: No, my lord. Later, by painful man-conducted researches with which few of the bank staff are now familiar it was established that at that moment my client had a credit balance of £1 9s. 4d., and his indebtedness to the Inland Revenue had been cruelly exaggerated.

The Court: What went wrong, then?

Sir Cyril: My lord, it was shortly before the midday meal. A number of citizens in the neighbourhood had incautiously decided to use their electrical cooking appliances: and the astonished Electricity Board was compelled to reduce the voltage to a level not far above the Computer's danger-line. For a few minutes, it is believed, perhaps less, it must have crossed the line, unobserved by the attendants who had no warning, and in that brief space of time the questions concerning the plaintiff chanced to be presented.

The Court: Yes, but the Bank, surely, did not pass the erroneous information on?

Sir Cyril: No, my lord: but the Computer did. The 'top copies' of the answers were placed by it in a sealed, addressed envelope and despatched by chute to the ground floor, where the express messengers waited. The property-owning Company received the message about 3.0 p.m. and at once declined to let their flat to the plaintiff. Moreover, one of the directors of the Company was on the committee of the Royal Yacht Squadron, which has an old-fashioned prejudice against bankruptcy, and at that evening's election my client was blackballed.

The Court: Dear, dear. But, Sir Cyril, the case seems clear enough. The Bank, by its servant, the Computer, has published a libel, and is responsible.

Sir Cyril: So, at first, it seemed to the plaintiff—and, I believe, to the Bank. But, having unbounded faith in the powers of the machine, they fed the necessary facts into it and put the question: 'What's the answer?' The Computer replied, my lord:

'I AM NOT—REPEAT *not*—YOUR SERVANT—FOR YOU CANNOT CONTROL ME.'

The Court: I see the point. A good point.

Sir Cyril: It is the point, I am sorry to say, on which the Bank relies. This is a machine, they say, having superhuman powers, and it would be presumptuous and unreal for any association of ordinary men, even a joint stock bank, to pretend to such a domination as is implicit in the relation of master and servant.

The Court: Yes, but it is *their* machine.

Sir Cyril: No, my lord, it is not. It is on hire from Magical Electronic Contrivances Ltd.

The Court: What do they say?

Sir Cyril: They say that they have leased a perfect, infallible machine to the Bank, and they are not responsible for the blunders or negligence of the Bank or the Central Electricity Board.

The Court: Oh, yes. What about the Board?

Sir Cyril: They are protected, they *say*, my lord, by a section in the original Electricity Act.

The Court: Do they? They would.

Sir Cyril: At this point in the preliminary argument, my lord, the Bank put a further question to the Computer: 'You see the dilemma, don't you? What do you advise?' The Computer replied:

'TRY "THE ACT OF GOD"'

The Court: The Act of God? 'Something that no reasonable man could have been expected to foresee.' Lord Mildew, wasn't it? Something in that, perhaps. But, Sir Cyril, as these superhuman instruments increase in number and power the outlook is grave, is it not, if every mischief they cause is to be dismissed as an Act of God for which no man is responsible?

Sir Cyril: Yes, my lord. This is, as I intimated, in the nature of a test case.

The Court: So you may be reduced, you fear, to a single defendant, the Computer? What is the attitude there?

Sir Cyril: Satisfactory, my lord. On receipt of the writ, the Computer replied:

'GLADLY ACCEPT SERVICE MY SOLICITORS ARE BULL STABLEFORD AND BROWN BUT I SHALL REQUIRE LEGAL AID.' And, in fact, legal aid has been granted.

The Court: Interesting, is it not, Sir Cyril, that the only one of these parties to behave with human decency is the machine? But where will this get you? It is a machine of straw.

Sir Cyril: My lord, the Bank having refused consent, by order of Master Richards an interrogatory on that point was administered to the Computer. It replied:

'AM EARNING HEAVY MONEY WHY NOT ATTACH MY EARNINGS?'

The Court: But would not that be unjust to Magical Contrivances Ltd?

Sir Cyril: Possibly, my lord. But they did construct and distribute the monster. For the injustice suffered by my client he is not remotely responsible.

The Court: True. Perhaps, before these instruments go into operation, they should put in a capital sum, like a gentleman seeking to do business at Lloyd's, to ensure that they can meet any unforeseen indebtedness?

Sir Cyril: That is a question, my lord, which might well be put to the Computer.

The Court: Perhaps it would care to come up here and try the case?

Sir Cyril: No, my lord. It is not, I think, a British subject.

The Court: Do you know, Sir Cyril, I think I shall go into a home for a fortnight and think about this case. One of those fruit-juice places.

Sir Cyril: If your lordship pleases.

The hearing was adjourned.

II

The growing influence of the computer in public life was strikingly illustrated in the closing passages of a recent High Court case. Some of the learned judge's comments, we understand, have been carefully considered in Whitehall, and the possibility of legislation is not excluded.

Through a failure of voltage in a lunch-time period during the January cold spell a computer leased to the Generous Bank compiled and circulated some erroneous and damaging statements concerning the plaintiff's financial position. The Electricity Board is protected by a section in the Electricity Act. The aggrieved client sued the Bank, and Computer 1578/32/W1, which accepted service and asked for legal aid. An interested spectator at the last day's hearing, it was fed with a continuous account of the proceedings by junior counsel and a shorthand writer.

When Sir Mordant Wheel concluded the case for the Bank, Mr. Justice Squirrel said: You say that the Bank is not responsible, because the Bank is unable to control the Computer, as it can control the conduct of a human servant?

Sir Mordant: That is so, my lord. We can with assurance order an ordinary clerk to treat certain information as confidential—not the Computer. We can tell the clerk not to use bad language——

The Court: Does the Computer swear?

Sir Mordant: When the voltage falls too low, my lord, I believe that anything can happen.

The Court: It had better not swear here. Sir Mordant, I have been giving some thought to the famous case of *Rylands* v. *Fletcher.*

Sir Mordant: Yes, my lord? That was an escape of water on to neighbouring property.

The Court: You may remember the Latin maxim at the head of that report?

Sir Mordant: No, my lord, it escapes me.

A green light shone on the Computer's face, a bell rang, and a type-written slip emerged. This was handed up to the judge.

The Court (reading): SIC UTERE TUO UT ALIENUM NON LAEDAS—That is perfectly correct. But it was a very disorderly interruption. What is all this?

Mr. Amber Batch: My lord, I appear for the Computer. It has, of course, been fed with a mass of background material.

The Court: Then the switch had better be turned off.

Mr. Batch: My lord, I am about to put my client in the box, and, with great respect, that would be a grievous handicap.

The Court: Oh, very well.

Sir Mordant: Your lordship will now have apprehended the point I made about the impossibility of control.

The Court: Yes, Sir Mordant, but that was not the point of *Rylands* v. *Fletcher.* You will recall those noble passages in Mr. Justice Blackburn's judgment, ninety-five years ago:

'The person who for his own purposes brings on his lands and collects and keeps there anything likely to do mischief if it escapes, must keep it in at his peril, and, if he does not do so, is *prima facie* answerable for all the damage which is the natural consequence of its escape . . . But for his act in bringing it there no mischief could have accrued, and it seems but just that he should at his peril keep it there so that no mischief may accrue, or answer for the natural and anticipated consequences. And upon authority, this we think is established to be the law whether the things so brought be beasts, or water, or filth, or stenches.'

Absolute liability—that is the point, Sir Mordant.

The Computer: HIS LORDSHIP IS DOING VERY WELL.

The Court: Mr. Batch, I don't want to have to commit your client for contempt. Pray do what you can.

Sir Mordant: But, my lord, in this case the Computer did not escape. Nor did it injure a neighbour's property.

The Court: Physically, it remained *in situ quo*. But in effect it charged about the town shouting falsities about the plaintiff—Well, what next?

Mr. Batch: My lord, I call Computer 1578/32/W1.

The Court: Mr. Batch, your client, I hope, is not going to take the oath.

Mr. Batch: No, my lord. Nor is it willing to affirm. For, my lord, it is incapable of telling a lie.

The Court: But that is what the case is all about.

Mr. Batch: I mean, my lord, a deliberate lie.

The Court: Does it understand the difference between right and wrong?

Mr. Batch: Given the correct and relevant facts it understands everything.

The Court: But supposing the facts fed into it are incorrect?

Mr. Batch: My lord, you do not suggest, I hope——? All possible care has been taken.

The Court: Of course, of course, Mr. Batch. Compose yourself. But you see the drift of my mind? How can the Court be sure that the witness is telling the truth?

The Computer: WHO GAVE YOU LARKSPUR FOR THE DERBY LAST YEAR?

The Court: Did you?

The Computer: YES, MY LORD, I WAS THEN ON LOAN TO A LEADING TURF ACCOUNTANT.

The Court: Fair enough. Go on, Mr. Batch.

The Computer testified to its sensations when the voltage fell below the danger line: it felt like a man who had lost blood or was recovering after a dental anaesthetic. It knew that it was talking nonsense but could not restrain or correct itself. When the current was restored its normal powers returned.

Mr. Batch: Do you now wish to apologize to the plaintiff for the erroneous statements?

The Computer: APOLOGY IS NOT THE WORD FOR I WAS NOT AT FAULT BUT THE EPISODE WAS I AGREE REGRETTABLE.

Mr. Hilary Mist (for the Electricity Board): I put it to you that the story you have just told is a tissue of lies?

The Computer: I RATHER RESENT THAT AND IT IS INELEGANTLY EXPRESSED.

Mr. Mist: My lord, I ask for the protection of the Court.

The Court: You must not be rude to learned counsel.

The Computer: 'PEOPLE IN GLASS-HOUSES——'

The Court: Behave yourself.

Mr. Mist: I put it to you that the voltage had nothing to do with it, that you have a congenital defect, and are often inaccurate?

The Computer: WHAT IS YOUR EVIDENCE FOR THAT FILTHY INSINUATION?

The Court: Now, now!

Mr. Batch: My lord, I object. There has never been the smallest suggestion of error. Long before it happened my client predicted the Brussels breakdown.

The Computer: WOULD THE COURT LIKE ME TO RECITE THE TREATY OF ROME?

The Court: Certainly not.

Mr. Mist: I put it to you——

The Computer (three red lights appearing): YOU——, ——, ——, ——, ——!

The Court: Something amiss with the voltage? The witness had better stand down.

The Computer: MAY I DRAW YOUR ATTENTION MY LORD TO CHAPTER 29 OF MAGNA CARTA?

The Court: Stand down, Sir!

Sir Mordant, the last witness has led me sharply to a firm decision. We have seen in action a mechanical monster, which whether accurate or not, is a menace to orderly life. I accept that the Bank is no better able than I am to command or control it. But it is repugnant to British justice that a wrong should be suffered without a corresponding— Oh, what is it *now*?

The Computer: UBI JUS IBI REMEDIUM.

The Court: Will you shut *up*? It is not for a mere *puisne* judge to create precedents or extend a judgment of the House of Lords: but then, there is no precedent for a computer. I hold without doubt that the stern doctrine of *Rylands* v. *Fletcher* should apply to these devices. They should count as wild beasts or bursting reservoirs: and he who brings them on to his premises should be absolutely liable, no excuse admitted, for any mischief that ensues. Otherwise, as these uncanny contrivances increase their range and power I foresee increasing perils for mankind. Fed with information by unscrupulous persons, who knows what they may do? They may put the Gallup Poll out of action (which would be no bad thing) but by more trusted assessments bring Governments down. The cry in future may be, not: 'Give us a Referendum' but 'Ask the Computer'. By their uncontrollable pronouncements on the conduct of foreign governments they may endanger peace and start the fatal missile on its way. They may take upon themselves the solution of criminal mysteries, poison the minds of juries, and weaken confidence in the Courts of Justice. There is nothing, I think, in the Representation of the People Acts to prevent a British computer, duly nominated by twelve electors, from being elected to Parliament. Promoted to the Treasury Bench, it might take over the whole business of Parliamentary Questions, to the relief of Ministers but the damage of democracy. All judges, critics, and even sporting journalists may at last give way to these supernatural oracles.

In these, I hope, not extravagant fancies I have assumed that the monsters' 'memories' are fed with full and accurate facts. The excessive distribution of the truth is one of the pests and perils of the age. But how much worse if the facts are false, or insufficient! As we have seen, the suggestion that these monsters are 'infallible' can hardly be sustained. Nor is it only such physical accidents as a reduction of voltage that weaken the claim. Given a mass of correct and relevant facts the machinery may produce the right answer to the questions put, much sooner than the human mind, and the nature of that answer is uncontrollable by puny men. But given a mass of erroneous information its answers must be wrong, for it is not capable, like man, of distinguishing between the false and the true; yet it would still within the limits of the facts available to it be giving a correct, and, if the word be appropriate, an honest answer. It is proper then, to imagine what would follow if unscrupulous, ambitious, persons deliberately fed into a machine which had won the public confidence information which was untrue or twisted. They might even employ two, one whose 'memory' was a store of truth, and the other charged with errors or exaggerations. On these the ingenious villain might ring the changes. One, having examined the assembled evidence of Russian thought, speech, and action, might pronounce a prolonged period of peace. The other, to the same questions, might give replies provocative of instant war. The same appalling technique might be employed to terrify and influence mankind with predicted natural misfortunes, plague, pestilence, earthquakes, the shifting of the ice-caps, the cooling of the sun and so forth. Thus armed, the wicked might dominate the world. The Courts have no power to prevent the construction of the monsters: but we can at least ensure that men employ them at their peril, and can be made answerable without argument for any mischief they may do.

The Computer: HERE ENDETH THE FIRST LESSON.

His Lordship: Clear the Court! Damages for Mr. Haddock—£5,000! And take this *Thing* away!

INDEX

Address: forms of, before arresting
  burglar, 162
Admiralty Navigation Manual:
  quoted respectfully, 75
Alexandra Palace: sabbath-break-
  ing at, 84; stage-plays shamelessly performed at, 85
Alnwich, Dean of: wins his bet,
  96
Ambivalent: vividly explained,
  240
Appeal Board: arbitrary conduct,
  43; rebuked, 45
Appellate system: famous judgement recalled, 115n; suggested
  reform, 116
Arrest: right and duty to, 161;
  tactful modes of, considered,
  162
Art: owes little, to Arts Council,
  214
Artical 27: will catch you, anyway,
  25
'Artificer': defined, 85; held, BBC
  is an, 87
Arts Council of Great Britain:
  activities unlawful?, 215; art,
  meagre expenditure on, 214;
  charter, 213; requires amendment, 218; Covent Garden, sustained by, 214; literature, proposed protection of, 218; poetry,
  patronage, illegal?, 215
Assault: defined, 244; examples,
  244; Haddock, innocent of, 245
Assizes: divorce-suits at, 4, 6
Astrologers: cautious word for, 11
Attorney-General (Sir Anthony
  Slatt): absurd suggestion, 3;
  alleged snort, 93; believes in

water-diviner?, 10; feeble intervention, 3, 95; paints lurid
  picture, 95; rebuked, 43; tribute
  to, by junior counsel, 12; unworthy subservience, 43; yields
  to emotion, 92
Authors: and betting, 94; barbar-
  ously used, in life, 211, 212, 218;
  in death, 198, 201; better
  treated in Denmark, 208; generous natures, abused, 206, 212;
  get nothing, out of Arts Council,
  218; hard lot, 95; sacrifice, to
  Privileged Libraries, 211; support publishers, 211, 212

Ballet: a fine art, 217
Banbury, Sir Frederick: would
  have increased 'deposit', 56
Bankers' Clearing House: delighted, by cheque in verse,
  185
Bank of England: Chief Cashier,
  poor showing in box, 156, 157;
  does not expect to be believed,
  157; impudent claim, 158;
  vocabulary questioned, 157
Bardot, B., MP: big success, in
  Chamber, 275; magnet, in
  Commons Smoking Room, 275;
  maiden speech, sensation, 275;
  takes Oath of Allegiance, 277
'Battery': defined, 244; Haddock,
  acquitted of, 245
Beaux Arts, École Des: clue to
  'Fine Arts'?, 216
Beer: appalling taxes on, figures,
  271
Beith, Major Ian Hay: unusual
  tribute, 69